Birnbaum's

Disneyland RESORT

Expert Advice from the Inside Source

Jill Safro EDITORIAL DIRECTOR

Suzy Goytizolo SENIOR EDITOR

Keith Groshans ASSOCIATE ART DIRECTOR

Tracey Randinelli PROJECT EDITOR

Erik Cucinelli EDITORIAL ASSISTANT

Alexandra Mayes Birnbaum CONSULTING EDITOR

Stephen Birnbaum FOUNDING EDITOR

THE OFFICIAL GUIDE

DISNEY EDITIONS AND HEARST BUSINESS PUBLISHING, INC.

For Steve, who merely made this all possible

Other 2002 Birnbaum's Official Disney Guides

Walt Disney World
Walt Disney World For Kids, By Kids
Walt Disney World Without Kids

Contents

Disney's California Adventure

95

From the glittering lights of Hollywood to the swells of the Pacific to the thrill rides of an amusement pier, Disney pays tribute to the glories of the Golden State in this compact theme park. Our exclusive coverage reveals all there is to see and do—follow our advice and Hot Tips on how to tour the area like a pro and be sure to catch all of the park's greatest hits.

Good Meals, Great Times

111

Whether it's a simple snack or a multicourse meal, the Disneyland Resort offers something for every palate and pocketbook. For a change of scenery, venture a bit farther afield into Orange County to Anaheim, other inland communities, or nearby beach towns. Our entertainment section reflects the area's wide range of possibilities, from the nightclubs in Downtown Disney to the dinner shows, concert halls, and lounges of Orange County.

Sports

131

Perhaps you dream of catching the perfect wave, hiking along cliffs above the Pacific coast, polishing your serve, or simply taking in a spectator sport. It's a cinch to fulfill your fondest athletic fantasies in the land of sun and surf.

Orange County & Beyond

137

Besides the Disneyland Resort and other family-oriented attractions, Orange County is home to impressive art museums, a presidential library, two seaside resort towns, a famous mission, a mammoth glass cathedral, and state-of-the-art performance venues. After you have thoroughly explored Disney's environs, why not plan a trip to see other parts of Southern California? The options are as diverse as the landscape itself.

A Word From The Editors

When his two daughters were growing up, Walt Disney often accompanied them to local amusement parks on Sunday afternoons. There he noticed that the youngsters entertained themselves quite easily, but the adults had little to do. To his way of thinking, a park should appeal to the sense of wonder and exploration in guests of all ages. His vision became a reality on July 17, 1955, when Disneyland opened in Anaheim, California.

Now, nearly a half-century later, Walt's original theme park is as popular and beloved as ever. While Disneyland Park is wonderfully familiar to us—practically a second home— Disney's California Adventure is a whole new

Editors Jill Safro (left) and Suzy Goytizolo at Disney's Paradise Pier Hotel.

playing ground, and finding the best ways to take it all in has been an adventure in itself. (Even now, a year after the park's grand opening, it remains a work in progress, as current attractions are constantly being tweaked and enhanced to further guest satisfaction.) You'll find some of the fruits of our labor in the form of a chapter dedicated to Disney's California Adventure, as well as sample schedules to guide you through the park.

Those familiar with the Disneyland property will find that Disney's California Adventure isn't the only recent addition to the area. There's also a dining, shopping, and entertainment district known as Downtown Disney, and Disney's Grand Californian Hotel. (To see how the pieces fit together, refer to the map on the inside back cover of this book.) Even some of the original names have changed. Walt Disney's first theme park, commonly known as Disneyland (though some may know it as the Magic Kingdom, while others simply remember it as The Happiest Place on Earth) is now officially named Disneyland Park, while the entire property— Disneyland Park, Disney's California Adventure, Downtown Disney, the Disneyland Hotel, Disney's Grand Californian Hotel, and Disney's Paradise Pier Hotel (formerly the Disneyland Pacific Hotel)—has been christened the Disneyland Resort. This year, we've eschewed our traditional terminology and chosen to use official Disney nomenclature. What does that mean? Any mention of "Disneyland," is a reference to the park formerly known as the Magic Kingdom, while a reference to the Disneyland Resort truly encompasses the whole property.

TAKE OUR ADVICE

In creating this book, we have considered every possible aspect of your trip, from planning it to plotting day-to-day activities. We realize that even the most meticulous vacation planner needs *detailed*, *accurate*, and *objective* information to prepare a successful itinerary. To that end, we have also packaged handy bits of advice in the form of "hot tips" throughout the book. This advice comes directly from the copious notes we've taken during our countless trips to the Disneyland Resort and the the surrounding Anaheim area. We've also used our "Birnbaum's Best" stamp of approval wherever we deemed it appropriate, highlighting *our* favorite attractions and restaurants — the crowd-pleasers we feel stand head, shoulders, and ears above the rest.

You, the reader, benefit from the combination of our years of experience and our independent voice — coupled with our access to up-to-date inside information from the Disney staff — that makes this guide unique. We like to think it's indispensable, but you be the judge of that 150 pages from now.

CREDIT WHERE CREDIT IS DUE

Both in the parks and behind the scenes been, Disneyland staffers have been a critical source of factual data. We hope we are not omitting any names in thanking Tom Brocato, Gail Kirkpatrick, Glen Miller, Tom Gaylem, Marie Chassot, Karlyn Moore, Tony Garrison, Ryan Burris, and John McClintock. Special thanks to Michele Nachum, who does so much to ensure the factual accuracy of *Birnbaum's Official Guide to Disneyland.*

We'd also like to thank our favorite off-site Disney expert, Wendy Lefkon, who edited these guides for many years and is still instrumental in their publication as executive editor at Disney Editions. Thanks, also, to Tim Lewis and Eric Huang at Disney Publishing.

Hats off to Michelle Magenheim, for her outstanding fact-checking, Tom Passavant and Shari Hartford, for their continued editorial support; and to Bob Rohr Sue Macy, and Sarah Jane Brian, special kudos for their proofreading panache.

Of course, no list of acknowledgments would be complete without mentioning our founding editor, Steve Birnbaum, whose spirit, wisdom, and humor still infuse these pages, as well as Alexandra Mayes Birnbaum, who continues to be a guiding light — to say nothing of a careful reader of every word.

THE LAST WORD

Finally, it's important to remember that every worthwhile travel guide is a living enterprise; the book you hold in your hands is our best effort at explaining how to enjoy the Disneyland Resort at the moment, but its text is no way etched in stone. Disney is constantly changing and growing, and in each annual edition we refine and expand our material to serve your needs better. Just before the grand opening of Disneyland, Walt Disney remarked that the main attraction was still missing — people. That's where you come in.

Have a wonderful time!

THE EDITORS

Don't Forget to Write!

No contribution is of greater value to us in preparing the next edition of this book than your comments on its usefulness and your own experiences at the Disneyland Resort. Drop us a postcard or send a letter to the address on the right.

Official Disney Guides
Birnbaum's Disneyland 2002
Disney Editions
114 Fifth Avenue, 12th Floor
New York, NY 10011

Getting Ready to Go

Anyone who visited the Anaheim area over the last few years was sure to see (and hear) evidence of the Disney Imagineers at work. Behind closed gates, construction went on day and night, and in early 2001, the results were finally unveiled—a brand new, 430-acre Disneyland Resort, with Disney's original theme park, Disneyland (although true Disney-o-philes may still refer to it fondly as the "Magic Kingdom"), at its heart. Besides this "Happiest Place on Earth," guests will find the just-opened Disney's California Adventure theme park, the Downtown Disney entertainment district, and Disney's Grand Californian Hotel—which brings Disney's on-property hotel count to a total of three. Of course, you'll want to do and see it all, but where should you start? When should you go? And then there are the all-important questions of how to get there and where to stay. Maybe you want to extend your vacation—perhaps you'll include a visit to (or a stay at) the beach or one of the other nearby attractions . . . .

That's a lot to think about. But don't worry. By the time you've read through this chapter, you'll have all the information you need to make smart decisions. So read on, and remember: A little advanced planning goes a long way.

WHEN TO GO

When you weigh the best times to visit the Disneyland Resort, the most obvious possibilities seem to be Christmas, Easter, and summer vacation—particularly if there are children in the family. But there are a few good reasons to avoid these periods—the major one being that almost everybody else wants to go then, too.

If you can only visit during one of these busy times and worry that the crowds might spoil your fun, there are some tactics for making optimum use of every minute and avoiding the lines—notably, go to the park early to get a jump on the day (and on the crowds), take advantage of any of the early-entry options that might be available to you, and remember that Disney keeps the parks open later during busy seasons, so pace yourself and stay until the park closes.

On the other hand, choosing to visit when the parks are least crowded may mean that you miss some of the most entertaining parades and special events. For instance,

Disneyland Park's Fantasmic! show and the fireworks might not be on the entertainment schedule, and certain attractions may be closed for annual refurbishment.

A wonderful time to visit the Disneyland Resort—when it's not too crowded but everything is still open—is the period between Thanksgiving and Christmas, when the park is decorated to the hilt, the Christmas parade takes place, and carolers add festive music to the mix. Other good times to visit are the period right after summer vacation—late September through early October—and soon after New Year's Day.

When *Not* to Go: If crowds make you queasy, keep in mind that Saturday is usually the busiest day of the week *year-round*. In summer, Monday and Friday are the next busiest. If you decide to visit the parks during a weekend, opt for Sunday. And remember that the week between Christmas and New Year's Day, Easter week, and the period from early July through Labor Day are packed.

Crowd Patterns

Least Crowded

- First week in January to Presidents' week

- Two weeks after Easter Sunday to Memorial Day week

- End of Labor Day week to Columbus Day

- End of Thanksgiving weekend to week before Christmas

Average Attendance

- End of Presidents' week to week before Easter

- Sundays in spring, autumn, and winter, except holiday weekends

- Memorial Day week to beginning of summer vacation

- Labor Day week

- Columbus Day to Thanksgiving weekend

- Week before Christmas

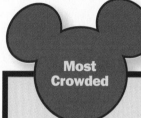

Most Crowded

- Any Saturday

- Sundays during summer and holiday weekends

- Presidents' week

- Week before and week after Easter Sunday

- Beginning of summer through Labor Day weekend

- Thanksgiving weekend (Thursday through Sunday)

- Christmas Day through New Year's Day

Keeping Disney Hours

With a new theme park, as well as an entertainment district, the Disneyland Resort has many more important hours to keep track of than ever before. Operating hours fluctuate according to the season, so call 714-781-4565, or visit *www.disneyland.com* for current schedules.

DISNEYLAND PARK (MAGIC KINGDOM): This park is typically open from 10 A.M. to 8 P.M. weekdays, 9 A.M. to midnight on Saturdays, and 9 A.M. to 9 P.M. on Sundays. Hours are extended in the summer and during holiday seasons.

DISNEY'S CALIFORNIA ADVENTURE: Hours at this park are subject to change and may extend if the park hits capacity during the day. The park generally opens at 8 A.M. and closes between 10 P.M. and midnight. Call 714-781-4565 for specifics.

DOWNTOWN DISNEY: Many of the shops and restaurants in this entertainment district open as early as the theme parks do (8 A.M.) and don't close until 2 A.M. Expect this area to start hopping around dinnertime and stay active until the early hours of the morning.

TRANSPORTATION: The monorail generally begins making its 2½-mile loop one hour before Disneyland opens, and continues running until about 30 minutes after the park closes. At press time, the trams transporting guests between the main parking structure or parking lots and the theme parks began picking up guests about 30 minutes before the first park opened, and continued transporting guests back to parking areas until the last group was dropped off, about an hour or so after the park closed.

EARLY-ENTRY DAYS: Disneyland frequently offers early-entry days—special mornings in which guests with appropriate tickets can enter the park 1½ hours before its official opening time (see page 18 for ticket qualifications) and ride some of the park's most popular attractions with little or no wait. Early-entry days are usually Monday, Tuesday, Thursday, Friday, and Saturday (call 714-781-4565 to determine the specific early-entry days during your visit). Also note that Disney's California Adventure theme park does not offer early-entry days at this time.

Disneyland Weather

If dry, sunny weather is your ideal, Anaheim may seem like a dream come true. Rainy days are few and far between, and generally occur between the months of November and April, which is also the coolest time of year. During this season, Santa Ana winds sometimes produce short periods of dry, crisp, warm desert weather and sparkling-clear skies that unveil distant mountains usually hidden by smog. In summer, thin, low morning clouds make it prudent to plan expeditions to the beach for the afternoon, when the haze burns off and the mercury rises. Mornings and nights are generally cool. The average daytime year-round temperature is 73 degrees.

	TEMPERATURE AVERAGE		RAINFALL AVERAGE
	High	Low	(INCHES)
January	65	47	3.12
February	67	49	3.11
March	68	50	2.66
April	70	53	1.09
May	72	56	0.31
June	77	60	0.06
July	82	64	0.01
August	83	65	0.06
September	81	63	0.24
October	77	59	0.49
November	73	52	1.39
December	67	48	2.58

Holidays & Special Events

Inside the Resort

The Disneyland Resort sponsors several special events during the year. Here are a few highlights. For more details, call Disney Guest Relations (714-781-4565) about three months before the event. In addition, you can find out about specific events at Disneyland Resort hotels by calling 714-956-6413.

JANUARY–FEBRUARY

Valentine's Day: Sweethearts will swoon over the romantic backdrop that Disneyland Park provides on this lovestruck holiday.

Mardi Gras: With its Creole and Cajun cuisine, and boutiques brimming with beaded necklaces, holiday hats, and parade masks, Disneyland's New Orleans Square offers the most traditional Mardi Gras setting. Meanwhile, the clubs at Downtown Disney keep the party going late into the night.

MARCH–MAY

Easter: The parks remain open late the week before and the week after Easter, making this a popular time to visit. At the Disneyland Hotel, "Alice in Wonderland's Easter Basket Buffet" takes place on Easter Sunday in the Wonderland-themed Grand Ballroom, where Alice, the White Rabbit, the Mad Hatter, and friends frolic. Reserve at least one month in advance (714-956-6413).

Mother's Day: Cinderella and other famous Disney princesses and their friends honor Mom during "Disney's Royal Buffet for Mother's Day" in the Disneyland Hotel's Grand Ballroom. The room is transformed with castles and other magical backdrops, creating a fairy-tale atmosphere. Reserve at least one month in advance (714-956-6413).

JUNE–AUGUST

Summer Flag Retreat: Disney's Collegiate All Star Band performs for nine weeks during the summer (usually beginning in mid-June), Tuesday through Saturday, at about 6:30 P.M. The performance takes place in front of the flagpole in Town Square; it includes patriotic Sousa marches and concludes with "The Star-Spangled Banner," which brings any guests not already standing to their feet.

Fourth of July: One of the busiest days of the year—and one to avoid if you're overwhelmed by crowds—this patriotic day features a bigger-than-usual fireworks display at Disneyland.

SEPTEMBER–DECEMBER

Disneyana Convention: This annual Disney-o-phile event is tentatively scheduled to be held at the Disneyland Resort's Florida counterpart (Walt Disney World) in 2002. To confirm the convention's location or reserve a package, visit *www.officialdisneyana.com*.

Thanksgiving Weekend: The four days of this holiday weekend are filled with musical entertainment and the first installments of Disneyland's Christmas Fantasy Parade and It's a Small World Holiday, both of which kick off on Thanksgiving Day. The parks observe extended hours. At the Disneyland Hotel, the characters host "A Disney Family Thanksgiving" buffet in the Grand Ballroom. Reserve at least one month in advance (714-956-6413).

Christmas Festivities: This may be the Disneyland Resort's most beautiful season. Main Street in Disneyland Park is festooned with greenery and hundreds of poinsettias in bloom, while a 60-foot Christmas tree decorated with about 6,000 colorful lights and ornaments further embellishes the scene. Carolers lead rousing sing-alongs in front of the tree, and during two nights early in the season, there's a candlelight ceremony involving a procession, Christmas music sung by a choir, and a reading of a Christmas story by a well-known entertainer. In Fantasyland, It's a Small World is transformed into a world of holiday magic, music, and color. The lively Christmas Fantasy Parade also takes place. Disney's California Adventure decks its halls as well. The week before the holiday ranks among the best times of year to visit. The week afterward, however, is one of the busiest, so wise guests will plan accordingly.

New Year's Eve: Fireworks and live entertainment are featured at this end-of-the-year bash, where a general admission ticket is your entrée to most of the festivities.

Elsewhere in Southern California

JANUARY–FEBRUARY

Tournament of Roses Parade and the Rose Bowl, Pasadena: An elaborate procession of floats covered in fresh roses, chrysanthemums, orchids, and even crushed seashells, this New Year's Day parade follows Colorado Boulevard through Pasadena. Afterward, another anticipated event occurs: the Rose Bowl, the annual college football game dating back to 1902. This year, the game will decide the national championship. Rose Bowl; 391 S. Orange Grove Blvd.; Pasadena, CA 91184; 626-449-4100; *www.rosebowl.com* or *www.tournamentofroses.com*.

MARCH–MAY

Festival of Whales, Dana Point Harbor: This event (held this year on three consecutive weekends in March) salutes the southward journey of the great California gray whales with a parade, street fair, and seaside musical performances, plus other special events and children's programs, and interesting displays of whale-related items. Dana Point Chamber of Commerce; Box 12; Dana Point, CA 92629; 949-496-1555 or 800-290-3262; *www.dpfestivalofwhales.com*.

Glory of Easter, Garden Grove: Held the two weeks before Easter at the Crystal Cathedral, this celebrated event is best known for its colorful array of costumes, live animals, flying angels, spectacular special effects, and theatrical interpretation of the crucifixion and resurrection. Crystal Cathedral; 12141 Lewis St.; Garden Grove, CA 97640; 714-544-5679 (for reservations); *www.crystalcathedral.org*.

Newport–Ensenada International Yacht Race, Newport Beach: This April event is the largest race of its kind in the world, and one of the oldest. More than 500 yachts of all sizes, classes, and varieties participate, and a spectators' boat follows the action. Newport Ocean Sailing Association; 949-644-1023; *www.nosa.org*.

Strawberry Festival, Garden Grove: Between 30,000 and 50,000 revelers show up on the Village Green for each day of Memorial Day weekend. The Strawberry Festival Parade of floats, bands, and equestrians is one of the highlights. Gourmands enjoy the cutting of an enormous strawberry shortcake, big enough to cover a whole stage and substantial enough to provide most festivalgoers with at least one portion. Radio and TV celebs are on hand for autographs. Garden Grove Strawberry Festival Association; Box 2287; Garden Grove, CA 92842; 714-638-0981; *www.strawberryfestival.org*.

JUNE–AUGUST

Festival of Arts/Pageant of the Masters, Laguna Beach: More than 50 years old, this highly regarded, seven-week-long event begins early in July and lasts through August. More than 150 artists take over Irvine Bowl Park to display and sell tapestries, paintings, sculptures, jewelry, and more. Meanwhile, at the concurrent Pageant of the Masters, live models re-create famous works of art onstage in two-hour-long "living pictures," accompanied by narration and a live orchestra. Weekend seats must be reserved in advance. Programs for children and other entertainment complete the festival. Festival of Arts; 650 Laguna Canyon Rd.; Laguna Beach, CA 92651; 949-494-1145; *www.foapom.com*.

SEPTEMBER–DECEMBER

Glory of Christmas, Garden Grove: Two hundred performers and a mini-menagerie of animals star in an annual nativity pageant performed up to three times daily, from the day after Thanksgiving through December. Crystal Cathedral; 12141 Lewis St.; Garden Grove, CA 97640; 714-544-5679 (for reservations).

Newport Harbor Christmas Boat Parade, Newport Beach: This event draws as many as 200 boats each night, all decked out with St. Nicks, angels, and other holiday images, plus enough lights to illuminate a score of oversize Christmas trees. Reflected in the inky waters of Newport Harbor—which hosts the event December 17–23 from 6:30 P.M. to 9 P.M.—all those stars create a spectacle worthy of Disneyland itself. Area waterfront restaurants book reservations for this period up to a year ahead. Newport Harbor Area Chamber of Commerce; 1470 Jamboree Rd.; Newport Beach, CA 92660; 949-729-4400.

Especially for Kids

December through April, whale-watching excursions draw squeals of delight from kids (949-248-7400, Dana Point; 949-673-1434, Newport Beach); mid-March through mid-April, Green Meadow Farm, at Irvine Park, in Orange, provides pony rides, hayrides, and close-up encounters with farm animals, including hands-on experiences with milk cows (714-289-0348); and late April through mid-May, the county-wide Imagination Celebration Festival focuses on culture and crafts for kids and families (949-833-8500); *www.icfestival.com*.

Celebrate 100 Years of Magic

It's not every day you celebrate the 100th birthday of the world's most famous magic-maker—and no, we're not talking about Harry Houdini. On October 1, 2001, the entire Walt Disney Company began paying tribute to Walter Elias Disney's century mark with an anniversary celebration called 100 Years of Magic. Although specific events at the Disneyland Resort were not finalized at the time we went to press, you may find remembrances of Disney's legacy throughout both theme parks. The festivities are sure to set the mood for the other magical elements the Disney Company has dreamed up for this monumental celebration.

> "I only hope that we never lose sight of one thing—that it was all started by a mouse."
>
> — Walt Disney

MAGICAL MILESTONES

1901
Walter Elias Disney is born on December 5 in Chicago, Illinois. He spends his boyhood in Marceline, Missouri.

1922
Walt and collaborator Ub Iwerks start Laugh-O-Gram Films, an animation studio located in Kansas City, Missouri. (The business lasts one year.)

1923
Walt and his brother Roy open the Disney Bros. Studio in Hollywood, California.

1928
Disney's studio introduces the world to the immortal Mickey Mouse with *Steamboat Willie,* the world's first cartoon with a synchronized soundtrack. (Walt Disney himself provides the voice for Mickey.)

1934
The Three Little Pigs wins the Disney Studios its first Academy Award, for cartoon short subject.

1937
Disney releases *Snow White and the Seven Dwarfs,* the world's first feature-length animated film.

1940
Great works of classical music meet Disney animation with the release of *Fantasia.*

1955
Disneyland opens its doors in Anaheim; while television's original *Mickey Mouse Club* begins a four-year run.

1971
Walt Disney World opens in Orlando, Florida.

1989
Disney animation experiences a renaissance of sorts with the release of the Studios' 28th animated film, *The Little Mermaid.*

1992
The Disney magic travels overseas with the opening of Disneyland Paris.

1994
Disney makes its Broadway debut, as *Beauty and the Beast* opens in New York to sold-out houses. (*The Lion King* would follow in 1997, and *Aida* in 2000.)

1996
Disney's kid-oriented radio station, Radio Disney, hits the airwaves.

2001
For the first time since its opening, the Disneyland Resort gets a new theme park: Disney's California Adventure.

GETTING READY TO GO

Weddings & Honeymoons

The Disneyland Resort's customized Fairy Tale Weddings program lets brides and grooms create an affair to remember at the Castle Garden inside Disneyland, or at one of the three Disney hotels—either indoors or out. Couples may go the traditional route or plan a themed event with invitations, decorations, souvenirs, napkins, and thank-you notes emblazoned with their favorite Disney character couples, including Cinderella and her prince and Mickey and Minnie Mouse.

One special spot for tying the knot is the gazebo at the Disneyland Hotel, in a picturesque garden setting where the bride or couple may arrive in a horse-drawn glass coach. Or they can take their vows at the poolside gazebo at Disney's Paradise Pier Hotel. Perhaps the most romantic choice is the courtyard area in the garden at Disney's Grand Californian. A Cinderella Fantasy reception may follow (at any of the three hotels), at which the newlyweds are greeted by a fanfare of trumpets provided by musicians clad in medieval attire as the couple steps onto a red carpet and through a re-creation of Cinderella's Castle. Here, they are serenaded by a string ensemble and greeted by some extra-special guests—assorted Disney characters dressed in their party finery.

A special-event coordinator will help make all the necessary arrangements for the wedding and reception—everything, that is, except providing Prince (or Princess) Charming.

The bridal salon at Disney's Grand Californian resort helps guests through the planning and preparation stages, and even through those pre-ceremony jitters.

For more information about creating a happy occasion in a happy location, contact the Disneyland Fairy Tale Weddings department, which coordinates events at all three hotels and in Disneyland; 714-956-6527.

PLANNING AHEAD

Collect as much information as you can about the attractions you're interested in from the sources listed below. Then consider all the possibilities before making any definite travel plans.

Information

For information about special events and performance times, the latest ticket prices, operating hours, rides under refurbishment, and other Disneyland Resort specifics, contact:

Disneyland Resort Guest Relations; Box 3232; Anaheim, CA 92803; 714-781-4565 or 213-626-8605 (for recorded information), or 714-781-4560 (to speak with a Disney employee); *www.disneyland.com*.

If you are staying at one of the Disneyland Resort hotels (see the *Accommodations* chapter), contact Guest Services at the hotel for help in planning your visit to both the parks and the surrounding area.

Inside the Disneyland Resort: Cast members (the friendly folks who work there) can answer questions on just about anything. Specific information stations in Disneyland Park include City Hall, on the west side of Town Square; the Bank of Main Street, on the east side of Town Square; and the Information Board on the west side of Central Plaza, at the far end of Main Street. In Disney's California Adventure, Guest Relations is located on the east side of the Entry Plaza before the Golden Gate Bridge, and Information Boards can be found by the sun icon at the far end of the Gateway Plaza and on the bridge leading to Paradise Pier. At any Disneyland Resort hotel, visit the Guest Services desk in the lobby for assistance.

www.disneyland.com

For up-to-date online information, head to *www.disneyland.com*, the official Disneyland Resort website. Using the handy Trip Wizard, you can actually plan your vacation, find out about the three Disneyland Resort hotels, book travel packages, and order park tickets, plus check park hours and show schedules. You can also book your Disneyland vacation online through *www.disneytravel.com*.

For other area information, contact these bureaus of tourism:

● **Anaheim/Orange County Visitor & Convention Bureau**; Box 4270; Anaheim, CA 92803; 714-765-8899 (ask about their coupon book and children's activities book). You can visit them at 800 West Katella Avenue. To order some free publications, call 888-598-3200; for a recorded message detailing current goings-on in the area, call 714-765-8899, ext. 9888; *www.anaheimoc.org*.

● **Laguna Beach Visitors Bureau**; 252 Broadway; Box 221; Laguna Beach, CA 92651; 949-497-9229 or 800-877-1115; *www.lagunabeachinfo.org*.

● **Newport Beach Conference & Visitors Bureau**; 3300 West Coast Hwy.; Newport Beach, CA 92663; 949-722-1611 or 800-942-6278; *www.newportbeach-cvb.com*.

● **Huntington Beach Conference and Visitors Bureau**; 417 Main St.; Huntington Beach, CA 92648; 714-969-3492 or 800-729-6232; *www.hbvisit.com*.

● **Los Angeles Convention & Visitors Bureau**; 685 Figueroa St.; Los Angeles, CA 90017; 213-689-8822, 213-624-7300, or 800-228-2452; *www.lacvb.com*.

● **Long Beach Area Visitors Bureau**; One World Trade Center, Suite 300; Long Beach, CA 90831; 562-436-3645 or 800-452-7829; *www.golongbeach.org*.

● **Orange Chamber of Commerce and Visitors Bureau**; 439 E. Chapman Ave.; Orange, CA 92866; 714-538-3581; *www.orangechamber.org*.

● **San Diego Convention & Visitors Bureau**; 11 Horton Plaza; San Diego, CA 92101; 619-236-1212; *www.sandiego.org*.

● **California Division of Tourism**; 916-322-2881; *www.gocalif.ca.gov*.

Reservations

With the Disneyland Resort's recent expansion, advance planning has become essential. To get your choice of accommodations, especially for visits during the busy spring and summer seasons, make lodging reservations as far in advance as possible—at least six months ahead, if you can, since area hotels fill up quickly during these months. For visits at other times of the year, check with the Anaheim/Orange County Visitor & Convention Bureau (714-765-8899) to see if any conventions are scheduled when you want to travel. Some of these events can crowd facilities enough to warrant altering your plans.

Travel Packages

The biggest advantage to purchasing a travel package is that it almost always saves you money over what you'd pay separately for the individual elements of your vacation, or it offers special options not available if you simply buy a ticket at the ticket booth. This is especially true the longer you stay. And there is the convenience of having all the details arranged in advance *by someone else*.

Finding the best package for yourself means deciding what sort of vacation you want and studying what's available. Don't choose a package that includes elements that don't interest you—remember, you're paying for them. And if it's Disney theming and extras you want, you should consider a Walt Disney Travel Company package.

The Walt Disney Travel Company offers packages that include a stay at a Disney hotel, a Resort Park Hopper Ticket, and choice of an extra, such as breakfast in the park or a guided tour of Disneyland, as well as admission to another Anaheim-area attraction, such as Sea World or Universal Studios Hollywood.

Besides booking guests into an official Disneyland Resort hotel, the Walt Disney Travel Company also works closely with more than 30 Good Neighbor hotels and motels (see page 42 for details), and they are included in its packages as well. To book a Disneyland Resort vacation package, call the Walt Disney Travel Company at 714-520-5050, or visit them on the web at *www.disneytravel.com*.

The Disneyland Resort is also featured in a wide variety of non-Disney run package tours, including those sponsored by individual hotels, Amtrak, airlines (United Vacations and Delta Vacations both offer fly-drive packages, for instance), and organizations. AAA Vacations packages are available to members and nonmembers alike, while AAA Disney Magic Moments packages represent savings and benefits for members only.

This book's selective guide to Anaheim-area hotels and motels can help you decide initially which property best suits your travel style, needs, and budget (see the *Accommodations* chapter). Pick one, then contact a travel agent or the desired hotel directly to make a reservation, or book a Disneyland Resort package. Happy hunting!

What to Pack

Southern California isn't so laid-back that you only need to pack a few pairs of shorts and a T-shirt. Nor is it a place that demands formal attire. Casual wear will suffice in all but the fanciest restaurants, and even there, men can usually wear sports jackets without ties. Bathing suits are an obvious must if you plan to take advantage of your hotel's swimming pool or go for a walk on a long, surf-pounded Pacific beach. It's also a good idea to bring along a bathing suit cover-up and sunglasses (and don't forget the sunscreen). Tennis togs or golf gear may be necessary if you plan to hit the courts or the course. The weather in summer can be hot, but because Southern California air-conditioning is often overefficient, take a lightweight sweater or jacket to wear indoors.

In winter, warm clothing is a must for evening; during nighttime visits to the parks, a heavy jacket may be a godsend. Whatever the time of year, come prepared for the unexpected: Pack an umbrella, a T-shirt, and a jacket—just in case the weather suddenly turns wet or unseasonably warm or cool.

Making a Budget

Vacation expenses tend to fall into five major categories: (1) transportation (which may include costs for airfare, airport transfers, train tickets, car rental, gas, parking, and taxi service; (2) lodging; (3) theme park tickets; (4) meals; and (5) miscellaneous (recreational activities, souvenirs, postcards, film, toiletries, and expenses such as pet boarding, etc.).

When budgeting, first consider what level of service suits your needs. Some prefer to spend fewer days at the Resort, but stay at a deluxe hotel like the Grand Californian or dine at pricier restaurants. Others want a longer vacation with a value-priced Good Neighbor hotel and less expensive meals. The choice is up to you. (Having said that, we do feel that a great deal of the Disney experience comes from staying on property, and recommend at least making room in your budget for accommodations at the more moderately priced Disneyland or Paradise Pier hotels.)

Once you've established your spending priorities, determine your price limit. Then make sure you don't exceed it when approximating your expenses—without a ballpark figure to work around, it's easy to get carried away.

Sample Budget

This is an example of a moderately priced budget for a family of four (two adults and two kids staying at the Disneyland Resort for four nights and five days, with a spending limit of $3,000). Totals include tax; theme park ticket prices are likely to increase in 2002.

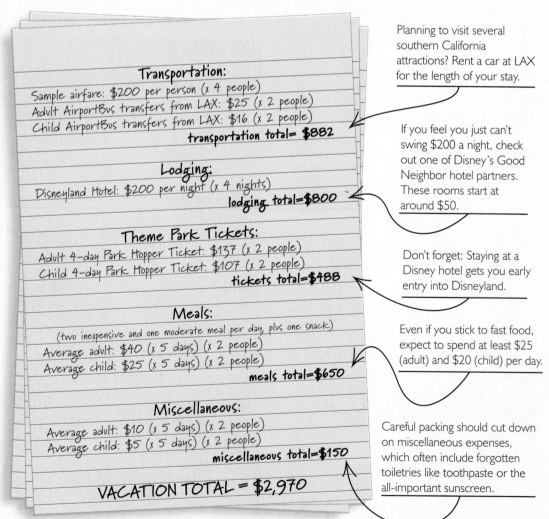

Transportation:
Sample airfare: $200 per person (x 4 people)
Adult AirportBus transfers from LAX: $25 (x 2 people)
Child AirportBus transfers from LAX: $16 (x 2 people)
transportation total= $882

Lodging:
Disneyland Hotel: $200 per night (x 4 nights)
lodging total=$800

Theme Park Tickets:
Adult 4-day Park Hopper Ticket: $137 (x 2 people)
Child 4-day Park Hopper Ticket: $107 (x 2 people)
tickets total=$488

Meals:
(two inexpensive and one moderate meal per day, plus one snack)
Average adult: $40 (x 5 days) (x 2 people)
Average child: $25 (x 5 days) (x 2 people)
meals total=$650

Miscellaneous:
Average adult: $10 (x 5 days) (x 2 people)
Average child: $5 (x 5 days) (x 2 people)
miscellaneous total=$150

VACATION TOTAL = $2,970

Planning to visit several southern California attractions? Rent a car at LAX for the length of your stay.

If you feel you just can't swing $200 a night, check out one of Disney's Good Neighbor hotel partners. These rooms start at around $50.

Don't forget: Staying at a Disney hotel gets you early entry into Disneyland.

Even if you stick to fast food, expect to spend at least $25 (adult) and $20 (child) per day.

Careful packing should cut down on miscellaneous expenses, which often include forgotten toiletries like toothpaste or the all-important sunscreen.

Money-Saving Strategies

Cost-Cutting Tips

LODGING: The most important rule is not to pay for more than you need or can realistically afford. Budget chains don't offer many frills, but they are usually clean and provide all the essentials; many even have a swimming pool, albeit a small one.

You can also save by checking the cutoff age at which children can no longer share their parents' room for free. Many of the hotels and motels in the Anaheim area allow children under 18 to stay free. Some places have a cutoff age of 12 or 16, so it's a good idea to find out before making a reservation. And always ask about special rates or discounts, especially if you are a California resident, a member of AAA or AARP, or are in the military.

Bed-and-breakfasts sometimes represent an excellent buy, though not so much for families, since they generally charge extra for more than two people in a room, regardless of age. While there are no bed-and-breakfasts in Anaheim proper, some charming ones are situated on the coast, within a half hour to an hour of Disney. (Refer to the "Bed & Breakfast Inns" section of the *Accommodations* chapter.)

Hostels and campgrounds also offer lower-priced lodging alternatives. Contact the Anaheim/Orange County Visitor & Convention Bureau at 714-765-8899 for a listing of those areas closest to the Disneyland Resort.

FOOD: The budget-minded should plan to have hot meals in coffee shops or fast-food restaurants, which are less costly than most establishments with table service, or save your splurges for the all-you-can-eat buffets, to get both your fill and your money's worth. If you want to try an upscale place, go at lunchtime; the entrées are often the same as those at dinnertime, but they usually cost less.

Pack a picnic and enjoy lunches outside. At the Disneyland Resort, there's a new picnic area just outside the main gates of the two theme parks.

You can also save significantly on meals by choosing lodging with kitchen facilities and opting to eat in some of the time. The savings on food, especially where a family of four or more is concerned, may more than cover the additional cost of accommodations.

In the Anaheim area, a number of places offer refrigerators or full kitchen facilities (look for suite hotels); some also provide complimentary breakfast.

TRANSPORTATION: When calculating the cost of driving to the Disneyland Resort, consider your car's gas mileage, the price of gasoline, and the expense of the accommodations and food en route. If you are thinking of

HOT TIP!
For a book of coupons to many of Anaheim's hotels, restaurants, and attractions, call 714-765-8899.

traveling by plane, don't forget about the cost of getting from your home to the airport and later to your hotel. Also factor in the cost of renting a car at your destination, if that's part of your plan. And remember to ask if your hotel charges for parking or shuttle transportation to the Disneyland Resort—these daily charges can tack a substantial amount onto a family's room bill.

Disney Discounts

DISNEY CLUB: Members of this organization (previously known as the Magic Kingdom Club) receive special savings on select theme park admissions, Disneyland Resort hotel accommodations, and merchandise (the discount is good toward purchases greater than $10), plus discounts from the Disney Store and the Disney Catalog, and more. Membership in the Disney Club costs about $40; join by calling 714-781-1550; *www.disneyclub.com.*

ANNUAL PASSPORT: Bearers are granted special savings on Disneyland Resort hotel accommodations; Disneyland Resort restaurants; select merchandise throughout the theme parks and Downtown Disney, in the Disney Stores, and from the Disney Catalog; and select guided tours; as well as complimentary parking at the theme parks.

AMERICAN EXPRESS: Members who present their American Express card for payment receive discounts at select restaurants, savings on merchandise over $50, significantly reduced prices on guided tours, and can purchase special vacation packages.

AUTOMOBILE ASSOCIATION OF AMERICA (AAA): Members can purchase discounted theme park tickets and special vacation packages through their local AAA office.

Theme Park Tickets

Along with the many changes to the Disneyland Resort comes a restructuring of the theme park ticketing system. Most admission media (with the exception of annual passes) are now called "tickets" rather than "passports." Two-Day Passports and Flex Passports are gone; taking their place are three- and four-day tickets that allow you unlimited park hopping between Disneyland and Disney's California Adventure. Two things haven't changed: Admission tickets to the theme parks include unlimited use of all attractions (except arcades) once inside, and ticket prices are subject to change.

HOT TIP!

Guests at a Disney hotel or those purchasing a vacation package at a Disney or Good Neighbor hotel can take advantage of special Resort Park Hopper Tickets, which include at least one early-entry day at Disneyland and an ESPN Game Zone Card. For details, call 407-956-6400.

Ticket Options

One-Day Tickets feature admission to one Disneyland Resort theme park, while Three- and Four-Day Resort Park Hopper Tickets (which expire 14 days after first use) allow you to "hop" between Disneyland and California Adventure.

Two main types of annual passports (one featuring admission to Disneyland only, the other featuring both parks), which include shopping and dining discounts, are available in Premium and Deluxe versions. The Premium Annual Passport is valid year-round and includes parking. The Deluxe Annual Passport is valid many days of the year but has block-out periods, such as each Saturday from March through June (passholders may enter the park on a blocked-out day by paying $20). An optional one-time parking fee, currently $35, is available to Deluxe Annual Passholders. In addition, the discounted California Annual Passport, with features similar to the Deluxe Annual Passport, can be purchased by guests with a state ID.

Early-entry tickets: This special ticket feature allows guests to enter Disneyland 1½ hours before official opening time on select days of the week (see page 9 for specifics).

Guests staying at a Disneyland Resort hotel receive complimentary early-entry privileges, while others can obtain the perk with certain Park Hopper Tickets purchased via the Walt Disney Travel Company.

Purchasing Tickets

Long lines have been known to form at the Disney ticket booths. Avoid the wait by purchasing your tickets ahead of time.

Where to Buy Tickets: One-, Three-, and Four-Day Tickets are sold at park ticket booths, the Downtown Disney monorail station, and West Coast Disney Stores. Special Resort Park Hopper Tickets are sold to guests at the Disney hotels, via the Walt Disney Travel Company, or through a travel agent.

Tickets by Mail: Send your check or money order and ticket request (along with a $10 handling fee for orders over $200), to Disneyland Ticket Mail Order Services; Box 61061; Anaheim, CA 92803. Allow five to ten business days for processing.

Tickets Online: Select tickets are sold online, at *www.disneyland.com*.

Tickets by Phone: Orders may be charged to a credit card by calling 714-781-4043. Allow four to five days for delivery; ten days during Christmastime.

How to Pay for Tickets: Cash, traveler's checks, personal checks, American Express, Visa, MasterCard, the Disney Credit Card, and the Discover Card are all accepted. Personal checks must be imprinted with your name and address, and accompanied by a government-issued photo ID card.

Ticket Prices

Although ticket prices are subject to change, the following will give you an idea of what you can expect to pay. Note that prices are likely to increase midyear. For current prices, call 714-781-4565 or visit *www.disneyland.com*.

	Adults	Children*
One-Day Ticket	$43	$33
Three-Day Ticket	$111	$87
Four-Day Ticket	$137	$107

	1 park	2 parks
Deluxe Annual Passport	$139	$199
Premium Annual Passport	$199	$299

*3 through 9 years of age; children under 3 free

CUSTOMIZED TRAVEL TIPS

Traveling with Children

When you tell your kids that a Disney vacation is in the works, the challenge is keeping them relatively calm until you actually arrive at the resort.

PLANNING: Get youngsters involved in plotting the trip from the outset, putting each child in charge of a small part of the vacation preparation—such as writing for travel brochures and the free 32-page *Kid's Guide to Orange County* activity and trivia book (request it and a coupon book for local attractions, dining, and lodging from the Anaheim/Orange County Visitor & Convention Bureau; Box 4270, Dept. K-B; Anaheim, CA 92803; 714-765-8899), choosing which attractions to see and in what order to see them, and deciding which other activities to include in your Southern California visit.

EN ROUTE: Certain resources can stave off the "Are we there yet?" chorus, such as travel games, books and magazines, and snacks to quiet rumbling stomachs. If you drive, take plenty of breaks along the way. If you fly, try to time your departure and return flights for off-peak hours and during the off-season, when chances are better that an empty seat or two will be available. During takeoffs and landings, encourage babies to suck on bottles and pacifiers to keep ears clear, and supply older children with chewing gum or a drink of water.

IN THE HOTELS: During the summer, several hotels offer special kids' programs at no (or low) charge. Some offer baby-sitting services or baby-sitting referrals year-round.

IN THE THEME PARKS: The smiles that light up your kids' faces as they enter a Disney theme park will repay you a thousandfold for any fuss en route. No place in the world is more aware of the needs of children—or their parents—than this one.

Favorite Attractions: Fantasyland and Mickey's Toontown in Disneyland Park are great places to start with small kids, who delight in the bright colors and familiar characters. In Disney's California Adventure, the watery *SS Rustworthy* play area in Paradise Pier and the Redwood Creek Challenge Trail in Golden State have the biggest kid appeal. If you have children of different ages in your party, you may have to do some juggling or split the group up for a few hours, so that older kids won't have to spend their whole vacation waiting in line for Dumbo. Some rides, like Snow White's Scary Adventures, may be too frightening for some youngsters; the guest waiting area sets the mood, so check your child's reaction before boarding.

Strollers: They can be rented for $7 ($12 for two) at the Stroller Shop, located to the right as you enter the main gate in Disneyland and on the right side as you enter Disney's California Adventure. If yours disappears while you're at an attraction, go to a replacement center (a Disney cast member can point the way), show your claim ticket, and get another.

Baby Care: Baby Care Centers feature toddler-size flush toilets that are quite cute — and functional. In addition, there are changing tables, a limited selection of formulas, strained baby foods, and diapers for sale, plus facilities for warming baby food and bottles. A special room with comfortable chairs is available for nursing moms.

The decor is soothing, and a stop here for diaper changing or feeding is a tranquil break for parent and child alike. The Baby Care Centers are located on the east side of the Central Plaza, at the Castle end of Main Street in Disneyland, and near Cocina Cucamonga in the Golden State at Disney's California Adventure.

Changing tables and diaper machines are also available in many of the women's and men's restrooms found throughout the Disneyland Resort.

Note: We recommend that parents of toddlers pack a few pairs of waterproof diapers. They'll come in handy for children who want to spend time splashing in the interactive water fountains at each of the parks.

Where to Buy Baby Care Items: Besides being at the Baby Care Centers, disposable diapers and baby bottles are sold at select shops throughout the parks.

Lost Children: When a child suddenly disappears or fails to show up on time, it's reassuring to know that Disney's security force and all cast members are carefully trained to follow specific procedures when they encounter a lost child.

Up to age 11, a youngster is taken to Child Services, adjacent to First Aid, where Disney movies and books provide temporary amusement. The child's name is registered in the lost children's logbook there. Kids 12 and older may leave messages and check in often at City Hall in Disneyland, or Guest Relations in the entrance area of Disney's California Adventure.

The telephone number for Lost Children is 714-781-4210; if you're calling from inside a park, dial extension 4210.

Height Ho!

At attractions with age and/or height restrictions, a parent who waits with a child too young or too small to ride while the other parent goes on the attraction may stay at the front of the line and take a turn as soon as the first parent comes off. This is called the "rider switch" policy, and if lines are long, it can save a lot of time. Be sure to ask the attendant, and he or she will explain what to do.

Traveling Without Children

The Disneyland Resort is as enjoyable for solo travelers and couples as it is for families for several reasons: Its ambience encourages interaction, if you're in the mood; cast members (Disney employees) are outgoing and helpful; and the attractions are naturally shared events.

PLANNING: Read Disney literature carefully before you arrive to familiarize yourself with the resort's layout and activities. Also request tourist information from other places in Southern California that you intend to visit.

IN THE THEME PARKS: Disney brings out the child in most adults, who suddenly find themselves donning Mouse ears and beaming after getting a hug from Minnie.

Park Tours: A good way to learn the lay of the lands in Disneyland is to take a walking tour. Led by a knowledgeable guide, the tour covers the whole park, and the price includes general park admission for the day (if you already have a park ticket, you pay an extra $16 for the tour itself), visits to six of the park's attractions (usually ones that don't have long waits), the services of a guide throughout the 4½-hour tour, and the run of the park for the rest of the day.

Walking tours depart every morning from City Hall in Disneyland; reservations are not necessary but are recommended for groups of 15 people or more. For details or to inquire about Disney's California Adventure tours, call 714-781-4773.

Food for Thought: Sightseeing takes energy, and only healthy meals can provide it at a consistent level. Don't try to save money by scrimping on food. Prices for meals at the parks (particularly at Disneyland) are reasonable, and there are many healthy options, even in the fast-food restaurants.

Health Matters: If you visit in summer, avoid getting overheated; August in particular can be sweltering. Protect yourself from the sun with a hat and plenty of sunscreen, rest in the shade often, and beat the mid-afternoon heat with a cold drink or a snack in an air-conditioned spot.

If you feel ill, speak to a Disney cast member or go to First Aid and lie down for a while. Above all, don't take unnecessary risks. If you have a back problem, heart condition, or other physical ailment, suffer from motion sickness, or are pregnant, you should steer clear of rough rides. Any restrictions are noted at the entrance to each ride in the park, as well as at the end of the individual listings in the *Disneyland Park* and *Disney's California Adventure* chapters of this book.

Lost Companions: Traveling companions do occasionally get separated. If someone in your party wanders off or fails to show up at an appointed meeting spot, head for City Hall in Disneyland or Guest Relations in California Adventure. Here you'll find a book in which guests can leave and receive messages for one another during the day.

Making Your Exit: If you are part of a bus tour, allow time to return to the coach at the end of the day. One tactic (and this holds true for anyone planning to leave the park at a particular time) is to save the entrance area sights for last. If you arrive at the main gate too far in advance of the group's meeting time, you can spend the extra minutes at those attractions. Expect the tram ride from the entrance of the park to the tour bus pickup point to take about 10 minutes, and plan accordingly.

MEETING OTHER ADULTS: Downtown Disney, with its mix of restaurants and nightclubs, is the best spot to mingle (especially once the sun goes down). With attractions such as the Golden Vine Winery's wine tastings, Disney's California Adventure attracts more grown-up guests than Disneyland. While each of Disney's three hotels has lounges worth visiting, those at the Grand Californian are perhaps the most sophisticated on-property.

SENIOR FUN DAYS AT DISNEYLAND: Specially priced ($41) one-day-only tickets are available to those 60 and older. Check with Guest Relations to confirm prices. Many Anaheim-area restaurants and hotels provide discounts for seniors, so be sure to ask.

Travelers with Disabilities

The Disneyland Resort is extremely accessible to guests with disabilities, and as a result, it makes an excellent choice as a vacation destination. But advance planning is still essential, and nothing is more useful than the free *Guidebook for Guests with Disabilities.* Allow enough time to order a copy and study the information in it before your trip (see "Park Resource," next page).

GETTING TO ANAHEIM

Probably the most effective means of ensuring a smooth trip is to make as many advance contacts as possible at every phase of your journey. It's important to make any necessary phone calls regarding transportation well before your departure date to arrange for any special facilities or services you may need en route.

The Society for the Advancement of Travel for the Handicapped (347 Fifth Ave., Suite 610; New York, NY 10016; 212-447-7284; *www.sath.org*) has member travel agents who book trips for travelers with disabilities, keeping their special needs in mind. (Send $5 to receive a listing of member agents; membership in the organization costs $45, or $30 for seniors 65 and older and for students.)

The following travel agencies specialize in booking trips for travelers with physical disabilities: Accessible Journeys, Ridley Park, PA (610-521-0339 or 800-846-4537) and Flying Wheels Travel, Owatonna, MN (507-451-5005 or 800-535-6790).

Avis (800-331-1212), Hertz (800-654-3131), and National (800-227-7368) have a limited number of hand-control cars available for rent in Southern California, most of which are available at Los Angeles International Airport.

Though slightly less convenient, it's also possible to access the area by public transportation. All buses operated by the Orange County Transportation Authority (714-636-7433), the public bus company that serves Orange County, are outfitted with lifts so that travelers in wheelchairs can board them easily. Many routes pass the Disneyland Resort.

Sightseeing tour buses are another option. Though only a few of them are wheelchair accessible, all have storage facilities for collapsible chairs, making this a possibility for travelers who have a companion to help them on and off the bus. Pacific Coast Sightseeing/Gray Line of Anaheim is wheelchair accessible (make reservations 72 hours in advance; 714-978-8855 or 800-828-6699); it offers tours to many Disneyland Resort area attractions.

LODGING

Most hotels and motels in Orange County have rooms equipped for guests with disabilities, with extra-wide doorways, grab bars in the bathroom for shower or bath and toilet, and sinks at wheelchair height, along with ramps at curbs and steps to allow wheelchair access. Unless otherwise indicated, all the lodging described in the *Accommodations* chapter provide rooms for travelers with disabilities.

INSIDE THE DISNEYLAND RESORT

Cars displaying a "disability" placard will be directed to a conveniently located section of each Disney parking lot, next to the tram pickup and drop-off area.

Wheelchairs and Electric Convenience Vehicles (ECVs) can be rented at the Stroller Shop just inside the main gate in Disneyland and across from Guest Relations in the Entry Plaza of California Adventure. The rental price ($7 per park per day for wheelchairs, $30 for ECVs) includes a refundable deposit of $20. A small number of wheelchairs are also available free of charge (the guest is charged if the wheelchair isn't returned) from Disney's three hotels; inquire at the front desk.

Most waiting areas are accessible, though some attractions have auxiliary entrances for guests with disabilities, who may be accompanied by up to five other party members using the special entry point.

Accessibility information is provided in the *Guidebook for Guests with Disabilities* (see "Park Resource" on this page). In all cases, guests with mobility disabilities should be escorted by someone who can assist as needed.

In some attractions, guests may remain in their wheelchair or ECV; in others, they must be able to transfer in and out of their wheelchair or ECV. In a few attractions, they must be able to leave their wheelchair or ECV and remain ambulatory during the majority of the attraction experience.

All the shops and food locations in the theme parks are completely accessible to guests in wheelchairs, with one exception: At Disneyland's River Belle Terrace, the stanchions designating the cafeteria line are spaced too closely together to permit wheelchair passage (otherwise, it is accessible).

For guests with visual disabilities: A tape recorder and cassette describing the park, along with the *Braille Guidebook*, are available upon request at City Hall in Disneyland and at Guest Relations in California Adventure. Service animals are allowed almost everywhere in the parks, except on attractions that involve a great deal of motion. In such instances, the service animal waits with a Disney cast member while the guest goes on the ride.

For guests with hearing disabilities: Several dozen attractions provide a written story line for guests to follow while they experience the attraction. Check at City Hall in Disneyland and Guest Relations in California Adventure for a list of attractions with written story lines.

Closed captioning is available in the pre-show areas of select attractions; contact Guest Relations for the use of a remote. Reflective captioning is available at several shows as well; inquire at each attraction.

Text typewriters (TTY) are located in Disneyland near the Guest Relations window at the main entrance (next to the kennel), and at the pay phones near the exit to Space Mountain. In Disney's California Adventure, TTYs can be found on the west side of the main entry area, in the Bay Area by Golden Dreams, and beside King Triton's Carousel. Sign language interpretation is available for some shows and attractions, but reservations must be made at least seven days in advance; to make this arrangement, contact Guest Relations at 714-781-4773. Volume-control telephones are located throughout the park.

Park Resource

The *Guidebook for Guests with Disabilities* describes accessibility to each theme park's shops, restaurants, and attractions, and tells where to find the wheelchair entrances. It is available at Guest Relations in Disneyland and Disney's California Adventure. It can also be obtained by writing to Disneyland Resort Guest Relations; Box 3232; Anaheim, CA 92803 (allow two to three weeks for delivery).

How to Get There

ost visitors to the Disneyland Resort arrive by car. Many of those who live nearby own an annual pass and drive down frequently to spend a day or weekend at the resort. But for those traveling any significant distance, it tends to cost less to fly than to drive, and certainly saves time. During your days at the Disneyland Resort, you can rely on Disney transportation (in the form of monorails, trams, and double-decker buses) to take you anywhere you want to go on-property. Plan to rent a car for the days you'll venture off-property, or rely on local tours to see the area sights. If you prefer to leave the driving to someone else altogether, traveling by bus or train are other alternatives.

By Car

SOUTHERN CALIFORNIA FREEWAYS: Driving almost anywhere in Orange County, or farther afield, requires negotiating a combination of freeways and surface streets. But once you familiarize yourself with a few names and numbers, navigating becomes much more manageable.

The freeways are well-marked and fast, barring (common) traffic snags. And locals are good drivers: slow to lose patience, but quick to apply their brakes when necessary. They tend to leave more than a full car-length space in front of them, knowing that abrupt lane switching is commonplace here.

Be forewarned that the proper names of most roads change depending on where you are. I-5, for instance, is called the Santa Ana Freeway in Orange County, but in the Los Angeles area it becomes the Golden State Freeway; to the south it's the San Diego Freeway. It's a good idea to learn both the name and the route number of any freeway on which you plan to travel. The exit signs will most likely indicate one or the other but not both.

It's also useful to have an idea of the overall layout of the freeways. Several run parallel to the Pacific coast and are intersected by others running east and west. While this scheme is fairly straightforward, it is complicated by a couple of freeways that squiggle diagonally across the map.

CALIFORNIA DRIVING LAWS: Under California law, seat belts are required for all front- and backseat passengers; right turns at red lights are legal unless otherwise posted, as are U-turns at intersections; and pedestrians have the right-of-way at crosswalks.

HOT TIP!

Freeway traffic updates can help you avoid a jam. Tune in to 1670 AM (Anaheim) or 980/1070 AM (Los Angeles).

AUTOMOBILE CLUBS: Any one of the nation's leading automobile clubs will come to your aid in the event of a breakdown en route (be sure to bring your membership card with you), as well as provide insurance covering accidents, arrest, bail bond, lawyers' fees for defense of contested traffic cases, and personal injury. They also offer useful trip-planning services—not merely advice, but also free maps and route-mapping assistance. AAA and the Auto Club of Southern California provide select free services to all Disneyland Resort guests (see page 33).

MAPS: Many car rental agencies provide helpful maps, but it's still wise to buy one before your trip. Or drop by a visitor information office; it can usually provide a map showing tourist attractions, major roads, and some minor streets. Local gas stations and bookstores often sell maps, as do some hotel gift shops. Routes can also be plotted ahead of time through *www.mapquest.com*.

By Air

Anaheim lies about 45 minutes southeast of Los Angeles by car. Most Disneyland Resort guests who arrive by plane disembark at Los Angeles International Airport (LAX), one of the busiest in the world. It handles approximately 1,900 departures and arrivals daily of more than 100 commercial airlines. Major carriers serving L.A. include American, Continental, Delta, TWA, and United.

Considerably closer to Anaheim, Orange County's pleasant and modern John Wayne Airport, in Santa Ana, is less than a half hour away from Disney and is served by 12 commercial airlines and more than 240 flights a day. It is sometimes possible to find the same fare to John Wayne/Orange County Airport as to LAX, and if it's a nonstop flight, so much the better. Long Beach Airport is also near Anaheim, but few airlines serve it on a nonstop basis.

HOW TO GET THE BEST AIRFARE: These days, airfares are constantly in flux, changing from day to day, seemingly hour to hour. That makes it important to shop around—or have your travel agent do so. It pays (literally) to keep these suggestions in mind:

• Find out the names of all the airlines serving your destination and then call them all. Tell the airline's reservationist how many people are in your party, and emphasize that you're interested in economy. Ask if you can get a lower fare by slightly altering the dates of your trip, the hour of departure, or the duration of your stay—or, if you live halfway between two airports, by leaving from one rather than the other or by flying into a different area airport.

• Fly weekends on routes heavily used by business travelers, and midweek on routes more commonly patronized by vacationers.

• Buy your tickets online. Airlines often offer lower fares or bonus frequent flier miles for tickets purchased through their website.

• Watch your local newspapers for ads announcing new or special promotional fares.

• Plan and pay as far ahead as possible. Most carriers guarantee their fares, which means you won't have to pay more if fares have gone up since you purchased your ticket. On the other hand, if you have *not* paid for your ticket, you *will* be required to pay the higher charge.

Similarly, if you change dates of travel or flight times and your ticket has to be re-issued, you'll have to pay the new fare, plus any penalties that may apply. If fares have come down in price since you paid for your ticket, the difference will be refunded to you by the airline, even if you've already paid the higher fare in full. Be sure to watch the newspaper ads and to call the airline to check for new, lower fares, since you have to request the refund to get it.

AIRPORT TRANSPORTATION: Frequent scheduled bus service is provided by AirportBus (714-938-8900 or 800-772-5299; *www.airportbus.com*). It not only goes to the Disneyland Resort hotels and the properties in Anaheim, but also Buena Park (seven miles away and the home of Knott's Berry Farm). The bus stops at each LAX airline terminal, outside the baggage claim area; look for the red BUS STOP signs on the center island and for the words DISNEYLAND/ANAHEIM displayed above the bus stop.

Those who fly into John Wayne Airport (named after one of Orange County's most famous residents), 16 miles from the Disneyland Resort, have an easier time of it. The ride into town takes half the time. From the baggage claim area, proceed to the AirportBus ticket booth across the street at the Ground Transportation Center and the designated AirportBus stop. Look for the AirportBus that has the words DISNEYLAND/ANAHEIM displayed above the windshield.

To Anaheim from the Airports

	AirportBus	SuperShuttle
Los Angeles International Airport	$14 ($25 round trip) per adult $9 ($16 round trip) per child 3–11	$13 per person
John Wayne Airport	$10 ($18 round trip) per adult $8 ($12 round trip) per child 3–11	$10 per person

Children under 3 ride free. Prices were accurate at press time, but are subject to change.

SuperShuttle (714-517-6600) also serves both airports. At Los Angeles International Airport, go to the curb outside the baggage-claim area to request pickup. A van should arrive within 15 minutes.

For passengers arriving at John Wayne Airport, in Orange County, SuperShuttle recommends 24-hour advance reservations; call 714-517-6600. Upon arrival, use a courtesy phone to request a pickup; the van should arrive outside the terminal within 15 minutes. To return to either airport, check with your hotel front desk the day before the departure for bus schedules and reservation information.

HOT TIP!

The SuperShuttle often carries a smaller group than the AirportBus. Expect it to make fewer stops before reaching your destination.

CAR RENTALS: Several major car rental agencies have locations at the airport, at many hotels, and elsewhere in Anaheim. Expect to pay around $200 a week for a midsize car, and $75 to $100 for a four-day weekend, with unlimited mileage included. Some rental companies to choose from are Avis (800-331-1212), Budget (800-527-0700), Dollar (800-800-4000), Hertz (800-654-3131), and National (800-227-7368).

It pays to call all the agencies to get the best available deal; be sure to ask about any special promotions or discounts (National offers discounts to Disney Club members). Collision damage waiver (CDW) insurance is essential for your protection in case of an accident, but it can add a hefty chunk to your bill (usually at least $9 a day). Most vacation packages that include a rental car do not include the CDW; if you choose not to take it, the agency may require a large deposit.

On a brighter note, an increasing number of credit-card companies offer free collision damage coverage simply for charging the rental to their card, and some may even provide primary coverage. That means your credit-card company may deal with the rental company directly in the event of an accident, rather than compensate you after your personal insurance has kicked in. It's worth a phone call to find out.

If you're renting a car at Los Angeles International Airport, the drive to the Disneyland Resort is only 31 miles, but it will take about 45 minutes with no traffic, or up to two hours if the roads are congested.

From John Wayne Airport, take I-405 north to Highway 55 north to I-5 north, exit at Katella, follow it to Harbor, and turn right. The drive takes about 25 minutes.

By Train

Amtrak (800-872-7245) and Metrolink (commuter service to and from Los Angeles; 213-808-5465) trains stop at Anaheim Station, only a mile from the Disneyland Resort. Taxis are available from the station.

Union Station in Los Angeles is served by a number of trains from the rest of the state, as well as the Northwest, the South, and the Midwest. To get to Anaheim from L.A., you can take Amtrak's *Pacific Surfliner* or rent a car. The major car rental agencies have phones at Union Station by which to arrange rental.

Amtrak also offers economical vacation packages to the Disneyland Resort. They feature transportation to Anaheim via the *Pacific Surfliner* and a one-day or multi-day Disney ticket. Call 800-872-7245 for details.

By Bus

Buses make sense if you're traveling a fairly short distance, if you have plenty of time to spend in transit, if there are only two or three people in your party, or if cost is a major consideration.

Direct buses make the trip from Los Angeles and San Diego, though they usually make a few stops along the way. Travel from most other destinations usually requires a change of vehicles in Los Angeles. The Greyhound terminal is located at 100 West Winston Road in Anaheim, about one mile north of the Disneyland Resort; 714-999-1256.

Car rental is not available, but taxis can transport you from the bus terminal to the Disneyland Resort or to any area accommodations. You can also walk if you don't mind the distance and have few bags to carry.

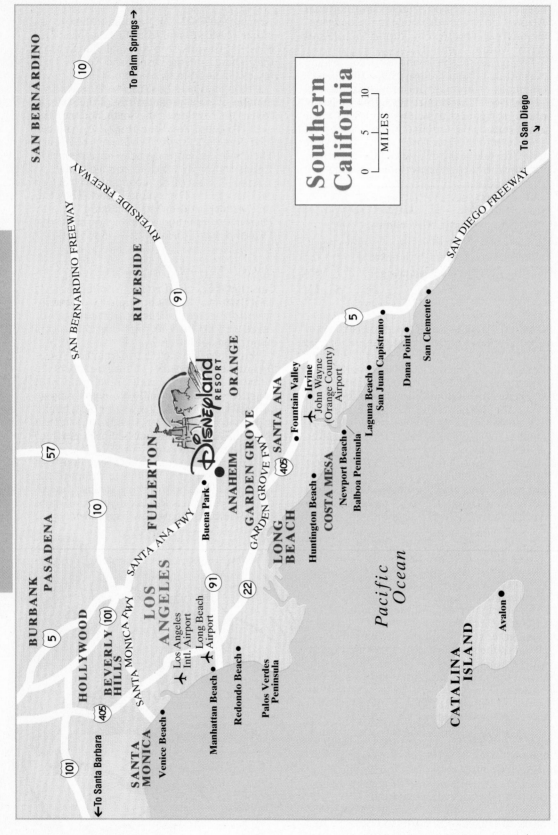

Southern California

0   5   10
MILES

To Palm Springs →

SAN BERNARDINO

RIVERSIDE

SAN BERNARDINO FREEWAY

RIVERSIDE FREEWAY

To San Diego ↗

SAN DIEGO FREEWAY

10

91

5

San Clemente

Dana Point

San Juan Capistrano

Laguna Beach

ORANGE

SANTA ANA

Irvine
John Wayne
(Orange County)
Airport

Fountain Valley

Balboa Peninsula

Newport Beach

COSTA MESA

Huntington Beach

Disneyland RESORT

FULLERTON

ANAHEIM

GARDEN GROVE

Garden Grove Fwy

LONG
BEACH

405

22

91

57

10

5

SANTA ANA FWY

BUENA PARK

Buena Park

Pacific
Ocean

CATALINA
ISLAND

Avalon

Palos Verdes
Peninsula

Redondo Beach

Manhattan Beach

Long Beach
Airport

Los Angeles
Intl. Airport

Venice Beach

SANTA MONICA FWY

LOS
ANGELES

HOLLYWOOD

BEVERLY
HILLS

BURBANK

PASADENA

SANTA
MONICA

101

101

405

To Santa Barbara ←

GETTING ORIENTED

Southern California's patchwork of small communities has undeniably blurred borders. The Disneyland Resort is in Anaheim, but you might not know if you were in that city or one of its immediate neighbors except for the signs. Buena Park lies to the northwest, Garden Grove to the southwest, Santa Ana to the southeast, and Orange to the east.

Farther south—in Huntington Beach, Newport Beach, Laguna Beach, and San Juan Capistrano—there's a bit more breathing room between communities. Heading northwest from Anaheim, you'll come to Los Angeles International Airport.

Proceeding north through Los Angeles, you'll pass Beverly Hills, Hollywood and West Hollywood (an independent municipality), Santa Monica (its own municipality as well), Malibu, Glendale, and Burbank, home of Walt Disney Studios. The San Fernando Valley lies farther north and a bit inland from L.A., while Santa Barbara, Southern California's northern boundary, is on the coast, about two hours to the north.

North–South Freeways: There are two. I-5 (the Santa Ana Freeway) runs from Vancouver, Canada, to San Diego, and is the principal inland route in Southern California, linking Los Angeles and San Diego. I-405 (the San Diego Freeway) sprouts from I-5 near Hollywood, veers toward the coast, then rejoins I-5 at Irvine, south of Anaheim.

East–West Freeways: Of the roads that intersect the two principal north–south arteries, one of the closest to Disneyland is Route 22, also known as the Garden Grove Freeway; it begins near the ocean in Long Beach and runs across the southern border of Anaheim. Route 91, called the Artesia Freeway on the west side of I-5 and the Riverside Freeway on the east, lies about eight miles north of Route 22.

The next east–west route as you travel north is I-10, called the Santa Monica Freeway from its beginning near the Pacific shore in Santa Monica to just east of downtown Los Angeles. At this point, it jogs north and then turns east again, becoming the San Bernardino Freeway. I-10 is located about 12 miles north of Route 91.

North of I-10 (anywhere from two to eight miles, depending on your location) is U.S. 101, which heads south from Ventura and then due east across I-405. West of I-405, it is known as the Ventura Freeway; at a point a few miles beyond the intersection with I-405, it angles south, becomes the Hollywood Freeway, and eventually crosses I-5.

HOW TO GET THERE: The Disneyland Resort is on Harbor Boulevard between Katella Avenue and Ball Road, 31 miles south of downtown Los Angeles and 87 miles north of San Diego. Many visitors drive to the resort from elsewhere in Southern California, while those who come from farther away fly into one of the area airports, rent a car, and drive from there. Once at their hotel, guests may prefer to use the hotel's shuttle for transportation to and from Disney.

Southbound I-5 Exit: To get to Disneyland, southbound I-5 (the Santa Ana Freeway) travelers should exit at Disneyland Drive, pass through Ball Road, and proceed to the theme park parking entrance.

Northbound I-5 Exit: Northbound travelers should exit I-5 at Katella Avenue, pass through Katella Avenue, proceed straight to Disney Way, and then follow signs to the theme park parking entrance, which will be on the left.

Travel Times

To/from the Resort	Approx. Distance	Drive Time
Balboa	30 miles	40 min.
Buena Park	7 miles	12 min.
Carlsbad	50 miles	60 min.
Costa Mesa	20 miles	30 min.
Dana Point	30 miles	40 min.
Garden Grove	5 miles	10 min.
Huntington Beach	15 miles	25 min.
John Wayne Airport	16 miles	25 min.
Laguna Beach	30 miles	45 min.
Las Vegas	280 miles	4–5 hrs.
Long Beach	20 miles	30 min.
Los Angeles (downtown and airport)	31 miles	45–60 min.
Newport Beach	20 miles	30 min.
Palm Springs	180 miles	2–3 hrs.
San Diego	87 miles	90 min.
San Juan Capistrano	32 miles	45 min.
San Simeon	270 miles	5–6 hrs.
Santa Ana	5 miles	10 min.
Santa Barbara	110 miles	2 hrs.

Drive times are under optimal conditions; rain or rush-hour traffic could increase—or even double—the time.

From John Wayne/Orange County Airport: San Diego Freeway (I-405) north to Newport Freeway (Route 55) north to Santa Ana Freeway (I-5) north. Take Katella Avenue exit, drive to Harbor Boulevard, and turn right into the parking structure.

From Los Angeles International Airport: San Diego Freeway (I-405) south, then Garden Grove Freeway (Route 22) east. Take Harbor Boulevard exit and go north about three miles to the Disneyland Resort.

Exit off Orange Freeway: Travelers on the Orange Freeway (Hwy. 57) should exit on Katella Avenue and proceed west to Harbor Boulevard, turn right on Harbor, and continue north about a quarter mile to the parking entrance on the left.

Note: When traffic is heavy, Harbor Boulevard and Ball Road and the freeways leading to them often get backed up. In this case, take the Katella Avenue exit off I-5. It'll put you a bit farther from the park, and may mean a slight detour for southbound drivers, but it allows easy access to the Disneyland Drive entrance, which is open on peak days.

For traffic updates, call the Disneyland Travel Advisory Hotline at 714-781-4400 or Caltrans at 714-724-2077 or 800-427-7623.

ANAHEIM-AREA SURFACE STREETS: The Disneyland Resort is in the center of Anaheim, bounded by Harbor Boulevard on the east, Disneyland Drive (a segment of West Street) on the west, Ball Road on the north, and Katella Avenue on the south (see maps on pages 42 and 132). Many of the city's hotels are located on these streets.

Ball Road near Harbor Boulevard is the most convenient place to pick up I-5 (Santa Ana Freeway) going north to Los Angeles. Katella Avenue between Harbor Boulevard and State College Boulevard is the most convenient entrance to southbound I-5 and to Newport Beach and points south.

Note: Be sure to park in a parking lot or feed the meter frequently. Fines run as high as $30 in Orange County.

LOCAL TRANSPORTATION: The Orange County Transportation Authority (OCTA; 714-636-7433) provides daily bus service throughout the area, with limited weekend service. Several lines stop at the Disneyland Resort, but keep in mind that public transportation can involve considerable waiting and transferring. Fares are $1 for a one-way fare or $2.50 for a one-day unlimited pass. Seniors 65 and older and people with disabilities pay 25 cents one-way or 50 cents for a one-day pass. Exact change is required.

HOT TIP!

Guests getting picked up or dropped off by car should arrange to meet their ride in the Disneyland Resort's short-term parking area. It's by the main entrance on Harbor Boulevard.

If you have wanderlust but lack wheels, your best bet is to sign up for a bus tour, such as one of those offered by Pacific Coast Sightseeing/Gray Line of Anaheim (714-978-8855). Hotel and motel desks can provide information on tour schedules and prices, sell you the tickets, and even arrange to have the sightseeing company come and pick you up at the hotel.

The Metropolitan Transportation Authority (MTA) serves Los Angeles County and the major attractions of Orange County (213-626-4455). Exact change is required.

TAXIS: The only licensed taxi company approved to serve the Disneyland Resort is Yellow Cab of North Orange County (714-535-2211). Cab fare to John Wayne Airport from the Disneyland Hotel runs about $33 with tip; from LAX, figure on $75 with tip. Prices for town cars are slightly higher. Taxis can be called to pick you up at the train and bus stations.

For those lucky enough to live in the Los Angeles/Orange County area, the Disneyland Resort offers the opportunity to return frequently. And over the past few years, Disney has given locals more incentive to do just that. With a second theme park and a shopping, dining, and dancing district, the "things to do" list at Disney has tripled in length since the turn of the millennium. Seasoned visitors and first-timers alike will do well to plan each step of their visit far in advance—make the travel arrangements as soon as vacation dates are set (refer to the "Trip Planning Time Line" below to make sure you don't miss any crucial steps), and then study the following chapters of this book to decide how you'd like to spend each day of the trip.

How many days should you spend with the Mouse? Well, that's up to you, but to experience the Disneyland Resort at its best, we recommend a stay of about four full days—you'll have enough time to see every attraction, parade, and show (plus revisit all of your favorites), lounge by your hotel's pool, enjoy a character meal, shop for souvenirs, and dance the night away. If you'd like to visit other area attractions, like Sea World, Universal Studios, or Hollywood, add on one day for each excursion. But don't try to cram too much into one visit; this is a *vacation* after all.

Once you've decided how many days you're going to dedicate to Disney, it's time to decide how you'll split up your time on-property. We suggest that you begin with a day at Disneyland Park (for the original and quintessential Disney experience), followed by a visit to Disney's California Adventure (to sample the rides and shows). On the third day return to Disneyland and hit the park's highlights, plus any attractions you missed on the first day, and save time for souvenir shopping. Day four should be dedicated to your preferred park and some downtime by the pool or in Downtown Disney's shopping plaza. Evenings can be spent in the park, if it's open late, or in Downtown Disney's clubs, lounges, and movie theaters. The options are plentiful.

On the next three pages, we've provided full-day schedules to guide you through four days in the theme parks (with special tips for families with young children and priorities for days when the lines are at their longest). The schedules are meant to be flexible and fun (not Disney boot camp) so take them at your own pace and plan breaks to relax: have a Mickey Mouse Ice Cream Bar, browse through the shops, feed the ducks, or just pick a bench and watch the crowds rush by.

Trip Planning Time Line

First Things First

- Make hotel and transportation reservations as far ahead as possible. Call 714-956-6425 to book a room at a Disney hotel (see page 38 for details); remember that a deposit must be paid within 21 days of the reservation. Log all confirmation numbers in the Trip Planner at the beginning of this book.
- Decide where you will be on each day of your vacation, and create a simple day-by-day schedule.

6 Months

- Unless you opted for a vacation package that includes theme park admission, it's time to purchase Disney tickets (see page 18 for ticket options and ordering methods). Your tickets should arrive in about a week.

3 Months

- Find out park hours, the attraction refurbishment schedule, and details on any special events that may be happening during your stay, by calling 714-781-4565 or by visiting *www.disneyland.com*; add this information to your day-by-day schedule.

1 Month

- Make dining reservations (they're only necessary at certain Disney restaurants), and add the information to your day-by-day schedule. Refer to the *Good Meals, Great Times* chapter for details on Disneyland Resort and Orange County dining options.

2 Weeks

- Airline tickets and travel vouchers should have arrived in the mail by now. Contact your travel agent or the travel company if they have not.

1 Week

- Reconfirm all reservations and finalize your day-by-day schedule.
- Add all your important telephone numbers (doctor, family members, house sitter) to the Trip Planner, and be sure to bring the Trip Planner and your day-by-day schedule with you!

Disneyland Park*
One-Day Schedule

- Disneyland's breakfast options are limited, so grab a bite to eat before entering the park.

- Take in the sights as you walk down Main Street, but don't stop to shop or snack now (you'll have time for that later). Instead, head straight to Adventureland's Indiana Jones[†], Jungle Cruise, Tarzan's Treehouse, and Enchanted Tiki Room, before making your way to Splash Mountain[†] and Country Bear Playhouse in Critter Country. **Note:** If you plan to dine at the Blue Bayou, be sure to stop at the restaurant first thing in the morning to make a reservation.

- Backtrack to New Orleans Square and visit the Haunted Mansion[†] and Pirates of the Caribbean[†] before breaking for an early lunch at a nearby eatery.

- Next, see the show at the Golden Horseshoe, take a relaxing river cruise on the *Mark Twain,* or raft over to Tom Sawyer Island before tackling Big Thunder Mountain[†] in Frontierland.

- Walk through the Castle into Fantasyland and visit Snow White, Pinocchio, Peter Pan, and Mr. Toad. Then see Alice, the Mad Tea Party, the Matterhorn, and It's a Small World.

IF YOU HAVE YOUNG CHILDREN

First, ride Dumbo, and then visit each Fantasyland attraction (note that some may be scary for small children) before heading to Animazement on the way to Mickey's Toontown.

Scope out a spot on a Main Street curb at least 30 minutes before the parade.

Cool off at *Donald's Boat* in Toontown or Cosmic Waves, in Tomorrowland.

Ride the Jungle Cruise, then see the Tiki Birds in Adventureland and the Country Bears in Critter Country before returning to your favorite rides.

LINE BUSTERS

When the park is packed, head to: the Disneyland Railroad, Enchanted Tiki Room, Pirates of the Caribbean, Haunted Mansion, Country Bear Playhouse, and The Walt Disney Story.

- Keep an eye on the time and try to fit a showing of Animazement and the afternoon parade into your schedule.

- Make your way to Mickey's Toontown and see as many of this land's attractions as you can, making Roger Rabbit's Car Toon Spin[†] a priority.

- Hop on the Disneyland Railroad and disembark in Tomorrowland (or Main Street) and head for dinner. **Note:** If the park is open late, board the monorail in Tomorrowland and dine in Downtown Disney before returning to the park.

- After dinner, catch a screening of Honey, I Shrunk the Audience, before riding Autopia[†], Space Mountain[†], Star Tours[†], or Astro Orbitor.

- Stroll back to Main Street. Shop, stop for dessert, see the Walt Disney Story, and watch the fireworks burst over the castle; or hustle over to Frontierland and catch Fantasmic!

- If there's time, take a second spin on your favorite attractions.

*Also known as the Magic Kingdom

[†]Fastpass is available for this ride. Retrieve your time-saving Fastpass before visiting the land's remaining attractions. To learn how the system works, see page 60.

Disneyland Delights

Short on time? These attractions form the quintessential Disneyland experience:

Indiana Jones Adventure • Pirates of the Caribbean
Haunted Mansion • Big Thunder Mountain Railroad
Splash Mountain • Peter Pan's Flight • Matterhorn Bobsleds
Roger Rabbit's Car Toon Spin • Star Tours
Honey, I Shrunk the Audience • Space Mountain

HOT TIP!

If you enter the park via monorail, you'll begin your tour in Tomorrowland. Hit the land's major attractions if you wish, and then ride the railroad to Main Street and follow this schedule from there.

Disney's California Adventure One-Day Schedule

- Begin your California adventure with a high-flying ride on Soarin' Over California[†]. Catch your breath and continue the lesson in aviation by navigating your way through the airfield's exhibits on history-making pilots and planes.

- Depart from Condor Flats and head into the Hollywood Pictures Backlot, via the Gateway Plaza. Refer to a park guidemap for the Hyperion Theater's[†] next showtime, and plan to arrive at the theater at least 30 minutes before the show. In the meantime, enjoy the in-your-face fun of Muppet*Vision 3-D[†] and Disney Animation.

- Break for lunch at one of Hollywood's entertaining eateries—the full-service ABC Soap Opera Bistro or the cafeteria-style Hollywood & Dine.

- Head to the Bountiful Valley Farm and don your bug eyes for a creepy-crawly screening of It's Tough to Be a Bug![†]

- Now it's time for a little mountain climbing: Make your way over to Grizzly Peak, and get set to get wet on the drenching Grizzly River Run[†] white water raft ride. If you're up for it (and properly shoed), next take the Redwood Creek Challenge Trail before viewing Golden Dreams.

- Keep an eye on the time and find a curbside spot in the San Francisco district about 20 minutes before the parade starts.

- Pick up some wine-pairing tips or sample Mondavi's finest at the Golden Vine Winery, and then settle in for an early dinner.

- Tour the micro-factories of the Pacific Wharf before proceeding on to Paradise Pier's daredevil rides.

- Work your way around the Paradise Pier Lagoon, stopping for each attraction, but making California Screamin'[†] and the Sun Wheel[†] your top priorities.

- Stroll along the boardwalk and try some Midway games, or enjoy a sweet treat, if you need to take a break from the action. Or head toward Hollywood and end the evening with Disney's Electrical Parade or the show at the Hyperion Theater, if you missed it earlier.

[†]Fastpass is available for this attraction. Retrieve your time-saving Fastpass before visiting the area's remaining attractions. To learn how the system works, see page 60.

IF YOU HAVE YOUNG CHILDREN

Compared to its sister park next door, California Adventure has considerably fewer attractions geared toward the five-and-under set.

Head straight to the Muppets. Next, maneuver young water-lovers through the sprinkler maze and gardens of the Bountiful Valley Farm. Note that It's Tough to Be a Bug! features a few familiar characters from the film *A Bug's Life*, but often frightens young children.

Try the kid-friendly obstacle course on the Redwood Creek Challenge Trail (save time for some campside story-telling).

Take a spin on the carousel and visit the *SS Rustworthy*, a water-spouting boat and play area before spending some time at the Paradise Pier Midway.

LINE BUSTERS

When lines abound at Disney's California Adventure, we suggest the following: the Golden State's micro-factories, Bountiful Valley Farm, Redwood Creek Challenge Trail, King Triton's Carousel, the *SS Rustworthy*, and Paradise Pier's Midway.

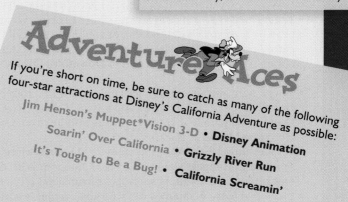

Adventure Aces

If you're short on time, be sure to catch as many of the following four-star attractions at Disney's California Adventure as possible:

Jim Henson's Muppet*Vision 3-D • **Disney Animation**

Soarin' Over California • **Grizzly River Run**

It's Tough to Be a Bug! • **California Screamin'**

A Second Day In Each Park

Returning for a second or third day in each of the theme parks means more time to savor the atmosphere, try any attractions you missed the first day, and revisit all the old and new favorites. Knowing that there will be a second day also makes for a much less harried pace on day one. Longer stays also allow time for full-day excursions to attractions like Universal Studios or Knott's Berry Farm (see *Orange County & Beyond* for some day-trip options).

DAY TWO IN DISNEYLAND PARK

- Start the morning with a character breakfast at the Plaza Inn (you can also share a morning meal with the characters outside the park at Goofy's Kitchen in the Disneyland Hotel, the Grand Californian's Storyteller's Cafe, or PCH Grill in Disney's Paradise Pier Hotel).
- Head to Tomorrowland and ride Space Mountain, Star Tours, and other favorite attractions.
- Hop on the train to Mickey's Toontown and see the sights before grabbing a seat for the next performance of Animazement.
- Visit It's a Small World and the nearby character greeting area, and then tour Fantasyland.
- Stroll, shop, and stop for lunch in Main Street, U.S.A. Have purchases sent to Package Express to be picked up as you exit the park.
- Watch the afternoon parade from the Main Street Railroad depot, or secure a curbside spot.
- Ride a Main Street Vehicle up to Town Square and then continue on foot toward Adventureland.
- Stop at Indiana Jones and the Jungle Cruise before heading on to New Orleans Square. Here the priorities are the Haunted Mansion and Pirates of the Caribbean. Visit them and move on to Splash Mountain or Country Bear Playhouse, in Critter County.
- Meander through the shops of New Orleans Square and then stop for a leisurely dinner at a nearby eatery. Riverbelle Terrace, the French Market, Cafe Orleans, and the full-service Blue Bayou are all excellent options.
- Select a spot lagoonside about 45 minutes ahead for the evening's performance of Fantasmic!
- Wait for the crowds to disperse at show's end, and make your way to Big Thunder Mountain for one last ride before the park closes.

DAY TWO IN DISNEY'S CALIFORNIA ADVENTURE

- Grab a quick breakfast before arriving at the park, so that your stomach will have time to settle before the big rides.
- Cut through the Golden State and head straight to Paradise Pier.
- Thrill-seekers will flip for California Screamin' and the Sun Wheel while King Triton's Carousel and Jumpin' Jellyfish offer less dizzying alternatives.
- Take a lunch break at Burger Invasion or Pacific Wharf Cafe; or, if the park is open late, head back to your hotel to relax or splash in the pool (remember to get your hand stamped before exiting, so that you can return to California Adventure later in the day). Another option is to spend the afternoon in Downtown Disney—the restaurants and shops will all be open by noon.
- Your California adventure picks up again with a tour of the Golden State, including Golden Dreams, It's Tough to Be a Bug!, Grizzly River Run, and Soarin' Over California.
- Stop for the parade if you haven't seen it already, and then make your way toward Hollywood Pictures Backlot.
- Wander through the Backlot, enjoying the impromptu entertainment, and catch the next showing of Muppet*Vision 3-D. Have dinner at ABC Soap Opera Bistro or one of the other star-studded dining spots (we recommend Hollywood & Dine).
- Line up at least 30 minutes early for the evening's performance at the Hyperion Theater.
- If time permits after the show, revisit some of your favorite attractions or search for last-minute souvenirs at the large shops in the park's Entry Plaza.

FINGERTIP REFERENCE GUIDE

BARBERS AND SALONS

Hair may be cut or coiffed at the Coral Tree, in the Anaheim Marriott (700 W. Convention Way; 714-750-6573). Besides haircutting and styling, the salon offers manicures and pedicures, and welcomes both men and women.

CAR CARE

AAA and the Auto Club of Southern California (ACSC) offer the following services free to all Disneyland Resort guests (not just to Auto Club members): assistance with stalled cars and flat tires, and towing up to three miles. Jump starts and lock-out services are provided by Disneyland. For assistance, contact any cast member. The Anaheim office of the ACSC is located at 150 West Vermont Avenue; 714-774-2392. For ACSC emergency roadside service, call 800-400-4222.

The Touring & Travel Services Center (operated by ACSC), located inside Disneyland Park adjacent to City Hall on Main Street, U.S.A., provides many services to guests, including the sale of annual AAA memberships.

DRINKING POLICIES

While there's a strict no-alcohol policy at Disneyland Park, drinking is an option at many of the dining spots in its sister park, Disney's California Adventure, as well as at Downtown Disney. Alcohol may also be purchased at the lounges and restaurants of the three Disney hotels. The legal drinking age in California is 21.

LOCKERS

Lockers of various sizes are available just outside the main entrance of the parks; inside Disneyland at the Lost and Found on Main Street (behind the Market House) and beside the Fantasyland Theatre; and inside Disney's California Adventure across from Guest Relations in the Entry Plaza. Prices are $3, $4, $5, or $6 per day, depending on the locker's size. The easy access of these storage facilities makes it convenient to intersperse frolicking on the attractions with shopping; just make your purchases, stash them in a locker, and go back to playing.

Locker availability is limited, and during busy periods all the space can be taken well before noon.

Not to worry: You can also take advantage of Package Express by having the theme park shops send your purchases to the pickup window outside the park entrance, or back to your hotel if you are staying on-property. Allow two hours for packages to arrive.

LOST AND FOUND

At any given time, a survey of the shelves of Lost and Found might turn up cameras, umbrellas, strollers, handbags, lens caps, sunglasses, radios, jewelry, and even a few crutches, false teeth, and hubcaps. Once, a wallet containing $1,700 in cash was turned in. The Disneyland Resort will return lost items to guests who fill out a report, at no cost to the guest.

If you find a lost item, you'll be asked to fill out a card with your name and address; if the object isn't claimed within 60 days, you have the option of keeping it. This system has a way of encouraging honesty, so if you lose something, don't fail to check at the Lost and Found office, located on Main Street behind the Market House in Disneyland, and in the Guest Relations building in Disney's California Adventure.

MAIL

Postcards are sold in gift shops all over Anaheim, in many shops and souvenir stands on Disney property, and at the three Disney hotels. Stamps are sold in the theme parks and hotels.

Cards and letters that are deposited in the small olive mailboxes positioned throughout the theme parks are picked up and delivered to the U.S. Post Office once a day, early in the morning. They are postmarked Anaheim, not Disneyland. (By the way, don't forget to arrange for your own mail to be held by the post office or picked up by a neighbor while you're on vacation.)

Post Office: The U.S. Post Office closest to the Disneyland Resort is Holiday Station, about a half mile from the parks (1180 W. Ball Rd.; Anaheim; 800-275-8777). It's open from 8:30 A.M. to 5 P.M. weekdays only.

MEDICAL MATTERS

Blisters are the most common complaint received by Disney's First Aid departments, located at the north end of Main Street adjacent to Lost Children in Disneyland, and by Mission Tortilla Factory in the Pacific Wharf area of Disney's California Adventure. So be forewarned and wear comfortable, broken-in shoes.

If you have a more serious medical problem while on-property, contact any Disney cast member. He or she will get in touch with First Aid to make further arrangements. First Aid, staffed by registered nurses, will store breathing machines and crutches for guests. It will not dispense medication to anyone under 18 without the consent of a parent or chaperone.

It's always a good idea to carry an insurance card and any other pertinent medical information. Those with chronic health problems should carry copies of all their prescriptions, along with their doctor's telephone number.

Prescriptions: The pharmacy at Sav-on Drugs, about a mile from Disney, is open 9 A.M. to 10 P.M. daily (1660 W. Katella Ave., at Euclid; Anaheim; 714-530-0500). Another Sav-on, three miles away, is open 24 hours daily (12031 Brookhurst St., at Chapman, Garden Grove; 714-530-5280).

Refrigerator Facilities: In the parks, insulin and antibiotics that must be refrigerated can be stored for the day at First Aid. (It does *not* store breast milk for nursing mothers, however.) Outside the parks, there are refrigerators in many of the area's hotels and motels. If your room doesn't have one, a fridge can usually be supplied at a nominal charge. Or the hotel or motel can store insulin in its own refrigerator. Inquire in advance.

MONEY

Cash, traveler's checks, personal checks, Disney Dollars, American Express, Visa, MasterCard, the Disney Credit Card, and the Discover Card are accepted as payment for admission to the theme parks, for merchandise purchased in shops, and for meals (except at food carts, where only cash is accepted). Checks must be imprinted with the guest's name and address, drawn on a U.S. bank, and accompanied by proper identification—that is, a valid driver's license and a major credit card. Department store charge cards are not acceptable identification for check-writing purposes. Disney hotel guests who have left a credit card number at check-in can charge most expenses in the theme parks to their hotel bill.

Disney Dollars: Accepted as cash throughout the parks, Disney Dollars are the equivalent in value of U.S. dollars. They are sold at the main entrances of the parks, as well as at City Hall in Disneyland, at select shops on-property, and at most Disney Stores nationwide. Kids love to use them; they also make good inexpensive gifts and souvenirs, and are accepted as cash at any Disney Store.

Financial Services: ATMs are located at each park's main entrance; in Disneyland at the Bank of Main Street, by the Fantasyland Theatre, in the Frontierland Stockade, and in the Starcade; in California Adventure at the Entry Plaza, by the Bay Area near Golden Dreams, beside Cocina Cucamonga, near Burger Invasion, and by Malibu-ritos; in Downtown Disney by Häagen-Dazs; and in all three Disneyland Resort hotels.

It's possible to cash a personal check made out to Disneyland for up to $100 at the main entrance to each park and at the Bank of Main Street; proper identification is required. The ATMs at the main entrance accept credit cards for cash advances.

AAA Services: The Touring & Travel Services Center, beside City Hall on Main Street, U.S.A. in Disneyland, provides many services to guests, including the sales of AAA memberships and traveler's checks, and help with

GETTING READY TO GO

booking rooms at Disneyland Resort hotels or Good Neighbor hotels (about 30 area hotels with which the Walt Disney Travel Company works closely).

American Express Cardmember Services: American Express cardholders can cash personal checks up to $1,000 per week ($200 in cash and the rest in traveler's checks) with a personal American Express card, or up to $2,500 per week ($500 in cash and the rest in traveler's checks) with a Gold Card. They can also get a cash advance of $1,000 on their Optima Card. All services are offered at the American Express Travel Agency, located in the MainPlace Mall (2800 N. Main St., Suite 600; Santa Ana; 714-541-3318).

This office can also exchange foreign currency (for a $3 fee, regardless of the amount) and replace lost cards or traveler's checks within 24 hours (for cards, 800-528-4800; for checks, 800-221-7282). Hours are 10 A.M. to 7 P.M. Monday through Saturday and 11 A.M. to 6 P.M. Sunday.

Banks in the area also sell American Express traveler's checks, usually for a one percent fee.

Other Major Credit Cards and Traveler's Checks: Cash advances on Visa credit cards can be arranged through the Western Union office, open from 9 A.M. to 5 P.M. Monday through Saturday (616 N. Anaheim Blvd.; Anaheim; 714-535-2291). To report lost Visa or MasterCard credit cards, guests in the Anaheim area should call 800-556-5678.

Most foreign currencies can be exchanged (for a fee) at the Thomas Cook office in the Disneyland Hotel; 714-502-0811.

PETS

Except for service animals, pets are not allowed in Disneyland or Disney's California Adventure. However, any nonpoisonous creatures can be boarded in the air-conditioned Disneyland Pet Care Kennel, which is located near Disney's main parking structure. Reservations are not necessary (the kennel rarely reaches capacity). Pets may be boarded for the day or for overnight stays. To inquire about kennel rates during your visit, call 714-781-4565.

Disney personnel do not handle the animals, so the pet owners themselves must put their animals into the cages and take them out again. Guests are encouraged to drop by to visit with and walk their pets several times a day.

Note: In busy seasons there may be a morning rush, starting about 30 minutes before the parks open, so you may encounter some delay in arranging your pet's stay.

Outside the Disneyland Resort: If you plan to stay at a Disneyland Resort hotel and want to board your pet nearby, contact

Animal Inns of America, 10852 Garden Grove Blvd.; Garden Grove; 714-636-4455; *www.thepetproject.com/animalinns.html.*

Some hotels and motels in the area accept well-behaved (preferably small) pets, but most of them do not allow guests to leave pets in the room unattended. The pet-friendly Anaheim Marriott (714-750-8000), within walking distance of the Disneyland Resort, is an exception.

To find out about other possibilities, contact the Anaheim/Orange County Visitor & Convention Bureau; 714-765-8888.

PHOTOGRAPHIC NEEDS

The Main Street Photo Supply Co. in Disneyland can do minor repairs and recharge most batteries (or you can bring your own charger and plug it in there). Disney's California Adventure offers similar services. For anything more serious, rent a camera (see below) and have a factory-authorized shop do the work on your own camera when you return home. If you've lost your lens cover, it's worth checking at Lost and Found; they may not have yours, but they often have extras.

Same-day film processing is available through Spectrum Photo Film Processing at select shops on-property. Allow two to three hours before picking up the prints.

A small store in the landscaped shopping area that fronts the Ramada Maingate Saga Inn, across the street from the Disneyland Resort, rents cameras for $10 a day and camcorders for less than $25 a day (about $17 per day for a multiple-day rental), with a cash or credit-card deposit. It also sells film, photo albums, and camera supplies, and offers one-hour photo processing; 1650-A Harbor Blvd.; 714-772-2250.

For a greater selection of film and camera equipment, go to Main Photo, 6916 Katella Ave.; 714-894-2526.

RELIGIOUS SERVICES

A number of religious services are held in the area surrounding the Disneyland Resort.

Baptist: The Garden Church; 8712 E. Santa Ana Canyon Rd.; 714-282-1899. Services, held on Sunday at 10 A.M., take place outdoors April through October. Sunday school and Bible study are at 9 A.M.

Catholic: St. Justin Martyr; 2050 W. Ball Rd.; 714-774-2595; about two miles from the Disneyland Resort. Weekday masses are at 6:30 A.M. and 8:30 A.M.; Saturday at 8:30 A.M. and 5:30 P.M. (English) and 7 P.M. (Spanish); and Sunday at 6:45 A.M., 8 A.M., 11 A.M., 12:30 P.M. and 5:30 P.M. (English) and 9:30 A.M. and 7 P.M. (Spanish). Holy day masses are at 6:30 A.M., 8:30 A.M., and 7 P.M.; holy day eve, 5:30 P.M. (English) and 7 P.M. (Spanish).

Episcopal: St. Michael's Episcopal Church; 311 W. South St.; 714-535-4654; about seven blocks from the Disneyland Resort. Sunday services are at 7:30 A.M. and 10 A.M. (English) and at 8:30 A.M. and noon (Spanish). Bible study is at 8:30 A.M.; Sunday school, at 10 A.M.

Jewish: Temple Beth Emet; 1770 W. Cerritos Ave.; 714-772-4720; less than a mile from the Disneyland Resort. Services are at 8:45 A.M. Mondays and Thursdays, 8 P.M. Friday, and 9 A.M. Saturday.

Lutheran: Prince of Peace Church; 1421 W. Ball Rd.; 714-774-0993; one mile from the Disneyland Resort. Sunday services are at 8 A.M. and 10:45 A.M. (traditional) and 9:15 A.M. (contemporary).

United Methodist: West Anaheim United Methodist Church; 2045 W. Ball Rd.; 714-772-6030; about two miles from the Disneyland Resort. Sunday services are at 10:30 A.M.; child care is provided during the service.

SHOPPING FOR NECESSITIES

It's a rare vacationer who doesn't leave some essential at home or run out of it midtrip. Gift shops in almost all the hotels stock items no traveler should be without, but they usually cost more than in conventional retail shops. One good source is Sav-on Drugs, about a mile from the Disneyland Resort; 1660 W. Katella Ave.; 714-530-0500.

Inside the theme parks, aspirin, bandages, antacids, suntan lotions, and other sundries are sold at a variety of shops; just ask a cast member to direct you to the closest one. Some items are also available at each park's First Aid location and Baby Care Center. A shop at each Disney hotel also offers a wide selection of sundries.

SMOKING POLICIES

State law bans smoking anywhere inside restaurants, bars, and cocktail lounges, but most establishments provide patios for puffing and often heat them on chilly evenings. At the Disney theme parks, smoking is permitted in designated smoking areas. Check a park guidemap for exact locations.

TELEPHONES

Local calls from most pay phones in Southern California cost 35 cents. Most hotels in the same area charge 75 cents or more for local, toll-free, and credit-card calls made from your room. So try to use a public pay phone whenever possible (it's worth making a trip to the lobby to do so).

For long-distance calls, policies vary from hotel to hotel, but charges are always higher than they would be for direct-dial calls made from a pay phone. It makes the most sense to use a calling card when dialing long distance.

Phone Cards: Disney offers AT&T pre-paid phone cards in values of $10 and $20. They can be purchased from machines in Disneyland and Disney's California Adventure, and at the Disneyland and Grand Californian hotels.

Weather Hotlines: Storm clouds have you worried? For Orange County weather, call 714-550-4636. The National Weather Service, which is based in Los Angeles, can provide Southern California forecasts; 213-554-1212.

TIPPING

The standard gratuities around Anaheim are about the same as in any other city of its size. Expect to tip bellhops about $1 per bag. Generally tip cabdrivers 15 percent; outstanding shuttle or tour bus drivers, $1. Valets usually get $1—when you pick up the car, not when you drop it off. In restaurants, a 15 to 20 percent gratuity is the norm.

Accommodations

The welcome sign is always out at the Disneyland Resort hotels, where themed meals, amenities, and decor are definitely in character and add to the fun of a Disneyland vacation. And the resort's newest hotel, the Grand Californian, takes staying in Disney-style to a whole new level of luxury and sophistication.

In addition to the three hotels located within the Disneyland Resort, there are about three dozen properties in Orange County, known as Disneyland Good Neighbor hotels, that the Walt Disney Travel Company has hand-picked to round out their Disney lodging options. We've selected 14 of these recommended hotels, based on services and proximity to the Disneyland Resort, to highlight in this chapter.

If the sole purpose of your trip is to visit Disney, plan to stay in Anaheim, either on Disneyland Resort property or at one of the surrounding hotels. Once you arrive and check in, you won't need your car again until you leave. Free transportation to and from the parks is provided by monorails, trams, and double-decker buses serving the Disneyland Resort, and by buses serving neighboring hotels, motels, and inns.

We've provided a variety of options in Anaheim, from old-fashioned to contemporary, simple to sublime. We've also included a selection of Orange County's seaside escapes and charming bed-and-breakfast inns, for those interested in venturing beyond the Disney region.

Disneyland Resort Hotels

With the addition of Disney's Grand Californian to the hotel scene, fans of the Disneyland Resort are faced with a difficult decision. It isn't whether or not to stay on-property (that's recommended if it's within the budget), but which of the three hotels to choose. Some factors to consider:

The whimsical pool area, large arcade, and ever-popular character meals continue to make the Disneyland Hotel, the first hotel built on Disneyland Resort property, appeal to the kids in the family (and the kid in us all).

Meanwhile, Disney's Paradise Pier Hotel (formerly the Disneyland Pacific Hotel) boasts a new facade to complement Disney's California Adventure. The sunny, splashy look is a warm welcome to all guests, especially those familiar with its previously conservative exterior. Inside, the Disney decor is still subtle, and the dining options are divine.

But the Disney design team has outdone itself with the Grand Californian. Located inside Disney's California Adventure, this hotel's theming and style touch every detail, right down to the floorboards.

Whichever hotel you choose, one thing's certain—a stay on-property is sure to complete the Disney experience. From a resort information TV channel to wake-up calls by Mickey himself, every detail reminds you that you're in Disney's land.

Exclusive benefits: Several perks are reserved exclusively for those guests staying on-property. Perhaps the most significant of these is guaranteed admission (with a ticket) to a theme park if it reaches capacity, while others, even if they have a ticket, will be asked to return later.

Guests staying on Disney property are able to buy special Resort Park Hopper Tickets—admission passes to both theme parks that include one early-entry day at Disneyland Park and an ESPN Game Zone Card. Those without this privilege must select one park for each day of their visit or purchase Three- or Four-Day Tickets, which allow them to "hop" between parks.

One of the most convenient perks is the ability to charge almost any expense incurred at a Disney theme park back to the hotel room, if a credit card imprint was taken at check-in. Purchases can be charged to the room from the time of check-in until 11 A.M. on the day of departure. (Note: This does not apply to most Downtown Disney purchases.)

Shoppers also enjoy the benefit of having purchases delivered directly to their hotel's Bell Desk, where they can pick up their packages at the end of the day (rather than having to carry them through the parks all day).

Check-in and Check-out: Officially, check-in begins at 3 P.M., but guests who arrive early can check in, store their luggage at the Bell Desk, and go have fun. A photo ID is required at check-in. Check-out is at 11 A.M., and, again, bags can be stored until guests are ready to depart. Express check-out is available by leaving a credit card imprint at check-in.

HOT TIP!

Nonsmoking rooms and rooms equipped for guests with disabilities are available at all three Disney hotels.

Prices: Room rates start at $200. They vary according to hotel, view, and season. Expect "regular" rates April 14–April 29, June 2–August 26, and December 22– December 31. Slightly discounted "value" rates apply from January 1–April 13, April 30–June 1, and August 27–December 21. Disneyland Resort room tax is 15 percent.

Deposit requirements: A deposit equal to one night's lodging is required *within 21 days* from the time the reservation is made. Reservations are automatically canceled if a deposit is not received in that time period. Reservations booked fewer than 21 days prior to arrival are held for about a week without deposit. Deposit payment can be mailed in the form of check or money order, or can be guaranteed by a credit card over the phone (in which case the card is not actually billed until check-in).

Cancelation policy: The deposit will be refunded if the reservation is canceled *at least 72 hours* before the scheduled arrival.

Additional costs: Room rates at all three hotels are based on double occupancy. While there is no charge for children under 18 sharing their parents' room, extra adults will each cost $15 extra per night. Note that there is no fee for rollaway beds, sleeping bags, or cribs.

A $5 per day resort service fee includes overnight parking, use of the fitness centers, and local telephone calls. Valet parking is available for $15 per day.

Discounts: Special savings are available to Disney Club members (see *Getting Ready to Go* for details). Annual Passport bearers are also rewarded with special rates.

Packages: The Walt Disney Travel Company offers several packages that feature a stay at one of the Disneyland Resort hotels. See "Travel Packages" in *Getting Ready to Go*, or contact the Walt Disney Travel Company at 714-520-5050.

DISNEYLAND HOTEL: This laid-back, family-oriented resort adjacent to Downtown Disney recently underwent a transformation. The familiar marina is gone, replaced by a Never Land-themed outdoor area with a 5,000-square-foot swimming pool that incorporates a 100-foot water slide, a pirate ship, and (waiting beside the ship) a comical sculpture of Tick Tock, the hungry crocodile from Disney's movie *Peter Pan*. A winding shoreline, lush flower gardens, rock formations, and a wedding gazebo add to the property's picturesque terrain.

The hotel has 990 rooms, including 62 suites, located in three high-rise towers. Most tower rooms have two double beds, and many can easily accommodate up to five people (one of them on a daybed). All the interior tower rooms have small balconies that are ideal for cooling off or catching a glimpse of the twice-nightly Fantasy Waters fountain show, which features music from favorite Disney films. The 11-story East Tower looks toward Downtown Disney and Disney's California Adventure on one side and the main pool on the other. The 14-story South Tower's rooms provide city views as well as windows overlooking the waterfall and koi fish pond. The 11-story North Tower offers rooms with pool views, but only on one side; guests on the other side look out over city rooftops. A monorail stop is located just out back, in neighboring Downtown Disney, which means extremely easy access to Disneyland (it drops guests off in Tomorrowland), an enormous convenience for guests who relish a break in their park-going with a quick trip to one of the hotel's pools; to the small beach, perfect for sandcastle-building and volleyball; or to Team Mickey's Workout, which features weight machines and aerobic exercise equipment. The workout room is featured in a $5-per-day package that also includes guest parking, local phone calls, and daily newspaper delivery.

Guests also enjoy Horseshoe Falls, a 165-foot-wide cascade that visitors can walk under. Nearby, a tranquil pool is filled with Japanese koi fish. The large arcade, a big draw for younger guests, is located in the shopping area that fronts the South Tower. The hotel's pools, beach, and Fantasy Waters show were all upgraded a few years back.

In the lobby of the North Tower, a large shop called Fantasia sells Disney souvenirs. Goofy's Kitchen, hosted by Chef Goofy and his Disney pals, is an extremely popular buffet open for breakfast, lunch, and dinner; Hook's Pointe & Wine Cellar features a mesquite grill and offers traditional cuisine and Never Land pool views; and Granville's Steak House serves savory steaks in a sophisticated setting. The Coffee House, Captain's Galley, and Croc's Bits 'n' Bites provide snacks and quick meals for guests on the go. Room service is available. (For more information about hotel dining, see the *Good Meals, Great Times* chapter.)

The convention and meetings area, adjacent to Goofy's Kitchen and linked to the lobby via a photo-lined passageway, deserves a look for its Disney-related artwork, including a floor-to-ceiling collage of Disney collectibles and milestones. Created entirely from old toys, souvenirs, name tags, and other memorabilia, it commemorates the colorful and unique history of Disneyland. The photo hall of fame depicts celebrities, members of royalty, and political figures who have visited the resort.

The hotel can provide safe-deposit boxes, currency exchange, and child-care referrals. An ATM is on the premises. Airport buses bound for the Orange County and Los Angeles airports make regular stops at the hotel, as do tour buses, city and county buses, and buses traveling to and from downtown Los Angeles.

Rates for doubles run $200 to $235, depending on the view and season, plus $15 for each extra adult (no charge for children under 18 staying in their parents' room); no charge for rollaways or cribs. For the outstanding concierge-level rooms and amenities, add $65 to $75. Suites are $450 to $2,500 (for the Marina Suite). Parking costs $5 per day for hotel guests ($15 for valet); others pay $2 per hour, with a $15 maximum for 24 hours. Disneyland Hotel; 1150 Magic Way; Anaheim, CA 92802; 714-956-6425 (for reservations and information) or 714-956-6400 (hotel switchboard); *www.disneyland.com*.

DISNEY'S GRAND CALIFORNIAN HOTEL:

This 750-room hotel sits at the heart of the Disneyland Resort, with its own entrance to Disney's California Adventure theme park (a Disney first) and easy access to Downtown Disney.

A border of trees surrounds the six-story hotel, built as a tribute to the arts-and-crafts tradition of the early 1900s—a style made famous by the striking designs of Frank Lloyd Wright. Rich cedar and redwood paneling decorate the lobby, where display cabinets filled with original art and quality reproductions introduce guests to that period of art, and a great hearth has a perennially lit fire. Furnishings throughout the hotel have warm colors and intricate textures. Even the hotel staff wears period costumes.

Each of the 702 deluxe guestrooms and 48 suites features a 27-inch TV, a safe large enough to fit a laptop computer, lighted wardrobe, desk with two-line telephone, a computer and fax-accessible data port, iron and board, and refrigerator. The bathroom has marble surfaces, a makeup mirror, and a hair dryer.

Most of the guestrooms in the hotel feature two queen beds, though 80 have a king bed, and 160 have one queen bed plus a bunk bed with a trundle (these rooms sleep five). The carved wooden headboards are designed to resemble vines on a trellis, the bedspreads have a stained-glass-like design, and Bambi appears subtly in the shower curtain pattern.

Guest services include 24-hour room service, same-day laundry and dry cleaning, a full-service business center, and a bridal salon. The concierge level offers upgraded amenities and services. Guests can relax at the quiet Fountain Pool or frolic in Redwood Pool (the two are connected), with its themed slide; or they can enjoy the two whirlpools, children's pool, clothing boutique and gift shop, child-care center called Pinocchio's Workshop, and Grizzly Game Arcade. The 4,000-square-foot fitness center incorporates a weight room, exercise classes, two massage rooms, dry and steam saunas, and lockers.

Among the varied dining options are the Napa Rose, which features California cuisine and wines, and the Storyteller's Cafe, open for breakfast, lunch, and dinner in an Old California setting and the backdrop for a character-hosted breakfast. A quick-service eatery, Whitewater Snacks, supplies specialty coffees, fast food, and baked goods; the poolside bar is good for a quick meal or snack. The Hearthstone Lounge doubles as a breakfast spot each morning, dispensing coffee and pastries to guests heading into the park.

HOT TIP!

Don't touch anything in a Grand Californian room's mini-bar unless you're sure you want it—you'll be charged whether or not you take the item.

The hotel can provide safe-deposit boxes and currency exchange. An ATM is on the premises. Airport buses bound for Orange County and Los Angeles airports stop here, as do tour buses, city and county buses, and buses traveling to and from Los Angeles.

Rates for regular rooms run $250 to $290, depending on the view and season, plus $15 for each extra adult (no charge for children under 18 staying in their parents' room); concierge rooms are $350; presidential suites, $2,500. There are no rollaways, but a sleeping bag with a pad can be supplied; no charge for cribs. Self-parking is $5 per day (this also includes local phone calls, daily newspaper delivery, and fitness center access); valet parking is $15. Disney's Grand Californian; 1150 Disneyland Drive; Anaheim, CA 92802; 714-956-6425 (for reservations and information) or 714-956-6400 (hotel switchboard); *www.disneyland.com*.

PHOTO BY KEITH GROSHANS

Two shops, including the spacious and well-stocked Mickey in Paradise, a congenial coffee bar with its own Mickey cappuccino machine, and two restaurants are on the ground level of the hotel. Disney's PCH Grill offers California cuisine and has a popular character breakfast, Minnie & Friends. The hotel's other restaurant, Yamabuki, contains the Disneyland Resort's first full sushi bar (see *Good Meals, Great Times*). Room service offers PCH Grill specialties. The hotel also has an exercise room, a small concierge lounge, and an ATM. A glass-enclosed elevator provides a bird's-eye view of both the lobby and Disney's California Adventure.

Guests at the hotel have an exclusive entrance into the Paradise Pier section of Disney's California Adventure. The hotel is also connected to the Disneyland Resort by a landscaped walkway. At press time, the Paradise Pier Hotel offered continuous transportation via double-decker bus to Downtown Disney. The bus stop is located in the turnaround next door to the hotel on Paradise Way. (Guests can also get to Disneyland by taking the monorail from the Downtown Disney station.) Rates for doubles run $200 to $235, depending on the view and the season (no charge for children under 18 sharing their parents' room), plus $15 per extra adult; no charge for rollaways or cribs. For concierge rooms and various amenities, add another $65 to $75. Suites run $850 to $1,200. Self-parking is $5 per day (that includes local phone calls, daily newspaper delivery, and access to the exercise room); valet parking is $15. Disney's Paradise Pier Hotel; 1717 Disneyland Dr.; Anaheim, CA 92802; 714-956-6400; *www.disneyland.com*.

DISNEY'S PARADISE PIER HOTEL:

When Disney's California Adventure rose on the plot of land across the street from the Disneyland Pacific Hotel, that property got a face-lift and a new name—Disney's Paradise Pier Hotel. Its facade now reflects the ambience and breezy, carefree California style of the Paradise Pier district of the new park, which it overlooks. This property, the smallest of the Disneyland Resort hotels, is generally popular with business people, vacationing adults, and families with older kids or teenagers.

The hotel's two high-rise towers—one 15 stories, the other 14 stories—are juxtaposed to create a central atrium, which cradles the lobby and a larger-than-life character sculpture. Mickey's familiar silhouette shows up extensively in the hotel's decor—in the artwork, the ceramics, and even the upholstery.

Each of the 502 rooms, including 12 suites, features Disney-themed furnishings, one king-size bed or two queen beds, plus a fold-out twin sofa bed in the sitting area (a particular convenience for families). The rooms on the cabana level open onto a large recreation area that also includes a split-level sundeck, swimming pool, whirlpool, children's play area, and snack bar. If you plan to spend a lot of time in or beside the pool, consider a concierge-level room on the third floor for direct access.

Disneyland Good Neighbor Hotels

With fewer than 2,500 rooms available at the Disneyland Resort and tens of thousands of guests pouring through the theme park turnstiles each day, it's no wonder that a majority of visitors must stay in one of the establishments located off Disney property. To make it easier for guests to narrow down their off-property choices, the folks at Disney have selected several local hotels and motels that meet the Disney standard and anointed them the "Disneyland Good Neighbor" properties. Before receiving the Disney seal of approval, hotels are graded on amenities, services, decor, guest satisfaction, price, and location.

Ranging from national chains to smaller operations, the Good Neighbor hotels proliferate along Harbor Boulevard, which flanks the resort on the east. From Harbor, it's easy to walk to the Disneyland Resort. A few properties are on Ball Road, the resort's northern boundary. Katella Avenue borders the resort to the south and leads to the Anaheim Convention Center and the city's major convention hotels. Divided into the categories of Suite, Superior, Moderate, and Economy, there are 38 Good Neighbor hotels in all. In the following pages we describe 14 of our favorites. For a rundown of the Good Neighbor properties not described in this listing, see "The Rest of the Best" on page 47.

Prices: Expect to pay $100 to $200, or more, per night for a hotel room for two adults and two children (kids usually stay in their parents' room for free), $50 to $120 for a motel room, and $25 to $55 for tent or RV camping. Prices drop a bit in winter; they are highest in the summer and over holidays. The room tax in Anaheim is 15 percent.

Additional costs: When comparing accommodation costs, consider hidden zingers, like parking. Big hotels usually charge for it ($6 to $10 a day; more for valet service). Most also charge an additional fee when more than two adults occupy a room. The cutoff age at which there is no charge for children varies; it's often 17 or 18 but can be as low as 12.

Savings: You can save money by staying in a hotel that offers complimentary breakfast. Discounts are sometimes offered to those who belong to an automobile or retirement association or to the Disney Club (to learn about the latter, refer to the *Getting Ready to Go* chapter).

Individual needs: What's essential for one vacationer—and worth the extra cost—might seem frivolous to another: room service, on-site restaurants, live music, a suite, a kitchen, concierge service and amenities, large swimming pool, exercise room, or a place that accepts pets.

Packages: The Walt Disney Travel Company offers packages in conjunction with each of the Good Neighbor hotels—representing potentially big savings for travelers. Refer to "Travel Packages" in *Getting Ready to Go*, or simply contact the Walt Disney Travel Company directly at 714-520-5050.

Good Neighbor Hotels

1 Embassy Suites Anaheim	21 WestCoast Anaheim Hotel
2 Residence Inn by Marriott	22 Candy Cane Inn
3 Hilton Suites Anaheim	23 Howard Johnson Plaza-Hotel
4 Embassy Suites Buena Park	24 Best Western Stovall's Inn
5 Hawthorn Suites Orange	25 Carousel Inn & Suites
6 Homewood Suites by Hilton	26 Portofino Inn & Suites
7 Hawthorn Suites LTD, Anaheim	27 Radisson Hotel Maingate Anaheim
8 Residence Inn Orange	28 Best Western Pavilions
9 Sheraton Anaheim	29 Quality Hotel Maingate
10 Crowne Plaza Resort	30 Hampton Inn & Suites
11 Hilton Anaheim	31 Holiday Inn Anaheim at the Park
12 Anaheim Marriott	32 Conestoga at Disneyland Park
13 Hyatt Regency Alicante	33 Tropicana Inn
14 Doubletree Hotel Anaheim/O.C.	34 Red Roof Inn Anaheim
15 Courtyard by Marriott Buena Park	35 Anaheim Travelodge International Inn
16 Best Western Park Place Inn	36 Ramada Maingate Saga Inn
17 Park Inn International	37 Red Roof Inn Santa Ana
18 Anaheim Fairfield Inn by Marriott	38 Anaheim Ramada Inn
19 Best Western Anaheim Inn	
20 Hilton Garden Inn	

ACCOMMODATIONS

PHOTO BY KEITH GROSHANS

Note: The following recommended establishments accept major credit cards and offer nonsmoking rooms and rooms for travelers with disabilities, unless otherwise indicated. Call the properties directly to inquire about deposit requirements and cancelation policies. Rates given were correct at press time but are subject to change and should always be confirmed by phone.

Suite Hotels

RESIDENCE INN BY MARRIOTT: This delightful 200-suite lodging is on a side street about two blocks from the Disneyland Resort. At first glance, the two- and three-story stucco buildings with tile roofs could easily be mistaken for an elegant condominium complex. The impeccably maintained grounds are landscaped with hibiscus, bougainvillea, lemon, sweet gum, and pepper trees, plus park-style benches and, we're convinced, the only remaining orange tree in Anaheim. Inside the inn, the living-room-like lobby is inviting, with comfortable couches, chairs, cocktail tables, fireplace, and television. Facilities include a swimming pool that's open 24 hours, a kids' pool, a whirlpool, Ping-Pong tables, and a single court for badminton, basketball, or volleyball. There is also a guest laundry.

Because the hotel is designed for long-term guests (short-term are always welcome), the suites, all recently renovated, are spacious and feature a 25-inch TV, pay-per-view movies, and Nintendo; a breakfast bar; and a fully equipped kitchen with a dishwasher, stove, microwave, and full refrigerator. Several room configurations are available. Complimentary services to guests include grocery delivery, daily housekeeping service, shuttle transportation to the Disneyland Resort and the convention center, a continental breakfast daily, and a social hour Monday through Thursday from 5 P.M. to 7 P.M. The hotel will accept one small pet in a suite for a minimal daily charge and a nonrefundable deposit.

Rates for a single studio start at $169 (or $99, if you're lucky and the occupancy rate is low when you visit); a one-bedroom suite, at $179; and a multi-room family suite, at $199. A rollaway costs $10; no charge for cribs. Lower long-term rates are also available.

Residence Inn by Marriott; 1700 S. Clementine St.; Anaheim, CA 92802; 714-533-3555 or 800-331-3131; *www.residence inn.com/snaah.*

Superior Hotels

ANAHEIM MARRIOTT: Across the street from the Anaheim Convention Center and the Hilton, the Marriott is a favorite among conventioneers. Most of the 1,030 rooms, located in two towers (one 17 stories, the other 19) and two four-story wings, have balconies. Each room has one king-size bed or two doubles and cable TV. The hotel restaurants—JW's Steakhouse and Cafe del Sol—are popular with locals and guests alike. For a quick bite, drop by the Pizza Hut or Starbucks on the premises. There are two pools, surrounded by lounge chairs (one pool is partially covered), as well as two whirlpools and a health club with an exercise room and two saunas. Guests enjoy the poolside and lobby bars, and concierge services.

The hotel, located a couple of long blocks from the Disneyland Resort (for many people, not within walking distance), provides free shuttle service to the park; transportation to all area airports is available. Rates for two run $119 to $235 (no charge for children under 18 sharing their parents' room); $220 to $1,250 for suites; $15 per additional adult. Rollaways and cribs are free. Special packages, including some for families, and discounted weekend rates are available. Self-parking costs $12 per day; valet parking is $17 per day. Pets are accepted at the hotel. Anaheim Marriott; 700 W. Convention Way; Anaheim, CA 92802; 714-750-8000 or 800-228-9290; *www.marriotthotels.com/LAXAH.*

HILTON ANAHEIM: The 14-story glass exterior of Southern California's largest hotel reflects the Anaheim Convention Center, just steps away, and the three-story atrium lobby invites the outdoors (and swarms of conventioneers) inside. The Hilton has 1,572 rooms, including 95 suites, decorated in soft, light colors, with wicker furniture and California art. Atop the hotel, the Executive Floor provides special services and amenities, as well as complimentary continental breakfast and hors d'oeuvres in its lounge.

The hotel's outdoor recreation center, on the fifth floor, features a heated swimming pool, four whirlpools, and three acres of sundecks and rose gardens. Cafe Express, open

PHOTO BY KEITH GROSHANS

18 hours a day, offers sandwiches, ice cream, and coffee. Other dining options include the *Casablanca*-style Cafe Oasis, serving breakfast, lunch, and dinner; the award-winning and elegant Hasting's Grill, featuring California cuisine; and Pavia, with Italian cuisine and live entertainment. Don't overlook the sushi bar and the sports bar with big-screen TV in the lobby. Note that the restaurants tend to be extremely crowded at lunchtime and during convention breaks.

Add to that a foreign-currency exchange, self-service post office, business center, and two levels of shops. The 25,000-square-foot Sports and Fitness Center has weight machines and exercise equipment, an indoor pool, basketball court, whirlpool, steam baths, sauna, aerobics classes, and massage. There's even an outdoor driving range.

Orange County Walk of Stars, the sidewalk entrance to the hotel, highlights local notables such as Gene Autry, Steve Martin, and Buzz Aldrin. Rates for a double room range from $88 to $330, plus $30 per extra adult (no charge for children, regardless of age, when sharing their parents' room); $800 to $1,325 for suites. Ask about special packages. There's no charge for cribs or rollaways. Self-parking costs $9 per day, valet parking $13. Pets are permitted. Hilton Anaheim; 777 Convention Way; Anaheim, CA 92802; 714-750-4321 or 800-222-9923; *www.hilton.com.*

HYATT REGENCY ALICANTE: The hotel, located in Garden Grove, is only a mile from the Disneyland Resort. Its dramatic, 17-story atrium encloses palm trees, fountains, and greenery, and houses Cafe Alicante, specialty shops, and a bar. Each of the hotel's 396 guestrooms features either a king-size bed or

two double beds and cherry-wood furniture that complements the modern interior design.

Each of the 16 spacious suites has a living room, dining room, wet bar, and an entertainment console. Business-plan rooms are equipped with a fax machine, coffeemaker, and an iron. All rooms have hair dryers. The hotel's impressive recreational facilities, located on a 25,000-square-foot, third-story roof, include a pool, whirlpool, exercise room, two tennis courts, and an arcade. Complimentary transportation to the Disneyland Resort is provided, and airport shuttle service is available.

Room rates run $89 to $210, with weekend rates of $99 to $109 (no charge for children under 18 occupying their parents' room), plus $25 for each additional adult; $350 to $1,095 for suites. There is no charge for rollaways or cribs. Self-parking is $6 per day, valet parking $8. Hyatt Regency Alicante; 100 Plaza Alicante; Chapman Ave. at Harbor Blvd.; Garden Grove, CA 92840; 714-750-1234; *www.hyatt.com.*

SHERATON ANAHEIM: With its turrets, towers, and Tudor design, this 489-room hotel looks more like a castle, surrounded by grounds that incorporate two peaceful courtyards, a rose garden, fountain, fish pond, and small waterfall. A stream runs through the lobby, which has a comfortable seating area around a stone fireplace, plus a restaurant, gift shop, bar, and deli that is open long hours. The reception staff and concierge get high marks for their helpfulness.

The 450 rooms and 39 suites are decorated in blue, green, and peach hues. The rooms—all large (500-plus square feet)—have two queen- or one king-size bed, cable television, in-room movies, voice mail, irons, ironing boards, hair dryers, and coffeemakers. Each suite has a sitting area with a sofa bed and wet bar. The concierge level offers personalized services and complimentary breakfast and cocktails in its lounge.

The hotel has an arcade, heated pool, whirlpool, exercise room, guest laundry, and conference rooms. It provides room service, valet service, and frequent complimentary shuttle service to the Disneyland Resort. Airport transportation is available. Rates run $150 to $195 for doubles (no charge for children under 18 sharing their parents' room); $150 to $345 for suites, plus $20 for rollaways; no charge for cribs. A refrigerator is available on advance request for $20 per stay. Sheraton Anaheim; 1015 W. Ball Rd.; Anaheim, CA 92802; 714-778-1700 or 800-331-7251; *www.sheraton.com/Anaheim.*

Moderate Hotels

ANAHEIM FAIRFIELD INN BY MARRIOTT: Fronted by palms and pines, this handsome, affordable 467-room hotel is situated across from the Disneyland Resort. The rooms are located in two towers (one tower is nine stories high; the other, eight). Each room has a king-size bed or two double beds, sofa bed, cable TV, an iron, hair dryer, refrigerator, and coffeemaker. The hotel is served by an outstanding family-style restaurant called Millie's.

Other facilities include a heated pool, whirlpool, gift shop, and Cafasia Snack Shop and Game Room. Delivery by Millie's and the neighboring McDonald's is available, as is complimentary transportation to the Disneyland Resort. The rooms may be occupied by up to five people, and rates range from $69 to $134; cribs are available. Fairfield Inn by Marriott; 1460 S. Harbor Blvd.; Anaheim, CA 92802; 714-772-6777 or 800-228-2800; *www.anaheimfairfieldinn.com.*

BEST WESTERN PARK PLACE INN: This three-story, 199-room inn with a jaunty striped awning is right across from the Disneyland Resort. The lobby is spacious, with a high ceiling and two cozy seating areas, a fireplace, and large windows looking onto Harbor Boulevard. Just off the lobby, a gift shop sells Disney souvenirs. Room configurations include a king-size bed and pullout sofa, two queen-size beds, or two double beds. Refrigerators are available for $5 a day, microwaves for $10.

Among the facilities are a pool with an adjacent whirlpool and sauna, and a guest laundry. Room service is available, with food supplied by Mom's Family Restaurant next door. Rates, which include continental breakfast at the inn or pancakes and eggs at Mom's Restaurant, run $89 to $129 for a double room in season; $75 to $99 the rest of the year (there is no charge for kids under 18 sharing their parents' room). Rollaway beds cost $15; there is no extra charge for cribs. Best Western Park Place Inn; 1544 S. Harbor Blvd.; Anaheim, CA 92802; 714-776-4800 or 800-854-8175, ext. 4; *www.bestwestern.com/parkplaceinn-minisuites.*

CANDY CANE INN: There's a lot to like about this sweet, two-story hotel with a fountain out front, relaxed ambience, wrought-iron touches, and flowers everywhere. Located just down the street from the Disneyland Resort's main entrance (a quick walk), the Candy Cane Inn is family-run, well-designed, and beautifully maintained.

Each of the 172 rooms, which are set far back from the street, has wooden shutters, new carpeting, a coffeemaker, and two queen beds with down comforters, dust ruffles, and European pillow shams. The deluxe rooms feature compact refrigerators and ceramic-tiled bathrooms with separate vanity areas. Add to that the guest laundry, swimming pool, gazebo-covered whirlpool, and kids' wading pool. A complimentary continental buffet breakfast is served daily. Sightseeing services are available, as well as complimentary shuttle service to and from the Disneyland Resort. Transportation to local airports can be arranged.

Rates for a double room with two queen-size beds range from $82 to $145, depending on the season. Rollaways are $10; no charge for cribs. The inn is conveniently located across the street from a small shopping area with fast-food eateries and one-hour photo processing. Candy Cane Inn; 1747 S. Harbor Blvd.; Anaheim, CA 92802; 714-774-5284 or 800-345-7057; *www.travelx.com/candy.html.*

HOLIDAY INN ANAHEIM AT THE PARK: About half a mile north of Disneyland's main entrance, this pretty, five-story hotel has one of the best landscaped pool areas in Anaheim, and—an added treat—the pool is heated and open 24 hours a day. All 253 guestrooms have coffeemakers, voice mail, pay-per-view movies, hair dryers, and irons. Other services and facilities include car rental, free parking, a gift shop, restaurant, room service, lobby bar, foreign currency exchange, guest laundry, valet dry cleaning, and complimentary shuttle to the Disneyland Resort, Knott's Berry Farm, and other area attractions. Kids eat free from a child's menu when accompanied by an equal number of paying adults. Rates for one to four people run $99 to $179, depending on season and occupancy (there is no charge for children under 17 sharing their parents' room). Rollaways are $12; no charge for cribs. Holiday Inn Anaheim at the Park; 1221 S. Harbor Blvd.; Anaheim, CA 92805; 714-758-0900 or 800-545-7275; *www.holiday-inn.com/anaheim-park.*

HOWARD JOHNSON PLAZA-HOTEL: This property has some of the lushest landscaping of any place in Anaheim, except for the Disney hotels, and that's a major reason to stay here. Birds-of-paradise, olive trees, and pines (some taller than the hotel's seven-story

tower) proliferate; a central fountain anchors the four two-story units. The hotel is close to the Disneyland Resort and popular local eateries. It offers shuttle service to and from the Disneyland Resort.

The 320 rooms are divided among six buildings on six acres; all have been completely renovated in recent years. Most have two queen beds, and all have a refrigerator, Sony PlayStation, and high-speed internet access. The rooms in the two-story units are all nonsmoking and feature in-room movies. All the rooms throughout the property are spacious, but the bathrooms (particularly in the Tower building) tend to be small. The top-floor rooms and suites have skylights; highly recommended Suite 1701 has two of them, plus floor-to-ceiling windows with a park view and a separate living room.

There are two outdoor heated pools (one oval-shaped), a whirlpool, and a kids' wading pool, as well as two laundry rooms, a gift shop, and an arcade. Acapulco Restaurant and Bar is adjacent to the property. Babysitting can be arranged. Room rates range from $69 to $109, depending on the season; suites are $169 to $189. Rollaways are $7; cribs are free. Ask about family packages. Howard Johnson Plaza; 1380 S. Harbor Blvd.; Anaheim, CA 92802; 714-776-6120 or 800-422-4228; *www.hojoanaheim.com.*

PARK INN INTERNATIONAL: Directly across the street—and just a short walk away—from the Disneyland Resort, this hotel, with its shingled roof, clock tower, turrets, and tidy window boxes, looks like something out of a Bavarian village. Each of the 121 rooms and suites has a refrigerator, coffeemaker, hair dryer, and an iron. The inn has a friendly, helpful staff and offers complimentary continental breakfast. It also has a pool (with a nice view of Disneyland's Matterhorn and fireworks); an outstanding gift shop called Cartoon Place, which sells Disney Unlimited clothing and souvenirs; a second shop that carries sundries and California mementos; and a guest laundry facility.

Although there's no in-house restaurant, many eating places, including Millie's restaurant, are within walking distance. Standard rooms, most with two queen-size beds, start at $89 year-round; suites start at $149 and can accommodate up to six people, but they have only one bath. Rollaways are $10; cribs are $7. Park Inn International; 1520 S. Harbor Blvd.; Anaheim, CA 92802; 714-635-7275 or 800-670-7275; *www.parkinn-anaheim.com.*

HOT TIP!
If you stay in the 1400 or 1500 block of Harbor Boulevard, you can cross the street and walk to the parks from your hotel.

WESTCOAST ANAHEIM HOTEL: This 14-story tower is easy to spot, and the 499 rooms and eight suites have full or small balconies that provide a nice view of the pool or Disneyland (and a great view of the fireworks). All rooms offer either one king or two queen beds, pay-per-view movies available anytime, Sony PlayStations, irons, coffeemakers, hair dryers, and baths with separate sinks.

A large gift shop is on the premises, as is a lobby bar, coffee shop, snack shop, and an espresso bar. Popular with groups, the Overland Stage restaurant (with furnishings from a Mississippi riverboat) serves steak, seafood, and pasta for dinner only and offers a kids' menu. The hotel also has a large L-shaped pool, whirlpool, poolside bar (in the summertime), and a sweeping expanse of lawn.

Car rental is available, along with free shuttle service to the Disneyland Resort. Rates run $129 to $195 for doubles, depending on occupancy and season; suites start at $320. Rollaways cost $15 extra; cribs are free. West-Coast Anaheim Hotel; 1855 S. Harbor Blvd.; Anaheim, CA 92802; 714-750-1811 or 800-426-0670; *www.westcoastanaheimhotel.com.*

Economy Hotels

BEST WESTERN STOVALL'S INN: What makes the inn unique is its topiary garden of deer, bears, elephants, and hippos. The property features 290 guestrooms, a pair of swimming pools (one is heated), two whirlpools, a wading pool, and a gift shop. Original artwork hangs in the lobby. Room configurations include a queen- or king-size bed or two double beds and a bathroom with a separate sink and plenty of counter space. Refrigerators are available for $8 a day. A complimentary shuttle bus takes guests to the Disneyland Resort. Rates for up to five people run $75 to $110 in season, $65 to $89 the rest of the year. Rollaways are $15; cribs are free. Best Western Stovall's Inn; 1110 W. Katella Ave.; Anaheim, CA 92802; 714-778-1880 or 800-854-8175; *www.bestwestern.com/stovallsinn.*

TROPICANA INN: Much bigger than it looks from the street, this hostelry with a sand-colored wood-and-stucco facade is situated right at the pedestrian crosswalk into the parks. Its 200 recently renovated rooms are decorated with light-wood furniture and pale colors. Each has a TV, coffeemaker (with coffee replenished daily), refrigerator, microwave, hair dryer, separate vanity, an iron, in-room movies, and either a king-size bed, two queens, or two doubles. A continental breakfast is included daily.

Although the inn has no restaurant, a well-stocked market on the premises sells fresh fruit, fried chicken, breakfast items, snacks and other food, wine, and travel supplies; a gift shop sells souvenirs and Disney merchandise (both shops conveniently stay open one hour after the parks close). McDonald's, IHOP, Millie's, Denny's, and other eateries are within walking distance. The inn has an outdoor pool, large whirlpool, and guest laundry. It provides a courtesy shuttle to the Disneyland Resort and the train and bus stations. Room rates range from $68 to $88; rooms with a kitchenette cost an additional $15. Suites accommodate four to six people and start at $120. Tropicana Inn; 1540 S. Harbor Blvd.; Anaheim, CA 92802; 714-635-4082 or 800-828-4898; *www.tropicanainn-anaheim.com.*

The Rest of the Best

Here's a roundup of the remaining Disneyland Good Neighbor hotels. They feature amenities and rates similar to those described in this chapter. However, some of these properties are located slightly farther from the Disneyland Resort (refer to the map on page 42).

Note: Hotels are subject to change; call 714-520-5050 for a list of current participants.

Suite Hotels

- Embassy Suites Anaheim; 3100 E. Frontera St.; Anaheim; 714-632-1221
- Embassy Suites Buena Park; 7762 Beach Blvd.; Buena Park; 714-739-5600
- Hawthorn Suites LTD Anaheim; 1752 S. Clementine St.; Anaheim; 714-535-7773
- Hawthorn Suites Orange; 720 The City Dr. South; Orange; 714-740-2700
- Hilton Suites Anaheim; 400 N. State College Blvd.; Orange; 714-938-1111
- Homewood Suites by Hilton; 12005 Harbor Blvd.; Garden Grove; 714-740-1800

Superior Hotels

- Courtyard by Marriott Buena Park; 7621 Beach Blvd.; Buena Park; 714-670-6600
- Crowne Plaza Resort; 12021 Harbor Blvd; Garden Grove; 800-227-6963
- Doubletree Hotel Anaheim/Orange County; 100 The City Dr.; Orange; 714-634-4500
- Hilton Garden Inn; 11777 Harbor Blvd; Garden Grove; 714-703-9100

Moderate Hotels

- Best Western Anaheim Inn; 1630 S. Harbor Blvd.; Anaheim; 714-774-1050
- Carousel Inn & Suites; 1530 S. Harbor Blvd.; Anaheim; 714-758-0444
- Hampton Inn & Suites; 11747 Harbor Blvd.; Garden Grove; 714-703-8800
- Portofino Inn & Suites; 1831 S. Harbor Blvd.; Anaheim; 714-491-2400
- Quality Hotel Maingate; 616 Convention Way; Anaheim; 714-750-3131
- Radisson Hotel Maingate Anaheim; 1850 S.Harbor Blvd.; Anaheim; 714-750-2801
- Residence Inn Orange; 3101 W. Chapman Ave.; Orange; 714-978-7700

Economy Hotels

- Anaheim Travelodge International Inn ; 2060 S. Harbor Blvd.; Anaheim; 714-971-9393
- Anaheim Ramada Inn; 1331 E. Katella Ave.; Anaheim; 714-978-8088
- Best Western Pavilions; 1176 W. Katella Ave.; Anaheim; 714-776-0140
- Conestoga at Disneyland Park; 1240 S. Walnut; Anaheim; 714-535-0300
- Ramada Maingate Saga Inn; 1650 S. Harbor Blvd.; Anaheim; 714-772-0440
- Red Roof Inn Anaheim; 1251 N. Harbor Blvd.; Anaheim; 714-635-6461
- Red Roof Inn Santa Ana; 2600 N. Main St.; Santa Ana; 714-542-0311

On the Coast

When it comes to upscale and elegant lodging, Orange County's coastal resorts are especially tempting—and they're only about a half-hour drive from the Disneyland Resort. Imagine spending the day in the park and then returning to your hotel for a stroll on the beach at sunset. Most coastal hotels do not offer regularly scheduled shuttle service to the Disneyland Resort (or anywhere else, for that matter), as the Anaheim hostelries do, so you'll need a car.

Laguna Beach

INN AT LAGUNA BEACH: Perched dramatically on a cliff overlooking Laguna Beach, the inn is within walking distance of Heisler Park, Main Beach, the Laguna Art Museum, and many galleries, shops, and cafes. Completely nonsmoking inside, it has 70 rooms, 52 of which have ocean views. Each room is furnished with a ceiling fan, artwork depicting local scenes, lamps with hand-painted shades, a TV, VCR (with selections from a video library), coffeemaker, hair dryer, an iron, a small refrigerator, bathrobes, CD players, feather beds, duvets, and books. Some rooms have two queen beds and a bathtub; others, a king bed, queen sleeper sofa, balcony, and shower. Four corner deluxe rooms, two of which are quite large, provide stunning views of the California coastline.

Guests enjoy free underground self-parking, a swimming pool, and whirlpool. In-room facials and massages are available on request. Complimentary continental breakfast is served in each guestroom; the inn treats guests to cookies and refreshments from 5 P.M. to 9 P.M. daily. The inn hosts changing art exhibits on the mezzanine level, curated by a local gallery owner, with a "Meet the Artist" reception the first Thursday of each month. The scenic Heisler Park cliffside walking trail winds right behind the inn. Rates in summer run $149 to $249 for village-view rooms and $299 to $589 for ocean-view rooms. The rest of the year, expect to pay $99 to $229 for village-view rooms and $199 to $499 for ocean-view. Ask about special travel packages. Inn at Laguna Beach; 211 N. Pacific Coast Hwy.; Laguna Beach, CA 92651; 800-544-4479; *www.innatlagunabeach.com.*

RITZ-CARLTON, LAGUNA NIGUEL: This magnificent Mediterranean villa-style resort sits on 18 acres, high on a bluff that overlooks the Pacific Ocean and Orange County's southern coast. The views from the lounge

and from many of the 363 guestrooms and 30 suites are sensational. On a clear day you can see Catalina Island, 37 miles away, and at night the sound of the surf lulls you to sleep. Each guestroom has French doors and a balcony or patio. The hotel's marble floors, Persian carpets, crystal chandeliers, and museum-quality 18th- and 19th-century European and American art and antiques make a visit here worthwhile even if you can't stay overnight.

In addition to a two-mile stretch of beach (which is open to the public), the hotel has two pools and two whirlpools; an 18-hole golf course designed by Robert Trent Jones, Jr.; four tennis courts; croquet, table tennis, and a beach volleyball court; and a fitness center with yoga and aerobics classes, lockers, whirlpool, two saunas or co-ed steam room, exercise room, massage center, and beauty salon.

The Dining Room, which is one of Orange County's finest restaurants, rates a visit in its own right, and the Club Grill and Bar features music and dancing. The Terrace Restaurant offers three meals a day, as well as a Friday night seafood buffet and Sunday champagne brunch. Afternoon tea is served in the library, and room service is available around the clock. Other amenities include

ACCOMMODATIONS

concierge and valet service, as well as a shuttle to and from the golf course and the beach.

Rates for doubles range from $375 to $645, depending on location and view (or $475 to $795 for Club rooms, with the addition of five culinary treats throughout the day), plus $50 per extra adult (no charge for children under 18 sharing their parents' room); cribs are free. Suites start at $515. Parking is valet only, $25 a day for overnight guests, $9 for other visitors. The hotel is a 40-minute drive south from the Disneyland Resort. Ritz-Carlton, Laguna Niguel; One Ritz-Carlton Dr.; Dana Point, CA 92629; 949-240-2000 or 800-241-3333; *www.ritzcarlton.com.*

SURF & SAND: Perched beside 500 feet of sandy beachfront less than a mile from the shops, galleries, and restaurants of Laguna Beach, this stylish hotel has 164 rooms, almost all with king-size beds and private balconies; six standard rooms share a courtyard patio. The accommodations fill three buildings. Elegantly decorated with furnishings the color of sand dunes, all provide in-room movies, CD players (management can supply CDs at no charge), robes, and a marble bath with a hair dryer.

Rooms in the nine-story Ocean Towers, the biggest and priciest except for the one- and two-bedroom suites, also have a sitting area. Because of its location, guests staying in the three-story Surfside building often have the sensation of being afloat when the surf rolls in. The five-story Seaview Terrace overlooks the pool and beach.

Casual Splashes restaurant has indoor and outdoor seating, serves breakfast, lunch, and dinner, and features primarily Mediterranean cuisine. Adjacent to it, Splashes Bar is particularly popular at sunset; both have direct access to the beach. The hotel also has a medium-size pool (with beach access, as well) and a well-stocked gift shop. Room service and concierge service are available.

A member of Preferred Hotels & Resorts Worldwide, the Surf & Sand is situated across the road from several art galleries and is a 40-minute drive south from the Disneyland Resort. Rates for doubles range from $240 to $450, depending on location, time of year, and time of week; suites start at $435 in winter and $475 in summer. The hotel has valet parking only, for $12 a day. Surf & Sand; 1555 S. Coast Hwy.; Laguna Beach, CA 92651; 949-497-4477 or 800-524-8621; *www.surfandsandresort.com.*

Newport Beach

BEST WESTERN BAY SHORES INN: The inn has that special ambience unique to small, family-run places (this one's been in the Pratt family for 20 years). Guests are encouraged to hang out in deck chairs on the roof; check out free videos; use the complimentary beach towels, umbrellas, boogie boards, pails, and beach toys; and grab fruit, coffee, or tea from the kitchen whenever the urge strikes. The three-story building has an elevator, a sundeck, breakfast room, and free parking. There's no pool or restaurant on the property, but the bay, ocean, and popular Crab Cooker restaurant are just a stroll away. The entire property is nonsmoking.

Most of the 25 rooms are furnished with a single queen bed, though a couple have

Where to Rent a Beach Bungalow

Newport Beach is brimming with cottages, condominiums, and duplex apartments waiting to be your beach home away from home. Some include patios with barbecue facilities, and many are situated right on the sand, within easy strolling distance of local restaurants and shops.

For additional information, contact the Newport Beach Conference & Visitors Bureau; 949-722-1611 or 800-942-6278; *www.newportbeach-cvb.com.*

two queens or two doubles. All feature corner armoires, hair dryers, and air conditioning, though the last is hardly necessary given the great ocean breeze. Double-paned windows muffle noise from the street. The Bay Suite has two queen beds (plus a pull-out couch in the living room), a balcony with a bay view, a kitchen, two baths, and a fireplace. Two one-bedroom annex suites contain two queen beds but no kitchen or view. Each suite sleeps six.

Rates include a breakfast of fresh muffins, pastries, bagels, toast, and hot or cold cereal; they range from $109 to $199 for a double room, depending on the season. Either annex suite runs $179 to $359; the Bay Suite is $259 to $439. Rollaways and cribs are not available. The hotel is about 20 minutes from the Disneyland Resort. Best Western Bay Shores Inn; 1800 W. Balboa Blvd.; Newport Beach, CA 92663; 949-675-3463 or 800-222-6675; *www.thebestinn.com.*

HYATT NEWPORTER: This local landmark (the first resort hotel in the Newport area), with a terra cotta exterior and French doors and windows, exudes a California-Mediterranean air of laid-back luxury. Its 405 guestrooms come in several settings: Some wrap around a courtyard, others look onto the golf course or Newport Bay, still others face one of the hotel's attractive pools. There are also four villas, each with three bedrooms, three baths, a fireplace, and a private yard with a swimming pool.

Besides a nine-hole golf course, three large swimming pools, and three whirlpools, the hotel has volleyball and shuffleboard courts, a health-and-fitness center, and 26 acres of lush, landscaped grounds. Guests have privileges at the adjoining private Palisades Tennis Club, which has 16 courts that are lighted for night play. The Jamboree Grill serves breakfast, lunch, and dinner in a gardenlike setting and on a terrace. Cantori

features a creative combination of international styles and fresh local flavors; its Newporter Sunday brunch features fresh seafood, carved meats, sushi, and a selection of tempting desserts. The Martini and Cigar lobby lounge offers the choice of a full menu or just drinks and cigars. Room service is also available.

The hotel provides complimentary transportation to Balboa Island, Fashion Island, and John Wayne Airport, where shuttle service to the Disneyland Hotel is available. Rates run $204 for doubles ($139 to $204 on the weekend); suites start at $300. There is no charge for children under 18 sharing their parents' room; $25 per extra adult; no charge for rollaways or cribs. Self-parking is $7, valet parking, $9. Pets are allowed. The hotel is a half-hour drive south from the Disneyland Resort. Hyatt Newporter; 1107 Jamboree Rd.; Newport Beach, CA 92660; 949-729-1234 or 800-233-1234; *www.hyattnewporter.com.*

HOT TIP!

Stay in Laguna if small inns and early-morning walks along the beach appeal to you. Choose Newport if you prefer resort hotels and nightlife. It's easier to get rooms in Newport than in Laguna on summer weekends.

NEWPORT BEACH MARRIOTT: The attributes of this 570-room property are many, but foremost among them are the views of Balboa Bay and the Pacific Ocean, the eight tennis courts (lighted for night play), two good-size swimming pools, two whirlpools, and the location across the street from Newport Center Fashion Island, with its 150 boutiques, department stores, and eateries.

The hotel boasts a fine restaurant with an open-air terrace, plus a pleasant bar. It also has concierge service, a gift shop, free transportation to John Wayne Airport, complimentary underground parking for 600 cars, and a health club that is free to all hotel guests. The guestrooms are located in two towers (one of which has a top-story cocktail lounge with a fabulous view of the Pacific Ocean) and in two low-rise wings; room configurations feature double, queen-, or king-size beds.

Small pets are permitted. Rates run $159 to $189 for doubles and $350 and up for suites; no charge for children under 13 sharing their parents' room or for cribs or rollaways. The hotel is a half-hour drive south from the Disneyland Resort. Newport Beach Marriott; 900 Newport Center Dr.; Newport Beach, CA 92660; 949-640-4000 or 800-228-9290; *www.marriott.com.*

Bed & Breakfast Inns

Economical, intimate, congenial. These are a few reasons fans give for choosing to stay in B&Bs. Guestrooms are often furnished with antiques, they may have fireplaces or fabulous ocean views, and private baths have become the norm. B&Bs get the day off to a fine start by supplying a filling breakfast in a serene setting. Most of Orange County's B&Bs are clustered along the coast.

BLUE LANTERN INN: On a bluff overlooking the Pacific, this upscale guesthouse has a slate roof, leaded glass doors, and cobblestoned pathways lined with flowers. Each of the 29 rooms features English or French country decor, a fireplace, large bathroom with whirlpool tub, refrigerator, coffeemaker, television, telephone, and robes. Most have their own private patio or balcony, with views of the Dana Point yacht harbor or the Pacific Ocean. The staff provides turndown service.

Breakfast is served in the sunroom, as are hors d'oeuvres later in the day. Guests chat and play games around a fireplace in the lobby's sitting area or in the library. Teddy bears proliferate in the public areas (and are for sale); the guestrooms, on the other hand, are more sophisticated and nearly bear-free. The inn has an exercise room; it also makes complimentary bikes available to guests.

Rates for doubles range from $155 to $500. It's one block west of the Pacific Coast Highway, well within walking distance of several restaurants, and a half-hour drive from the Disneyland Resort. Because of the location, it's a particularly good choice for those who plan to visit both Anaheim and San Diego. Blue Lantern Inn; 34343 Blue Lantern Dr.; Dana Point, CA 92629; 949-661-1304 or 800-950-1236 (reservations); *www.foursisters.com.*

CASA LAGUNA INN: This has got to be one of Southern California's best-kept secrets, tucked atop a hill overlooking the ocean, just south of Laguna's galleries and restaurants. More enclave than inn, it has five patios, where guests enjoy a large buffet breakfast and afternoon refreshments and hors d'oeuvres—unless they choose to socialize in the inn's newly restored, landmark Mission House (1920). Also on the grounds are a heated pool and spa landscaped with exotic flowers, and a bell tower with an observation deck.

The 20 rooms and suites on the property are individually decorated with a mix of turn-of-the-century furnishings in wicker and wood. Each one has a private bathroom with shower (some have a whirlpool tub), a ceiling fan (some rooms have air conditioning), cable television, telephone, and small refrigerator. The one-bedroom Cottage, which dates from 1932 and is a favorite of honeymooners, features original stained glass, a sitting room with a fireplace, a living room area with a piano, and a private wraparound deck. The Cottage and some of the suites have full kitchens.

The courtyard-room rates for doubles are $105 to $135; the slightly more spacious balcony rooms, $125 to $195; suites, $175 to $295; and the Cottage, which sleeps up to four, $225 to $295. Kids under 13 stay for free in their parents' room. There is free parking behind the inn, which is across the highway from white-sand Victoria Beach and Moss Point Beach. It's about a 45-minute drive south from the Disneyland Resort. Casa Laguna Inn; 2510 S. Coast Hwy.; Laguna Beach, CA 92651; 949-494-2996 or 800-233-0449 (reservations); *www.casalaguna.com.*

DORYMAN'S OCEANFRONT INN: Situated across the street from the ocean and pier in a charming part of Newport Beach, this B&B is elegant, romantic, and Victorian. Each of the ten guestrooms is beautifully appointed with French and American antiques, a queen- or king-size bed, a fireplace, and modern amenities, including Italian marble showers that double as sunken tubs, a pedestal sink or one tucked into an oak cabinet, plus television and telephone. Half the rooms overlook the ocean, and a couple have whirlpool tubs. Complimentary champagne is provided; rose petals on the bed and chilled grapes by the bath are a luxurious touch.

The inn has lamp- and skylighted passageways, wood paneling, a breakfast room, and a patio (three rooms open directly onto it) that is perfect for sunbathing and sunrise and sunset watching. Rates range from $175 to $325.

Take the elevator to the second floor, where the reception area and the rooms are located. The inn is a half-hour drive south from the Disneyland Resort. Doryman's Oceanfront Inn; 2102 W. Ocean Front; Newport Beach, CA 92663; 949-675-7300.

EILER'S INN: The reception area of this European-style hostelry fills a corner of the living room, a comfortable gathering spot with couches, local art, a large coffee table, and fireplace; wine and cheese are served here daily from 4 P.M. to 7 P.M., and a classical guitarist performs on Saturday.

Twelve rooms occupy two floors and surround a flower-filled, brick courtyard. Each has country decor complete with antique chest and mirror, floral bedspread and wallpaper, and a private bath with shower (some baths are short on counter space; no TVs or telephones in the rooms). Most rooms have a king or queen bed; one has two double beds. Two rooms provide an ocean view.

The inn also has a sundeck and a small game and TV room. Breakfast—an event, with homemade breads or cakes, boiled eggs, fruit, fresh-squeezed juice, and hand-ground coffee—is served in the courtyard or by the fireplace. The innkeepers supply iced tea and coffee throughout the day; they also keep a stash of fruit and candy at the reception desk.

Rates for doubles range from $95 to $165, depending on the room and time of the year and week (they tend to be higher in the summer and on Friday and Saturday year-round).

B&B Line

For more information about numerous bed-and-breakfast accommodations throughout the state, contact Bed & Breakfast International of California (408-867-9662 or 800-872-4500; *www.bbintl.com*).

The suite, which has a living room, bedroom, and kitchenette, goes for $185 to $255; add another $20 for each person in the suite beyond two. The inn is four blocks from the center of town; it's a 40-minute drive south from the Disneyland Resort. Limited parking. Eiler's Inn; 741 S. Coast Hwy.; Laguna Beach, CA 92651; 949-494-3004.

SEAL BEACH INN AND GARDENS: On a quiet street a block from the beach and the heart of picturesque Seal Beach, this secluded B&B is also only a 10-minute drive from much livelier Long Beach. All 23 rooms are filled with fine Victorian antiques, framed prints, Oriental carpets, and luxurious fabrics.

PHOTO BY ALICE GARRARD

Accent pieces include brass chandeliers from old houses in New Orleans and stained-glass windows from Scotland. Most rooms have built-in bookcases and fully equipped kitchens; several have whirlpools; and some of the larger rooms can accommodate more than two guests.

A red telephone booth from England, lampposts that stood on the streets of Long Beach in the 1930s, and a 300-year-old iron fountain from France decorate the grounds. Behind the inn is a small heated swimming pool, and colorful gardens bloom throughout the year.

A complimentary breakfast is served in the Tea Room on tables covered with lace cloths. In the late afternoon, tea and snacks are served here beside the fireplace, and guests read vintage books and play chess, checkers, or Scrabble in the adjoining library. The inn's staff provides concierge service, helping plan itineraries and making reservations at area restaurants.

Rates start at $169; the elegant penthouse goes for $399. For a real treat, ask about the Gondola Getaway packages. The inn is a 25-minute drive southwest from the Disneyland Resort. Seal Beach Inn and Gardens; 212 Fifth St.; Seal Beach, CA 90740; 562-493-2416 or 800-443-3292; *www.sealbeachinn.com*.

Disneyland Park

When you wish upon a star, your dreams come true. So says the song, and it's always possible in Disneyland Park (also known as the Magic Kingdom), Walt Disney's own dream come true. He envisioned "a place of warmth and nostalgia, of illusion and color and delight." The result: A place where imagination is given free rein, grins and giggles are encouraged, and everyone can see the world through a child's eyes.

The undisguised pleasure on the faces of park-goers reveals that they have fallen under the spell of a turreted pink castle; the oompah of a band marching down Main Street, U.S.A.; the sound of a train conductor's voice calling "All aboard!"; a close-up encounter with Mickey and Minnie; or a nighttime spectacle more fantastic than the most elaborate dream.

Those who first entered Disneyland as kindergartners now return with their own children—or even grandchildren—to find the theme park of their memories unchanged in spirit and heart. Attractions have come and gone since the park opened in 1955, of course, and whole new "lands" have been added. Most recently, Tomorrowland underwent a near-total transformation.

But the enchantment guests feel when they walk through the portals of "The Happiest Place on Earth" remains constant. That may well be Disneyland's most enduring accomplishment.

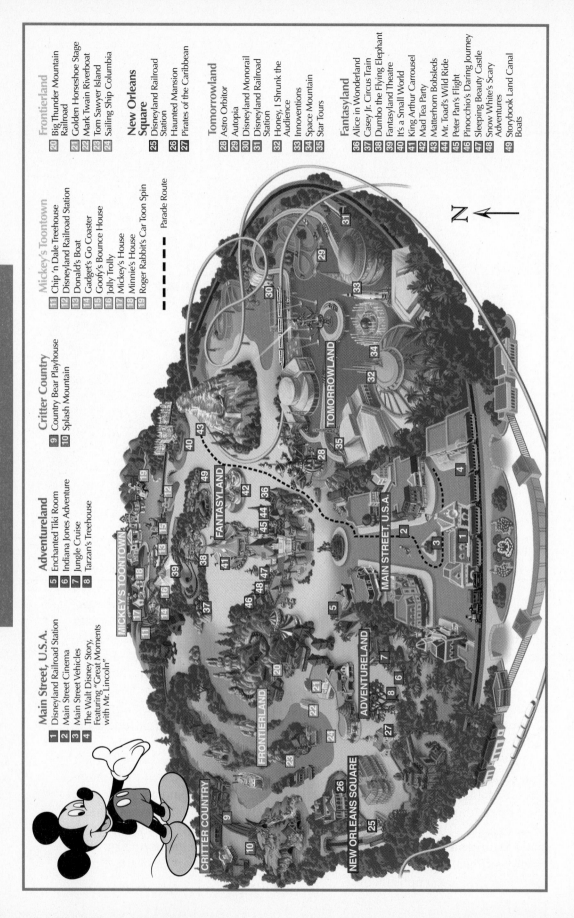

Main Street, U.S.A.

1 Disneyland Railroad Station
2 Main Street Cinema
3 Main Street Vehicles
4 The Walt Disney Story, Featuring "Great Moments with Mr. Lincoln"

Adventureland

5 Enchanted Tiki Room
6 Indiana Jones Adventure
7 Jungle Cruise
8 Tarzan's Treehouse

Critter Country

9 Country Bear Playhouse
10 Splash Mountain

Mickey's Toontown

11 Chip 'n Dale Treehouse
12 Disneyland Railroad Station
13 Donald's Boat
14 Gadget's Go Coaster
15 Goofy's Bounce House
16 Jolly Trolly
17 Mickey's House
18 Minnie's House
19 Roger Rabbit's Car Toon Spin

Frontierland

20 Big Thunder Mountain Railroad
21 Golden Horseshoe Stage
22 Mark Twain Riverboat
23 Tom Sawyer Island
24 Sailing Ship Columbia

New Orleans Square

25 Disneyland Railroad Station
26 Haunted Mansion
27 Pirates of the Caribbean

Tomorrowland

28 Astro Orbitor
29 Autopia
30 Disneyland Monorail
31 Disneyland Railroad Station
32 Honey, I Shrunk the Audience
33 Innoventions
34 Space Mountain
35 Star Tours

Fantasyland

36 Alice in Wonderland
37 Casey Jr. Circus Train
38 Dumbo the Flying Elephant
39 Fantasyland Theatre
40 It's a Small World
41 King Arthur Carrousel
42 Mad Tea Party
43 Matterhorn Bobsleds
44 Mr. Toad's Wild Ride
45 Peter Pan's Flight
46 Pinocchio's Daring Journey
47 Sleeping Beauty Castle
48 Snow White's Scary Adventures
49 Storybook Land Canal Boats

- - - - Parade Route

N

54

GETTING ORIENTED

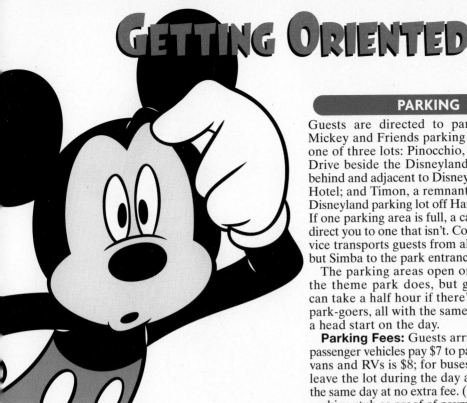

Disneyland Park's layout—a basic hub-and-spokes configuration—is simple, but it was innovative when the park opened in 1955. The design makes getting around easy, though it's not altogether effortless, since the numerous nooks, crannies, and alleyways can be confusing at first.

The hub of the theme park's wheel is Central Plaza, which fronts Sleeping Beauty Castle. From it extend five spokes leading to eight "lands": Main Street, U.S.A.; Adventureland; Frontierland; New Orleans Square; Critter Country; Fantasyland; Mickey's Toontown; and Tomorrowland.

As you face Sleeping Beauty Castle, the first bridge to your left takes you to Adventureland; the next one, to Frontierland and New Orleans Square. To your right, the first walkway goes to Tomorrowland, and the next one—known as Matterhorn Way—leads directly into Fantasyland, and on to Mickey's Toontown. If you cross the Castle's moat and walk through the archway, you'll also end up in Fantasyland. Critter Country occupies its own cul-de-sac extending north from New Orleans Square.

Study the map at left to familiarize yourself with the layout of Disneyland *before* you actually set foot in it. When you arrive at the park, ask for a Disneyland guidemap, which contains the same map, along with information about the times and locations for the day's scheduled entertainment and where to see the characters. It also supplies a list of special services available in the park.

PARKING

Guests are directed to park in Disney's Mickey and Friends parking structure or in one of three lots: Pinocchio, on Disneyland Drive beside the Disneyland Hotel; Simba, behind and adjacent to Disney's Paradise Pier Hotel; and Timon, a remnant of the original Disneyland parking lot off Harbor Boulevard. If one parking area is full, a cast member will direct you to one that isn't. Courtesy tram service transports guests from all parking areas but Simba to the park entrance.

The parking areas open one hour before the theme park does, but getting a space can take a half hour if there's a long line of park-goers, all with the same idea of getting a head start on the day.

Parking Fees: Guests arriving in regular passenger vehicles pay $7 to park. (The fee for vans and RVs is $8; for buses, $9.) You may leave the lot during the day and return later the same day at no extra fee. (Hold on to your parking stub as proof of payment.)

Lost Cars: Even if you take careful note of where you parked your car, you might have trouble remembering or recognizing the exact spot when you return hours later. Hundreds more vehicles will likely be parked around yours. If this happens, contact a cast member and tell him or her approximately when you arrived. With that little bit of information, parking lot personnel can usually figure out the car's general location, and someone will then comb the lanes for it on a scooter.

GETTING AROUND

The Disneyland Railroad's five narrow-gauge trains make a 20-minute loop around the perimeter of the park, stopping at stations in Main Street, U.S.A.; New Orleans Square; Mickey's Toontown; and Tomorrowland. Horse-drawn streetcars, horseless carriages, and a motorized fire engine make one-way trips up and down Main Street.

To travel to points outside of Disneyland, consider the sleek Disneyland Monorail, which glides effortlessly between Tomorrowland and Downtown Disney, a five-minute round-trip. From Downtown Disney, you can easily walk to any of the three on-property hotels—the Disneyland Hotel, Disney's Paradise Pier Hotel, and Disney's Grand Californian. Disney's California Adventure theme park is just a few steps from the entrance to Disneyland (the two parks require separate admission, unless you have a Three- or Four-Day or Resort Park Hopper Ticket).

PARK PRIMER

BABY FACILITIES

The Baby Care Center, on Main Street, U.S.A., by First Aid, provides changing tables, high chairs, toddlers' toilets, and a nursing area. Baby food can be warmed here, and baby powder, diapers, formula, and food are sold. There are no napping facilities or baby-sitting services.

EARLY-ENTRY DAYS

Select attractions in the park typically open 1½ hours early several days a week, depending on the season. However, this is subject to change, so always call ahead. Participating hotels post early-entry days, and those guests who are eligible to take advantage of them definitely get a jump on the day. Guests of a Disneyland Resort hotel are eligible for early admission whenever it is offered; certain Resort Park Hopper Ticket holders get one early entry during their stay.

FIRST AID

First Aid is located at the north end of Main Street, next door to the Main Street Photo Supply Co. A registered nurse is on duty during park operating hours.

GUIDED TOURS

There are no signs pointing the way to attractions at Disneyland, which can make it a daunting, albeit delightful, place for first-time visitors. The four-hour guided walking tour, which starts at Town Square, in Main Street, U.S.A., and ends in Tomorrowland, is an excellent way for newcomers to familiarize themselves with the park. Besides describing what and where everything is, the guide answers questions and accompanies tour guests on six attractions (yes, you do have to wait in line with the other park guests).

Guests who are familiar with Disneyland but would like to know more about it should try the 2½-hour guided tour, "A Walk in Walt's Footsteps." Packed with anecdotes, history, and culture, it starts at Town Square, in Main Street, U.S.A., and ends near Pirates of the Caribbean, in New Orleans Square.

Tickets for either tour cost $14 for adults and $12 for children under 12; they are available at the ticket booths at the main entrance or at City Hall. The tours usually depart at 10:30 A.M. from City Hall.

HOURS

Disneyland is open daily. Weekday hours are generally from 10 A.M. to 8 P.M., with extended hours during the summer. Saturday hours are typically 9 A.M. to midnight. Sunday hours are usually 9 A.M. to 9 P.M. For specific park hours, call 714-781-4565, or check online at *www.disneyland.com*.

During the busy summer and Christmas holiday seasons, it's especially wise to arrive first thing in the morning so that you can visit the popular attractions before the lines get long. If you arrive at Disneyland too late, the parking structure and surrounding lots could be more crowded than usual; this is almost always the case in the summer months and during the last week of December.

For more timing tactics, see "Hot Tips" in this chapter and "Crowd Patterns" in the *Getting Ready to Go* chapter.

INFORMATION

Cast members at Disneyland Information Centers in City Hall and at Central Plaza can answer any questions you might have (or help plot your day so that you can make the most efficient use of your time and see what attractions truly interest you). Specifics on special services and safety considerations have been compiled in Disneyland's guidemap; ask for it when you enter the park.

Information Board: An invaluable resource for planning the day, the Information Board is set up permanently at the north end of Main Street, U.S.A. Located in a grassy spot near the Plaza Pavilion and the entrance to Adventureland, it lets you know how long the waits are for most of the popular attractions, what (if anything) is not operating that day, and where and when park entertainment will take place. The board is updated every hour. Cast members who are stationed there will also answer specific questions and provide information about the restaurants and hotels in the Disneyland Resort.

MONEY MATTERS

Cash and traveler's checks are accepted at all food and merchandise locations throughout Disneyland. American Express, Master-Card, Visa, the Disney Credit Card, and the Discover Card are accepted at all shops, cafeterias, fast-food eateries, snack bars, and full-service establishments (cash only at vending carts). Traveler's checks are sold at the Touring & Travel Services Center on Main Street, U.S.A. Personal checks with your name and address printed on them, drawn on U.S. funds, and accompanied by a government-issued photo ID are also accepted as payment for meals and merchandise. Disneyland Resort hotel guests may charge almost any purchase made in the theme park back to their hotel bill if they gave a credit card number at check-in.

Guests may buy Disney Dollars in $1, $5, and $10 denominations from any park entrance ticket booth, the Bank of Main Street, and City Hall. Disney Dollars are accepted at the three Disney hotels, Downtown Disney, California Adventure, and throughout Disneyland. They can be redeemed for real currency at any time.

PACKAGE EXPRESS

There's no need to lug bags around. You can have purchases sent free of charge to the Package Express pickup point, at the Newsstand at the entrance to Disneyland (on the right as you exit the park). Allow at least two hours between purchase and pickup; for retrieval, just show your sales slip. Guests at the Disneyland Hotel, Disney's Paradise Pier Hotel, or Disney's Grand Californian Hotel can have packages delivered to the bell-services desk for pickup at the hotel.

SAME-DAY RE-ENTRY

Guests who wish to leave the park and return later the same day may do so by getting their hand stamped upon exiting. The stamp will survive numerous hand washings.

SMOKING POLICY

At Disneyland, smoking is only permitted in designated smoking areas; refer to a park guidemap for specific locations. It is prohibited inside all attractions, waiting areas, shops, and indoor and outdoor dining areas.

STROLLERS & WHEELCHAIRS

Strollers and wheelchairs may be rented for $7 just inside the turnstiles of Disneyland, with a $20 deposit. Electric Convenience Vehicles (ECVs) cost $30 for the day, with a $20 deposit. Lost strollers may be replaced at the main entrance and at The Star Trader, in Tomorrowland.

DISNEYLAND PARK

Ticket Prices

Although ticket prices are subject to change, the following will give you an idea of what you can expect to pay. Note that prices are likely to increase midyear. For current prices, call 714-781-4565 or visit *www.disneyland.com*. Refer to page 18 for complete details on ticket options and benefits, including annual passports and Resort Park Hopper Tickets.

	Adults	Children*
One-Day Ticket	$43	$33
Three-Day Ticket	$111	$87
Four-Day Ticket	$137	$107

*3 through 9 years of age; children under 3 free

MAIN STREET, U.S.A.

This pretty thoroughfare represents Main Street America in the early 1900s, complete with the gentle clip-clop of horses' hooves on pavement, melodic ringing of streetcar bells, and strains of nostalgic tunes such as "Bicycle Built for Two" and "Coney Island Baby."

The sounds of brass bands, barbershop quartets, and ragtime piano fill the street. An old-fashioned steam train huffs into a handsome brick depot. Rows of picturesque buildings with mansard roofs, dormer windows, and wrought-iron accents line the street. Authentic gaslights, which once lit the city of Baltimore, flicker at sundown in ornate lampposts lining the walkways, and the storefronts—painted in a palette of pastels—could not be more inviting. Disney was a master of detail: Throughout Main Street, U.S.A., even the doorknobs are historically correct.

To make the buildings appear taller, a set designer's technique called forced perspective was employed. The first floor is seven-eighths scale (this allows guests to enter comfortably); the second story is five-eighths scale; and the third, only half size. The dimensions of the whole are small enough for the place to seem intimate and comforting, yet the proportions appear correct. (Forced perspective was also used to make the Matterhorn and Sleeping Beauty Castle, the park's visual centerpiece, seem taller than they actually are.)

The shops that line Main Street, U.S.A., draw guests back repeatedly during their Disneyland visit (see the "Shopping" section of this chapter and you'll understand why).

The following attractions are listed in the order in which you'll encounter them while walking from the main entrance up Main Street to the Central Plaza, toward Sleeping Beauty Castle.

CITY HALL: Before strolling up Main Street, stop briefly at the Information Center at City Hall, on the west side of Town Square, to find out when and where to catch up with the singers and musicians who perform all over the park. City Hall is also a great meeting place if members of your party separate and plan to congregate later.

FIRE STATION: Next door to City Hall, this was Walt Disney's home away from home during the construction of Disneyland. His apartment, on the top floor, is decorated just as he left it, but is not open to the public. A light burns in the window in his memory. Kids love—and are welcome—to climb on the fire wagon parked inside the Firehouse. It's authentic (from the early 1900s) and provides a wonderful photo opportunity.

BANK OF MAIN STREET: The bank offers foreign-currency exchange and an ATM, and sells Disney Dollars, but is used primarily to process annual passports. (If you see a long line outside, that's why.)

DISNEYLAND RAILROAD: Walt Disney loved trains so much he actually built a one-eighth-scale model, the *Carolwood Pacific*, in the backyard of his home. So it was only natural that his first park include a railroad—five narrow-gauge steam trains that circle Disneyland in 20 minutes, making stops in Main Street, U.S.A.; New Orleans Square; Mickey's Toontown; and Tomorrowland.

BIRNBAUM'S ★BEST★

Stamps like this one indicate the attractions that we find superlative in one and usually more of the following ways: state-of-the-art technology, theming, beauty, novelty, thrills and spills (make that splashes), and overall whimsy. Each "Birnbaum's Best" promises to deliver a dynamite Disneyland experience!

Main Street just wouldn't be Main Street without the sound of the trains chugging in and out of the station and the conductors calling "All aboard!" The voice may sound familiar, but the name won't: It's that of Thurl Ravenscroft, who growled "They're great!" for Kellogg's Tony the Tiger.

Two of the locomotives were built at the Walt Disney Studios; three had other lives before coming to Disneyland. All five trains are powered by oil-fueled steam boilers and must stop several times a day to take on water.

Guests who ride the train between Tomorrowland and Main Street, U.S.A., are in for a couple of surprises. In 1958, Walt Disney added a diorama of the Grand Canyon, depicted from its south rim on a seamless, handwoven canvas that is 306 feet long and 34 feet high, and covered with 300 gallons of paint. The fauna and foliage depict deer, a

HOT TIP!

The Disneyland Railroad is wheelchair-accessible at New Orleans Square, Mickey's Toontown, and Tomorrowland stations.

mountain lion, a golden eagle, wild turkeys, skunks, porcupines, and desert mountain sheep, surrounded by quaking aspens and piñon and ponderosa pines, with a snowfall, a storm, a sunset, and a rainbow thrown in for good measure. The accompanying music is the "On the Trail" section of American composer Ferde Grofé's *Grand Canyon Suite*.

Adjacent to the Grand Canyon, yet eons away, the Primeval World diorama—a scene of misty swamps, deserts, rain forests, erupting volcanoes, and 46 prehistoric creatures inspired by Disney's 1940 film *Fantasia*—opened in 1966, after an interim stop at the Ford Pavilion at the New York World's Fair.

THE WALT DISNEY STORY, FEATURING "GREAT MOMENTS WITH MR. LINCOLN":

The Disneyland Opera House makes the perfect backdrop for a tribute to the life and accomplishments of Walter Elias Disney. A 15-minute film about him is shown continuously, and the actual offices he used in the Burbank studio for 26 years are on view. His briefcase and models of his personal planes, the Mickey I and the Mickey II, rest in this office, just as they did when he worked there. Adjacent to it, in his formal office, is the baby grand on which Leopold Stokowski previewed music for *Fantasia*. Other memorabilia include letters from celebrities and politicos. Note that the offices and memorabilia may not be on display during your visit.

Mr. Lincoln: Besides Walt Disney, the other star here is the Audio-Animatronic version of America's 16th president. After a brief slide show about the Civil War, a seated "Mr. Lincoln" comes center stage. He stands up and discourses on liberty, the American spirit, dangers facing the country, and duty—all the while nodding, gesturing, turning, and shifting his weight in a realistic, if slightly stiff, fashion. His speech is composed of excerpts from talks he gave in Baltimore, New York City, and Springfield, Illinois, from 1852 to 1864. One was part of a eulogy honoring Henry Clay.

DISNEYLAND PARK

Save Time in Line!

For those of us who'd prefer not to waste time standing in line for theme park attractions, Disney's Fastpass is nothing short of a miracle. Basically, the system allows guests to forego the task of waiting in an actual line for a number of theme park attractions. How? Simply by walking up to the Fastpass booth (located near the entrance of participating attractions) and slipping their park ticket into the Fastpass machine. In return, guests get a slip of paper with a time printed on it (in addition to the safe return of their park ticket). That time, for example 4:05 P.M. to 5:05 P.M., represents the window in which guests are invited to return to the attraction and practically walk right on—without standing in a long line! Once you use your Fastpass to enter an attraction (or the time on it has passed), you can get a new Fastpass time for another attraction. It's also possible to get a Fastpass for a second attraction two hours after the first one is issued. For example, if one pass was issued at 2 P.M. you can get a Fastpass for another attraction at 4 P.M. Sound confusing? It won't be once you've tried it.

Disney's Fastpass service is free and available to everyone bearing a valid theme park ticket. It should be available during peak times of the day and all peak seasons. We've placed the Fastpass logo (FP) beside the listing for all of the attractions that were participating at press time. However, since more attractions are scheduled for inclusion, check a park map for an up-to-the-minute listing of Fastpass attractions.

Note that all Disney attractions continue to offer the option of standing in a traditional line. If you happen to enjoy the standing-in-line experience, by all means, go for it. Otherwise, take our advice: Fastpass is the way to go!

MAIN STREET VEHICLES: Main Street's motorized fire wagon, horseless carriages, and horse-drawn streetcars give the thoroughfare a real touch of nostalgia, while at the same time giving guests a lift from one end of the street to the other. The fire truck is modeled after those that might have been found on an American main street in the early 1900s, except that it has seats where the hose would have been carried.

The horse-drawn streetcars, inspired by those in 19th-century photographs, carry 30 passengers each. Most of the horses that pull the cars are Belgians (characterized by their white manes and tails and lightly feathered legs) and Percheron draft horses.

MAIN STREET CINEMA: This small theater was dark for much of last year while the attraction underwent refurbishment. Now back in operation, the theater features a new cartoon classic starring Mickey Mouse.

PENNY ARCADE: This place is now more candy shop than arcade, but the air of nostalgia remains. Those who have frequented it in the past will be happy to find Esmeralda front and center, as before, ready as always to tell your fortune. The arcade still has Mutascopes, machines that feature hand-cranked moving pictures and require a penny to operate. Save some change for the arcade's nine penny presses. You insert a penny (plus a few other coins to pay for the service), and the penny will be flattened and imprinted with the image of Sleeping Beauty Castle or the face of one of the Disney characters.

CENTRAL PLAZA: Main Street, U.S.A., ends at Central Plaza, the hub of the park, and four of the park's lands are directly accessible from here. At its center stands the Walt and Mickey Partners Statue, a life-size bronze sculpture surrounded by diminutive companion likenesses of Pinocchio, Dumbo, Pluto, Minnie Mouse, Donald Duck, Chip and Dale, the White Rabbit, and Goofy—it's one of the park's most popular picture spots.

One of Disneyland's two Information Centers is located here, near the entrance to Adventureland. Besides the information desk, there is a handy Information Board, updated hourly, that posts wait times for many attractions, what (if anything) is not operating that day, and where and when park entertainment will take place. Cast members stationed here can answer specific questions.

PLAZA GARDENS: Visiting performers fill the small stage here in the afternoons, and guests dance to live bands Saturday evenings year-round and Friday evenings in summer. Food is no longer served, but this is a fine spot to bring a snack and relax.

ADVENTURELAND

For someone who grew up in Marceline, Missouri, around the turn of the twentieth century, as Walt Disney did, the far-flung regions of the world must have seemed terribly exotic and exciting. So it's not surprising that when he was planning his new park, he designated one area, called Adventureland, to represent all the (then) remote and mysterious corners of the world.

The original South Seas-island ambience all but disappeared with the opening of the Indiana Jones Adventure in 1995, and Adventureland became a 1930s jungle outpost. Today the entrance to the Jungle Cruise is a walk-through headquarters, with period photographs and radios playing big-band music interrupted by news flashes about Professor Jones' latest exploits and discoveries. Shops here now sell wares that appeal to modern-day adventurers. And it's not at all uncommon to see guests wandering around in safari hats à la Indy.

ENCHANTED TIKI ROOM: Introduced in 1963, this was the first of the park's Audio-Animatronic attractions and the precursor of more elaborate variations, such as "Great Moments with Mr. Lincoln" and the above-mentioned Dr. Jones. Housed in a vaguely Polynesian complex situated at the entrance to Adventureland, the 15-minute show is admittedly a bit dated, but it's vintage Disney, nonetheless.

The stars are four feathered emcees (José, Michael, Pierre, and Fritz), backed up by a sextet of pastel-plumed, long-eyelashed parrots (Collette, Fifi, Gigi, Josephine, Mimi, and Susette), and an eclectic chorus of orchids, carved wooden tiki poles, tiki drummers, singing masks, bird-of-paradise flowers, macaws, Amazon parrots, toucans, fork-tailed birds, cockatoos, and several other species.

The 225 performers all sing and whistle and drum up a tropical storm with so much animation that it's hard to resist a smile. Their repertoire includes "In the Tiki, Tiki, Tiki Room" (the show's theme song), "The Hawaiian War Chant," "Let's All Sing," and "Aloha to You." The courtyard waiting area holds a few surprises, so plan to arrive early and watch them unfold.

JUNGLE CRUISE: The spiel delivered by the skipper on this seven-minute river adventure has its share of corny jokes, but your navigator may turn out to be a natural comic with a genuinely funny delivery. Anyway, you get to glimpse the Temple of the Forbidden Eye (part of the Indiana Jones Adventure) early in the cruise and drift peacefully under a waterfall.

As jungle cruises go, this one is as much like the real thing as Main Street, U.S.A., is like life in a real small town—long on loveliness and short on the visual distractions and minor annoyances that constitute the bulk of human experience. There are no mosquitoes, no Montezuma's revenge. And the Bengal tiger and two king cobras at the ancient Cambodian ruins, and the great apes, gorillas, crocodiles, alligators, elephants, hippos, and lions in the water and along the shores represent no threat to passersby—though according to maintenance crews, they are almost as much trouble as real ones.

Movie buffs should note that Bob Mattey, who helped develop these jungle creatures, also worked on the giant squid from the Disney film *20,000 Leagues Under the Sea*, the man-eating plants in many Tarzan movies, and the menacing mechanical shark in *Jaws*.

The large-leafed upright tree in the Cambodian ruins section of the attraction is a *Ficus religiosa*, the same species of tree under which Buddha received enlightenment in India many centuries ago.

TARZAN'S TREEHOUSE: The 70-foot-high *Disneydendron semperflorens grandis*, or "large, ever-blooming Disney tree," which cradled the Swiss Family Treehouse from 1962 to mid-1999, now embraces another lofty dwelling: Tarzan's Treehouse, inspired by the book by Edgar Rice Burroughs and Disney's animated feature *Tarzan*. Overlooking the Jungle Cruise and the Temple of the Forbidden Eye (the setting for Indiana Jones's misadventures), this moss- and vine-covered "high-rise apartment" shelters Tarzan; his adoptive mom, the ape Kala; and his companion, Jane.

An interactive play area at the base of the tree has been designed around the scientific equipment that Jane and her father brought to the jungle. (Guests are welcome to experiment with some of it.) Nearby, a makeshift wooden staircase crafted from

shipwreck salvage and a weathered suspension bridge provide easy access to the treehouse itself.

Jane's drawings, displayed throughout the compound, reveal the amazing story of Tarzan's survival and coming-of-age in the wild. (But could there be trouble in paradise? That lout of a leopard, Sabor, is lurking in the tree!) By the time guests plant their feet on terra firma once more, they will have hit new heights, not unlike a certain high-flying hero himself, and gotten acquainted with some of the characters—human and animal—who have shared in his exploits.

INDIANA JONES ADVENTURE: FP Hidden deep within the dense jungles of India, the Temple of the Forbidden Eye was built long ago to honor the powerful deity Mara. According to legend, Mara could "look into your very soul" and grant the "pure of heart" one of three gifts: unlimited wealth, eternal youth, or future knowledge. But legend also issues a stern warning: "A terrible fate awaits those who gaze upon the eyes of Mara!" Dr. Jones would only comment, "Records indicate that many have come, but few have returned."

BIRNBAUM'S **BEST**

Now you can take an expedition through the ancient temple ruins in this attraction based on the George Lucas-Steven Spielberg film trilogy. The whole experience, including the pre-show and queue area, can easily take more than an hour (without a Fastpass), though the ride itself lasts 3½ minutes. You follow the jungle path through Dr. Jones's cluttered encampment, then enter the temple via the path marked by his original team. In the queue area, a newsreel tells of Jones's latest expedition. What it does not reveal is that he has entered the temple and disappeared.

Following in his footsteps, you will see warning signs that indicate there still may be booby traps that have not yet been disarmed. (The fun is in paying no heed to the warnings and letting the spikes fall where they may.) Once inside the temple, guests board 12-passenger off-road vehicles reminiscent of 1930s troop transports. One person takes the wheel and serves as the expedition driver, but not until all are securely fastened in their seats for the twists and turns ahead. Hold on to your belongings!

The search for Indiana Jones is on, and an encounter with the fearsome Mara is unavoidable. The trip reveals an underworld of screaming mummies, glowing fires, falling lava, worrisome snakes, and poisonous darts. Surprises lurk around every bend, and escape is only temporary (just as in the movies), as you suffer an avalanche of creepy crawlies, traverse a quaking suspension bridge, and, best of all, find yourself face-to-face with a gigantic rolling ball that threatens to flatten everyone in its path. At the end of the ride, Indy himself is waiting for you, with a flippant parting remark such as "That wasn't so bad" or "Next time you're on your own."

Thanks to the wizardry and cunning of the Disney Imagineers, no two rides are exactly the same, so each time you enter the Temple of the Forbidden Eye, the experience will be slightly different.

Note: Pregnant women and guests who suffer from heart conditions, motion sickness, weak backs, and other limitations should not ride. Children must be at least three years old or at least 46 inches tall to board; those under seven must be accompanied by an adult.

NEW ORLEANS SQUARE

Though New Orleans Square did not figure in Disneyland layout until 1966, it's certainly among the park's most evocative areas. This would be true even if it were home only to the superb Haunted Mansion and Pirates of the Caribbean. But there's also its picturesque site on the shores of the Rivers of America, and its architecture, a pastiche of wrought-iron, pastel stucco, French doors, and beckoning verandas.

Not to be missed are the pleasant open-air dining spots; the romantic Blue Bayou restaurant overlooking the moonlit lagoon stretch of Pirates of the Caribbean; the unique assortment of shops; and the music, lively jazz and Dixieland, performed in traditional New Orleans style.

As you sit here on a warm evening, snacking on fritters and hot chocolate, images of Disneyland-as-amusement-park evaporate. Just as Main Street, U.S.A., makes the theme park a great place to shop, New Orleans Square makes it a fine spot to spend a few relaxing hours. Those click-click sounds emanating from the railroad station are the Morse code version of the actual speech Walt Disney gave on the opening day of Disneyland.

The attractions described below are listed as you encounter them when strolling from east to west in New Orleans Square.

PIRATES OF THE CARIBBEAN: FP One of

BIRNBAUM'S *BEST* the most swashbuckling adventures you'll find at Disneyland, this 16-minute boat ride transports guests through a series of sets portraying a rowdy pirate raid on a Caribbean village. Bursting with cannon fire, stolen loot, a gluttonous feast, and a raucous band of unruly mercenaries, Pirates of the Caribbean has entertained more people than any theme park attraction in history. It was the last attraction on which Walt Disney worked extensively.

The experience begins with a short excursion through a bayou, where will-o'-the-wisps glow just above the grasses. Fireflies twinkle nearby, while stars spangle the twilight-blue sky overhead. The attention to detail nearly boggles the mind. The Audio-Animatronic cast of 64 human figures and 55 animals includes drunken pigs whose legs actually twitch in their soporific contentment, chickens so realistic that even a farmer might be fooled at first, and a piccolo-playing pirate whose fingers move and cheeks puff as he toots a little ditty. Notice the realistic details, like the hairs on the leg of one swashbuckler perched atop a bridge overhead.

The attraction's theme song, "Yo-Ho, Yo-Ho; a Pirate's Life for Me," manages to transform what is actually a picture of some blatant buccaneering into a rousing time for all. A must—again and again.

Note: Pirates of the Caribbean is one of the highest-capacity attractions at the park, so the line tends to move quickly, even when it appears long.

THE DISNEY GALLERY: The stairways on either side of the entrance to Pirates of the Caribbean lead to this French Quarter-style suite of rooms, originally designed to be the private apartment of Walt Disney. Dignitaries often visited the park, and he wanted an elegant place in which he and his brother, Roy, could meet and greet them. Today, the gallery has changing exhibits of original artwork, focusing mainly on the concepts and drawings for specific Disney projects. Cast members give gallery tours upon request.

The inviting interior patio is climate controlled year-round because Walt Disney planned to do a lot of entertaining there. Guests can bring a snack or coffee and enjoy it there or on the balcony. In the evenings, the balcony holds up to 18 guests for VIP seating for each showing of Fantasmic! (reservations are necessary; for more information, see "Entertainment" at the end of this chapter).

Look carefully at the wrought-iron grillwork surrounding the balcony; the initials WD and RD (for Walt and Roy Disney) are woven into the design.

HAUNTED MANSION: FP In a British radio interview, Walt Disney once explained how sorry he felt for those homeless ghosts whose hauntable mansions had fallen to the wrecker's ball. Feeling that these lost souls sorely needed a place of their own, he offered this Haunted Mansion, unquestionably one of Disneyland's top attractions. From its stately portico to the exit corridor, special effect is piled upon special effect to create an eerie, but never terrifying, mood. Just frightfully funny.

PHOTO BY KEITH GROSHANS

Judicious applications of paint and expert lighting heighten the shadows that play ghoulishly on the walls outside. The jumble of trunks, chairs, dress forms, and other assorted knickknacks in the attic are left appropriately dirty, and extra cobwebs, which come in convenient liquid form, are strung with abandon. The eerie music and the slightly spooky tones of the Ghost Host often set small children to whimpering, and soon their Mickey Mouse ears have been pulled tightly over their eyes. Some members of the crews who work in the mansion at night find themselves jumping at sudden noises. Still, the spirits that inhabit this house on the hill—999 in all—are a tame lot for the most part, though they are always looking for occupant number 1,000.

What makes the seven-minute attraction so special is the attention to, and abundance of, details—so many that it's next to impossible to take them all in during the first, or even the second or third, time around. In the Portrait Chamber, a roomful of fearsome-looking gargoyles that adjoins the chandeliered and lace-curtain-adorned foyer, it's fun to speculate on whether the ceiling moves up or the room moves down. (It's one way here and the opposite way at the mansion's counterpart at Walt Disney World's Magic Kingdom.)

Once in your Doom Buggy, look for the raven that appears again and again as you go through the house, the bats' eyes on the wallpaper, the TOMB SWEET TOMB plaque, and the rattling suit of armor in the Corridor of Doors. Can you spot the Hidden Mickey in the haunted dining room?

Then there are the dead plants and flowers and broken glass in the Conservatory, where a hand reaches out of a half-open casket; the

HOT TIP!
Repeat visitors to the Haunted Mansion occasionally enjoy shouting out the words of the Ghost Host and screaming in mock terror. This may scare younger guests.

terrified cemetery watchman and his mangy mutt in the Graveyard; the ghostly teapot that pours spectral tea; the ectoplasmic king and queen on the teeter-totter; the bicycle-riding spirits; the transparent musicians; and the headless knight and his supernatural Brunhilde. Nice stuff all.

The mansion was constructed in 1963, based on studies of houses around Baltimore; the attraction itself opened in 1969. The music "Grim Grinning Ghosts" was composed especially for the Haunted Mansion attraction.

FRONTIERLAND

PHOTO BY KEITH GROSHANS

This is the America experienced by the pioneers as they pushed westward: rough wilderness outposts, dense forests, rugged mountains delineating the skyline, and rivers lapping at the shore.

The sights in Frontierland are just about as pleasant as they come at Disneyland, and the atmosphere as relaxing. That's especially true in the afternoon, when the riverboat *Mark Twain*, with its elaborate wooden lacework trim, pulls majestically away from its dock for a cruise along the Rivers of America.

The following Frontierland attractions are described in the order in which visitors encounter them while moving counterclockwise from the Central Plaza gateway toward Big Thunder Mountain.

FRONTIERLAND SHOOTIN' EXPOSITION:

This shooting gallery, set in an 1850s town in the Southwest Territory, is completely electronic. Eighteen rifles are trained on Boothill, a mining town complete with a bank, jail, hotel, and stables. They fire infrared beams that trigger humorous results whenever they strike the red reactive targets. The most challenging target is the moving shovel, which, when struck, causes a skeleton to pop out of a grave.

Note: Disneyland tickets do not include use of the arcade. Pay 50 cents for 20 shots—then fire away.

BIG THUNDER MOUNTAIN RAILROAD:

BIRNBAUM'S **BEST** FP Inspired by peaks in Utah's Bryce Canyon, Big Thunder Mountain is entirely a Disney creation. The name comes from an old Indian legend about a sacred mountain in Wyoming that thundered whenever men tried to excavate its gold. The attraction took five years of planning and two years of construction, and it cost about as much to build as the rest of Disneyland put together—$16 million.

As roller coasters go, this one is relatively tame. It's short on steep climbs and precipitous drops that put hearts in throats and make stomachs protest, but long on tight curves that provoke giggles of glee. Adding to the appeal of this thrill ride is the scenery that the runaway mine train passes along the way: a pitch-black bat cave, giant stalactites and stalagmites, a waterfall, a canyon inhabited by coyotes, a natural-arch bridge that affords fine views over the Big Thunder landscape, and mine walls ready to cave in.

The queue area sets the scene of the quaint mining town, with two hotels, a newspaper office, dance hall, saloon, and general store. If you listen closely, you may hear a local barmaid flirting with a miner to the tune of "Red River Valley" or "Listen to the Mockingbird."

As you proceed toward the loading area, notice the brownish stone walls on each side of you. They were created from a hundred

tons of real gold ore from the former mining town of Rosamond, California, which also yielded the ten-foot-tall stamp mill designated BIG THUNDER MINE 1880.

This is an extremely popular ride, so try to get to it first thing in the morning, during a parade, or just before park closing, when the lines are shorter. For the best of both worlds, ride twice—once by day, to see the scenery, and again after dark, for the pleasure of hurtling through the cool night (you might catch a glimpse of the Fantasmic! show).

Note: Pregnant women and guests who have heart conditions, motion sickness, weak backs, and other limitations should not ride. Children must be at least three years old and a minimum of 40 inches tall to board. Kids under seven years old must be accompanied by an adult.

MARK TWAIN RIVERBOAT: One of the original Disneyland attractions and the first paddle wheeler built in the United States in half a century, this five-eighths-scale vessel circumnavigates Tom Sawyer Island. Along the way, it passes the River Belle Terrace, the Royal Street Veranda, the docks for the Tom Sawyer Island Rafts, piney Critter Country, a waterfall, abandoned railroad tracks, and lovely dense woods full of the alders, cottonwoods, maples, and willows that might have been found along the Missouri frontier more than a century ago. Moose, elk, and (real) ducks complete the passing scene.

On a busy day, this 14-minute ride offers a pleasant respite from the crowds. And if you manage to get one of the few chairs in the bow, the *Mark Twain* also provides a rare opportunity to put your feet up.

GOLDEN HORSESHOE STAGE: Tongue-in-cheek humor and western flair are the key ingredients in the musical and specialty acts featured at this entertainment venue. The hall itself is resplendent with chandeliers, polished floors and banisters, and a long

DID YOU KNOW...

Walt and Lillian Disney celebrated their 30th wedding anniversary on July 13, 1955, with a party aboard the *Mark Twain* riverboat. Disneyland officially opened four days later.

brass railing. Supposedly, it was inspired by the Golden Horseshoe Saloon, which flourished in a bygone era in New York City. Walt Disney kept a private box here, just to the left of the stage, on the upper level.

Billy Hill & the Hillbillies, brothers who mix bluegrass music and wacky comedy, are regular performers at the Golden Horseshoe Stage (for specifics, see page 90). Performance times may vary throughout the year; your best bet is to check your Disneyland guidemap's entertainment schedule or drop by one of the Information Centers when you arrive at the park.

There is no assigned seating inside; all of the seats are good, though those up front or on the balcony are perhaps the best.

SAILING SHIP COLUMBIA: A full-scale replica of the ten-gun, three-masted "Gem of the Ocean," the *Columbia* operates seasonally and on higher-attendance days at Disneyland. The original ship, constructed in Plymouth, Massachusetts, in 1787 and christened the *Columbia Rediviva* ("freedom reborn"), was the first American craft to circumnavigate the globe. (Back then, that took three years to do.)

Disney's *Columbia*, dedicated in 1958 and renovated in 1984, was the first of its kind to be built in more than a century, and it circumnavigates the Rivers of America in 15 minutes. It has a steel hull and a deck planked with Douglas fir, and measures 110 feet from stem to stern, with an 84-foot mainmast. Usually moored at Fowler's Harbor, opposite the Haunted Mansion, the ship towers majestically over the treetops below.

Below Decks: The *Columbia*'s maritime museum, open only when the ship is operating, illustrates the way sailors lived on the original vessel during its later voyages, as reported in the ship's log and in letters between the captain and the owners.

TOM SAWYER ISLAND: The landfall that the *Mark Twain*, the *Columbia*, and Davy Crockett's Explorer Canoes circle as they ply the Rivers of America was at one time the highest point in Disneyland. Its archetypal treehouse, complete with spyglasses and peepholes, lets would-be branch dwellers gaze out over the treetops to the *Mark Twain* docked across the river. But the treehouse is only one of the many wonders on Tom Sawyer Island.

On another wonder, the floating Barrel Bridge, it's nearly impossible to maintain a stride more decorous than a lurch. Nearby, kids scramble up a small hill studded with log steps. Then there's Castle Rock Ridge—a fantastic group of boulders that includes the mightily spinning Merry-Go-Round Rock, the aptly named Teeter-Totter Rock, and (inside the Ridge) the spacious Pirate's

HOT TIP! Cool, dark, and spooky inside, the labyrinthine Injun Joe's Cave is one of the best spots on Tom Sawyer Island.

Den and smaller Castle Rock Dungeon. The latter is full of niches and cul-de-sacs just the right size for the island's youngest explorers, but so narrow and low-ceilinged in places that grown-ups who don't bend down or turn sideways risk getting stuck, just like Winnie the Pooh.

At the island's southernmost point, not far from where visitors disembark, there's a perpetually creaking old mill; at the opposite end stands Fort Wilderness.

Small signs point to all the places of interest on the island, and even though the footpaths are decidedly well-trodden, any time spent here is worthwhile, and could encompass some of your happiest getaway moments at Disneyland.

Note: Tom Sawyer Island closes at dusk. Check at the dock for excursion times, particularly the last departure.

L ush shady forests of pines, locusts, white birches, coastal redwoods, and ever-green elms surround Critter Country, one of the most pleasant corners of Disneyland. In 1972, this land debuted as Bear Country, the backwoods home of the perennially popular Country Bear Playhouse. From 1956 through 1971, the area was called the Indian Village, complete with teepees and a dance circle, and was part of Frontierland.

In 1989, the bears were joined by foxes, frogs, geese, rabbits, crocodiles, and many of the other critters that make up the Audio-Animatronic cast of Splash Mountain. To make their neighbors feel welcome, the bears (in cahoots with a handful of Disney Imagineers) rechristened the area Critter Country. Observant guests will spot scaled-down houses, lairs, and nests tucked into hillsides and along the river.

Attractions are described here according to their east-to-west locations.

SPLASH MOUNTAIN: FP

BIRNBAUM'S
★BEST★

The fourth peak in Disneyland's mountain range of thrill rides—along with Big Thunder Mountain, the Matterhorn, and Space Mountain—Splash Mountain is unlike the other three attractions, where passengers ride roller coaster-style cars down tubular steel tracks. In this nine-minute ride, they board hollowed-out logs and drift on a waterborne journey through backwoods swamps and bayous, down waterfalls, and finally (here's where the speed picks up), over the top of a steep spillway at the peak of the mountain into a briar-laced pond five stories below.

Splash Mountain is based on the animated sequences in Walt Disney's 1946 film *Song of the South*, and the principal characters from the movie—Brer Rabbit, Brer Fox, and Brer Bear—appear in the attraction courtesy of Audio-Animatronic technology. In fact, Splash Mountain's stars and supporting cast of 103 performers number almost as many as those in Pirates of the Caribbean, which has 119 Audio-Animatronic characters.

HOT TIP!

If you want to get soaked on Splash Mountain, sit in the front of the car; the spray has less of a dampening effect in back.

Comparisons to Pirates of the Caribbean are particularly apt, as Splash Mountain was consciously designed to be a "How do we top this?" response to the popular, long-running pirate adventure. Splash Mountain breaks new ground on several counts. Besides setting a record for total animated characters, it also boasts one of the world's tallest and sharpest flume drops (52½ feet at a 47-degree angle). It's one of the fastest rides ever operated at Disneyland Park.

One other twist makes Splash Mountain unique in the annals of flumedom: After hurtling down Chickapin Hill, the seven-passenger log boats hit the pond below with a giant splash—and then promptly sink underwater (or seem to), with just a trace of bubbles left in their wake.

Splash Mountain's designers didn't only borrow the attraction's characters and color-saturated settings from *Song of the South*. They also included quite a bit of the film's Academy Award-winning music. In

fact, the song in the attraction's finale, "Zip-A-Dee-Doo-Dah," has become something of a Disney anthem over the years. The voice of Brer Bear is performed by none other than Nick Stewart, the same actor who spoke the part in the film when it was released in 1946.

Keep in mind: The hotter the day, the longer the lines, so go early or late.

Note: You must be at least 40 inches tall and three years old to ride the Splash Mountain attraction.

DAVY CROCKETT'S EXPLORER CANOES: Of all the boats that circle the Rivers of America, these 35-foot fiberglass craft may offer the most fun, at least for the stalwart. They're real canoes, and no, they are definitely not on tracks. Though the helmsman and the sternman are strong enough to handle the rowing, guests' contributions are also vital when it comes to completing the 2,400-foot voyage.

Note: This attraction operates only on certain days, and it closes at dusk. Check at the landing for excursion times.

COUNTRY BEAR PLAYHOUSE: It's just about impossible to sit through this 16-minute country-and-western hoedown without cracking a smile. Ostensibly dreamed up by one Ursus H. Bear at the end of an especially good winter's nap, it is presented, with rib-tickling results, by an assortment of 18 Audio-Animatronic bruins. Among them are Henry, the lively seven-foot-tall master of ceremonies; the big-bodied pianist, Gomer; the Five Bear Rugs (Fred on mouth harp, Zeke on banjo, Zeb on fiddle, Ted on white lightning jug, and Tennessee picking the guitar-like one-string "thang"); and the ample Trixie, lamenting lost love after being jilted at an ant-plagued picnic.

Dressed in a yellow slicker, rain bonnet, and red galoshes, Teddi Barra floats down from the ceiling crooning "Singin' in the Rain." (Fittingly, her Swingin' Arcade is next door; see below.) Bubbles, Bunny, and Beulah, in sweet harmony, sing "Wish They All Could Be California Bears." Completing the cast are Wendell, the "overbearing baritone"; Liver Lips McGrowl; and last but never least, the show-stopping Big Al, one of the few Audio-Animatronic figures in the park with a following great enough to create a demand for his likeness on postcards and plush toys. There's a penny press in the lobby.

Note: At Christmastime, the bears put on a special holiday show.

"THOTFUL SPOT": Winnie the Pooh and his friends like to linger in a peaceful forest enclave in Critter Country. They call it the "Thotful Spot." The location changes from time to time but is usually by the exit to Country Bear Playhouse. It's the perfect place for snapping some pictures or having a keepsake photo taken by a Disneyland photographer (see "Pooh & You Photos" on page 86).

TEDDI BARRA'S SWINGIN' ARCADE: This small entertainment center, named for the female star of the Country Bear Playhouse, provides the opportunity to duel western-style with Johnny Rio or Fast Draw, and to take aim at a multitude of moving targets.

FANTASYLAND

Walt Disney called this a timeless land of enchantment. Village lanes twist between houses built of half-timbers, brick, stone, and stucco, often embellished with brightly colored folk paintings.The skyline, dominated by the peak of the Matterhorn, bristles with chimneys and weather vanes, turrets and towers. At the center of it all, as if deposited here by an itinerant carnival, is the King Arthur Carrousel.

When Walt Disney created Snow White's Scary Adventures, Mr. Toad's Wild Ride, and Peter Pan's Flight, the black light and glow-in-the-dark paints he used (so popular during the psychedelic sixties) were great novelties. But in recent decades the palette of available hues and the spectrum of special-effects techniques have taken quantum leaps forward, and Fantasyland has benefited from these remarkable advances. Thanks to fiber optics, rear projection, holography, and other advanced special-effects techniques (developed in the course of constructing Epcot at Walt Disney World and Tokyo Disneyland), it has become even more of a visual treat.

Note: Parents of young children should be aware that some of Fantasyland's attractions take place in the dark. These include Peter Pan's Flight, Mr. Toad's Wild Ride, Alice in Wonderland, Snow White's Scary Adventures, and Pinocchio's Daring Journey.

Attractions are described here as you come upon them when moving roughly counterclockwise from Sleeping Beauty Castle.

SLEEPING BEAUTY CASTLE: Rising above the treetops at the end of Main Street, U.S.A., it could be a figment of your imagination or a mirage created by Tinker Bell's pixie dust. Closer inspection proves this architectural confection is as real as the swans in the moat surrounding it. A composite of medieval European castles, primarily in the French and Bavarian styles, Sleeping Beauty Castle, the gateway to Fantasyland, is constructed of concrete, with towers that rise 77 feet above the moat. Trimmed in 22-karat gold leaf, it appears shiny even on gray days. The structure seems larger than it really is due to the use of forced perspective, down to the bricks.

From the Central Plaza, you're actually looking at the back of the castle; Walt Disney decided it was prettier that way and had the builders turn it around. The drawbridge, lowered when the park first opened in 1955, functions like a real one—though it has been raised (and lowered again) only once since then, in 1983, at the rededication ceremony for the "new" Fantasyland.

Inside the castle, a Walk-Thru Tour tells the story of Sleeping Beauty scene by scene in diorama form. Outside, juniper is planted around the water's edge; it's one of the few green plants that the swans won't eat. One of the two graceful trees to the right of the drawbridge bears hundreds of tiny yellow flowers in spring, and the other is covered with fragile lavender flowers for several weeks in early summer.

ARIEL'S GROTTO: The Little Mermaid spends most of the day in a grotto just a few steps north of her father's garden. Here she visits with guests, who often ask her to sign their autograph books or pose for a photograph. She's happy to oblige. You can take as many shots as you like with your own camera or purchase a five-by-seven ($10) or eight-by-ten ($15) photo taken by one of Disneyland's photographers. The photos may be picked up at the Main Street Photo Supply Co.; allow a few hours for processing.

TRITON GARDEN: This diminutive oasis, located between the castle and the entrance to Tomorrowland, is filled with landscaped walkways, tide pools, rock outcroppings, and succulent plants. But the big lure at Triton Garden is the jets of water that leap from rock to rock and catapult over the bridge. Kids can't resist matching wits with them. At

PHOTO BY KEITH GROSHANS

MR. TOAD'S WILD RIDE: Based on the 1949 Disney film *The Adventures of Ichabod and Mr. Toad*—which was inspired by Kenneth Grahame's classic novel *The Wind in the Willows*—this zany attraction, housed in an English manor bristling with ornate chimneys that really smoke, takes guests on a riotous ride from the perspective of the eccentric but lovable Mr. Toad.

DID YOU KNOW...

There is a shadow of Sherlock Holmes (complete with pipe and cap) in the second-story window of the manor that houses Mr. Toad's Wild Ride.

night, the interplay of lights, colors, and fountain spray transforms the garden into a particularly beautiful spot.

SNOW WHITE GROTTO: Tucked off Matterhorn Way, at the eastern end of the moat around Sleeping Beauty Castle, this is one of those quiet corners of the park easily overlooked by guests. If you stand by the wishing well, you might hear Adriana Caselotti, the original voice of Snow White, singing the lovely melody "I'm Wishing," written for Disney's Oscar-winning 1937 film. While she sings, jets of water rise and fall in the waterfall fountain on the other side of the walkway, and a quartet of small fish rises up from the bottom of the pool at the base of the cascade to swim around in little circles. Any coins tossed into the well go to charity.

PETER PAN'S FLIGHT: This attraction is one

BIRNBAUM'S BEST

of the park's loveliest—and most popular. Based on the novel by Sir James M. Barrie about the boy who wouldn't grow up, by way of Walt Disney's 1953 animated feature, the ride's special effects soar to celestial heights. Pirate ships carry travelers through the clouds and into a sky filled with tiny fiber-optic stars.

Water ripples and gleams softly in the moonlight; the lava on the sides of a volcano glows with almost the intensity of the real thing. After an ephemeral few minutes, the ships seem to drift through a waterfall and back into reality, an unloading area that is all the more jarring after the magic of the trip through Never Land.

Of the approximately 350 miles of fiber optics found throughout Fantasyland, the majority is used in this ride. The twinkling London scene is an enlarged model of an authentic map of the city.

Unfortunately, he is as inept a driver as you might expect a toad to be. During the excursion, you crash through the fireplace in his library, scattering embers everywhere; burst through a wall full of windows; careen through the countryside; charge headlong into a warehouse full of TNT; lurch through the streets of London; then ram into a pub and veer out again. During the two-minute journey, you'll also be berated by a judge in court, nearly collide head-on with a railroad train, and even be banished to a fiery inferno.

DISNEYLAND PARK

71

ALICE IN WONDERLAND: Traveling in over-size caterpillars, visitors fall down the rabbit hole and embark upon a bizarre adventure in that strange world known as Wonderland. They come face-to-face with Tweedledum and Tweedledee, a garden filled with singing roses, the Cheshire Cat, the Queen of Hearts and her playing-card soldiers, the White Rabbit, and other characters from Lewis Carroll's beloved story *Alice in Wonderland*. At the end of the nearly four-minute ride, the giant "un-birthday" cake explodes, providing a suitable climax to this sweet interlude.

MAD TEA PARTY: The sequence in Walt Disney's 1951 release *Alice in Wonderland* in which the Mad Hatter hosts a tea party for his "un-birthday" is the theme for this attraction—a group of oversize pastel tea-cups whirling wildly on a spinning tea table. Festive Japanese lanterns hang overhead. The park's original thrill ride back in 1955, it lasts only 1½ minutes, so if the line is long, come back later.
   Note: The teacups may look mild, but it's a good idea to let a reasonable interval pass after eating before you take one for a spin.

MATTERHORN BOBSLEDS: Though it's 100 times smaller than the actual peak, Disney's version of the Matterhorn is still a credible reproduction. The use of forced perspective makes the snowy summit look much loftier than the approximately 147 feet it does reach. Even the trees and shrubs help create the illusion. Those at the timberline are far smaller than the ones at the bottom.

BIRNBAUM'S **BEST**

   The ride itself, like the more sophisticated Space Mountain and Big Thunder Mountain Railroad attractions, has to be counted among the most thrilling at Disneyland. At the time the Matterhorn Bobsleds were dedicated, in 1959, they were considered an engineering novelty because their dispatch system allowed more than one car to be in action at once. The ride begins with a long climb into the frosty innards of the mountain, then makes a speeding, twisting, turning descent through a cloud of fog and past giant icicles and ice crystals. The wind howls as you hurtle toward a brief but inevitable encounter with

HOT TIP!

There are two Matterhorn ride experiences. At the left queue, the wait is shorter, and the two-minute ride is more thrilling. The right queue leads to a smoother, more scenic ride that lasts 2½ minutes.

the Abominable Snowman. The speed of the downhill flight away from the creature seems greater than it really is because much of the journey takes place inside tunnels. Splash-down is in an alpine lake.
   Note: Pregnant women, children under the age of three, and guests who suffer from weak backs, heart conditions, motion sickness, and other physical limitations should not take the ride.

IT'S A SMALL WORLD: The background music for this attraction is cheerful and sing-song, sometimes maddeningly so. It does grab your attention, starting with the pastel facade, embellished with stylized representations of the Eiffel Tower, the Leaning Tower of Pisa, Big Ben, the Taj Mahal, and other world landmarks. The 30-foot-tall mechanized clock with the loud ticktock and the syncopated swing is frosting on the architectural cake. The whirring of gears that marks every quarter hour alone warrants a trip to the attraction's plaza on the edge of Fantasyland and adjacent to Mickey's Toontown.
   Boats carry guests into a land filled with more than 300 Audio-Animatronic dolls representing children from 100 regions

of the world. It's a pageant for the eyes, even if the ears grow weary. (If you find yourself humming "It's a Small World" for the next several hours, you can blame Richard M. and Robert B. Sherman, the Academy Award-winning composers of the music for *Mary Poppins*, among many other Disney scores.) Topiary figures in the shapes of a giraffe, elephant, rhinoceros, lion, horse, and other friendly beasts bid guests a fond farewell at the end of the ride.

Note: It's a Small World is transformed inside and out between Thanksgiving and New Year's to become as close to a winter wonderland as you're likely to find in Southern California. The dolls even sing "Jingle Bells" along with "It's a Small World."

STORYBOOK LAND CANAL BOATS: This seven-minute cruise past miniature scenes from classic Disney animated films is not one of Disneyland's major attractions, yet few who take the trip deny that the journey is one of the park's sweetest, filled with intricate, evocative settings. No detail was spared, from the home of the Three Little Pigs to the Old English village of Alice in Wonderland (where the White Rabbit boasts his very own mailbox) to the London park that Peter Pan and Tinker Bell flew over with Wendy, John, and Michael Darling on their way to Never Land.

Other storybook locales include Agrabah and the marketplace where Aladdin met Princess Jasmine, the Seven Dwarfs' home and jewel mine, and Cinderella's castle. At the end of the cruise, the boat drifts past the three mills from the film *The Old Mill*, Geppetto's village, Prince Eric and Ariel's castle, and King Triton's castle.

DUMBO THE FLYING ELEPHANT: As beloved a symbol of Fantasyland as Sleeping Beauty Castle, this ride reminds all who see it of the baby elephant immortalized in the 1941 Disney film. Dumbo discovers, after drinking from a bucketful of champagne, that his inordinately large ears, which have been such a source of embarrassment, actually enable him to fly.

A mechanical marvel, Dumbo the Flying Elephant is full of filigreed metalwork, with cogs, gears, and pulleys galore. Brass pipes spew water from the base, and music is supplied by a vintage band organ housed in a small, ornate structure nearby. That figure atop the ride is Timothy Mouse, who became Dumbo's manager after the little elephant was hired to be a star by the same circus folk who once teased him. The topiary figures pay tribute to the little guy with the floppy ears.

CASEY JR. CIRCUS TRAIN: One of the key sequences in the movie *Dumbo*, in which an engine named *Casey Jr.* pulls a circus train up a steep hill, became the inspiration for this 3½-minute train ride that circles Storybook Land. The Story-book Land Canal Boats are better for viewing the landscaping and miniature details there, but it's worth a ride inside one of the wild-animal cage cars. Each train has two of them—plus a real caboose. Listen as the engine chugs "I think I can" and then "I thought I could" as it negotiates the hill.

SNOW WHITE'S SCARY ADVENTURES: Ornamental stone ravens perch on carved stone skulls atop a stone tower and hearts pierced through with swords lie at the base of the twisted pillars that support this brooding building. All this might lead you to expect an attraction as frightfully elabo-

PHOTO BY KEITH GROSHANS

rate as the Haunted Mansion. It isn't. That said, the two-minute ride includes several fairly menacing scenes. In one, the Queen changes into a scraggly-haired, wart-nosed old hag before your eyes; in another, this wicked green-eyed crone has the nerve to offer *you* a poisoned apple.

After passing a brief and joyful scene in the Seven Dwarfs' cottage, the cars travel through a creepy dungeon, visit a workshop

Who's Who?

In the cottage scene at the beginning of Snow White's Scary Adventures, that's Grumpy playing the organ, Sleepy on fiddle, Bashful on guitar, Happy on accordion, Doc on mandolin, and Dopey on Sneezy's shoulders.

where the Queen labors over her bubbling caldron, and then venture into the Frightening Forest, where moss-draped trees point talon-like branches at passersby. The visit to the jewel mines, where the Seven Dwarfs labor, is more beautiful than scary, because of the topaz, emeralds, rubies, and sapphires glowing benignly in the darkness.

Thankfully, it all ends in true storybook fashion: As the evil Queen attempts to roll a stone down the side of a mountain to crush the dwarfs below, she tumbles over the edge of a cliff, leaving Snow White, the handsome prince, and their seven sidekicks to live together happily ever after, as depicted in the mural near the exit. The music is taken from rare recordings used to create the film's original sound track.

Note: This attraction can be too intense for small children.

PINOCCHIO'S DARING JOURNEY: Based on Walt Disney's 1940 animated feature, this is a small, three-minute morality play of sorts, with Jiminy Cricket, conscience personified, serving as host and guide. Pinocchio, who is the creation of the toy maker Geppetto, visits Pleasure Island to discover the right way to live. This is a land of popcorn and candy-cane Ferris wheels.

Then almost imperceptibly, the ride vehicles move to the seamy world of Tobacco Road, where Pleasure Island hues are supplanted by drab, dirty shades of brown and gray. Here, little boys are turned into donkeys and sold to the salt mines.

Pinocchio escapes that fate, nearly becomes supper for Monstro the Whale, and winds up back home in the care of Geppetto—another happily-ever-after ending. The final tableau, in which the dazzling Blue Fairy turns into a cloud of sparkles before your eyes and then disappears, leaving a smattering of pixie dust on the floor, is partially accomplished via fiber optics.

KING ARTHUR CARROUSEL: Guests come upon this graceful park landmark as they stroll toward the Sleeping Beauty Castle passageway into Fantasyland. One of the few attractions in the park that is an original rather than a Disney adaptation, the carousel contains 72 horses—all movable, as Walt Disney wished. Carved in Germany over a century ago, no two alike, they are as pampered as the live Belgian horses on Main Street. The ornamentation on them is gold, silver, and copper leaf.

The faces on the inside and outside of the carousel are gold leaf. The shields on the lances supporting its big overhead canopy are those of the Knights of the Round Table and other, less illustrious, crests. Nine hand-painted panels on top of the carousel's main face re-create the story of Sleeping Beauty.

MICKEY'S TOONTOWN

Disneyland lore tells us that when Mickey Mouse burst onto the movie scene in 1928 in *Steamboat Willie*, the first sound cartoon, his success was so great that his busy schedule demanded he practically live at the Walt Disney Studios. Thirty cartoons later, in the early 1930s, he was one tired mouse, so he moved into a quiet residence in a "toon only" community south of Hollywood. Over the years, many toon stars gravitated to Mickey's Toontown, as it quickly became known. Minnie Mouse, Pluto, Goofy, Roger Rabbit, Chip, Dale, and Gadget all live here, and Donald Duck docks his boat, the *Miss Daisy*, on Toon Lake.

HOT TIP!

There are no full-service restaurants in Toontown, just a few fast-food places with window service and limited outdoor seating. So don't plan on having a big meal here.

One afternoon in the early 1950s, while Mickey and his close friend Walt Disney were relaxing on Mickey's front porch, Walt revealed his idea for a theme park that would appeal to "youngsters of all ages." Mickey suggested that he build it next to the secret entrance to Toontown, and the rest is history. Disneyland opened to the public in 1955, but little did anyone realize when they were drifting through It's a Small World that they were right next door to Mickey's Toontown.

In 1990, Mickey and his friends decided to open up their neighborhood and their homes to non-toons, and in preparation, all of Toontown received a new coat of ink. The grand opening took place in January 1993, marking the first new "land" to debut at Disneyland since Critter (originally Bear) Country opened in 1972.

Legend aside, the development of Toontown was a real challenge: to create a three-dimensional cartoon environment without a single straight line. Yet as topsy-turvy as it is, Mickey's Toontown is a complete community, with a downtown area, including a commercial center and an industrial zone, plus a suburban neighborhood. The best part is that everything is meant to be touched, pushed, and jumped on. Kids do just that, while adults relish the attention to detail and the assortment of jokes and gags. Much of what's here is interactive, from the mousehole covers to the public mailboxes.

This booming toontropolis is home to ten attractions, two shops, and three fast-food eateries. The rides are described in the neighborhood sections that follow; the shops, in the "Shopping" section later in this chapter; and the eateries, in the *Good Meals, Great Times* chapter.

Guests enter this colorful land by walking under the Toontown train depot. The attractions are listed as they are encountered when strolling counterclockwise.

Downtown Toontown

In Toontown's "business" zone, an animated taxi teeters off the second-floor balcony of the Cab Co. A runaway safe has crashed into the sidewalk, and crates of rib-ticklers, ripsnorters, slapsticks, and wisecracks wait for passersby to lift the lids. At the Fireworks Factory, a plunger sets off quite a response when pressed; it's a good thing the Toontown Fire Department is located right next door.

Lift the receiver of the police phone outside the Power House (home to all sorts of electrifying gizmos—open the door at your own risk), and you might hear a voice over the toon police car radio announcing "Someone put mail in the box, and the box doesn't like it. Please respond post haste." Or step on the mousehole cover near the Post Office, and you might hear "How's the weather up there?" or "Is it time to come out now?"

You never know what to expect in Toontown, except that it's bound to be "goofy."

ROGER RABBIT'S CAR TOON SPIN: FP

BIRNBAUM'S ★BEST This chaotic, rollicking ride combines the technology of the Mad Tea Party teacups (cars here spin 360 degrees) and the tracks of Fantasyland attractions such as Mr. Toad's Wild Ride. Benny the Cab and Roger Rabbit join the dizzying chase, which takes guests through the back alleys of the toon underworld made famous in the film *Who Framed Roger Rabbit*. The mission of each car is to save Jessica Rabbit from the evil weasels while avoiding the dreaded Dip.

ROGER'S FOUNTAIN: In this funny fountain, a statue of Roger Rabbit is suspended in midair, afloat on a column of water erupting from a broken fire hydrant that he has seemingly crashed into. He's still holding the steering wheel from the cab he was driving. Surrounding the hydrant, four floating cab tires serve as inner tubes for fish spouting arcs of water into the air.

JOLLY TROLLEY: Transportation around Mickey's Toontown is supplied by a rocking-and-rolling trolley that weaves its way on figure-eight rails. Providing a one-way ride to or from either end of Mickey's Toontown, it stops outside Roger Rabbit's Car Toon Spin and Mickey's House. A large gold windup key on top of the engine turns as the trolley makes its rounds.

POST OFFICE: Each audacious mailbox actually speaks in the voice of the character whose mail it receives—Mickey Mouse, Minnie Mouse, Roger Rabbit, Jessica Rabbit, Donald Duck, and Goofy. It can be quite a cacophony. Outside, the letter box pipes in with comments like "Don't just stand there; mail something!"

Toon Square

Located between the downtown area and the residential section of Toontown, this district is home to local businesses and institutions, including the Toontown Skool, the Department of Ink & Paint, and the 3rd Little Piggy Bank. Toontown's three eateries—Clarabelle's Frozen Yogurt, Pluto's Dog House, and Daisy's Diner—stand side by side on the square.

CITY HALL: Toon residents emerge from this municipal building and proceed to the bandstand out front to greet their guests, entertain them with their antics, and provide more relaxing photo opportunities than are often available elsewhere in Disneyland. When a character is about to arrive, the colorful "Clockenspiel" high above City Hall comes to life: Mallets ring bells, gloved toon hands pull whistles, and figures of Roger Rabbit and Mickey Mouse pop out of cannons, blowing shiny horns that, in turn, produce bouquets of flowers.

GOOFY'S GAS: From the looks of it, any traveler would think twice about refueling at this station. On the other hand, it *does* house Toontown's public restrooms and telephones, and that's an important location to know (though we don't recommend making any important business calls here).

Pedestrians can now refuel here, too. A seasonal candy stand, called Goofy's Tuneup Treats, offers sweet snacks, and is also a convenient locale to purchase souvenirs. The water fountain beside the station dispenses funny but refreshing drinks.

Mickey's Neighborhood

The homes in this district sit at the base of the 40-foot-tall Toon Hills, which have their own version of the Hollywood sign. The attractions are described as a guest would pass them walking counterclockwise from Mickey's Fountain.

MICKEY'S FOUNTAIN: A statue of the world's most famous mouse stands at the center of a pool surrounded by toon-style musical instruments, creating a whimsical centerpiece for the Toontown residential area.

MINNIE'S HOUSE: This lavender-and-pink creation has a sweetheart theme for the sweetheart inside. The top window, welcome mat, and weather vane are heart-shaped, while the mailbox looks like Minnie. Inside,

guests can visit Minnie's living room with its chintz sofa and magazines (*Cosmousepolitan* and *Mademouselle*) on the coffee table. There are messages from Goofy and Mickey on the answering machine. Guests get to create new fashions for Minnie on an interactive computer in her dressing room.

In Minnie's kitchen, a cake in the oven rises when a knob is turned, pots and pans clank out a melody when the stove is switched on, and the dishwasher churns when a button is pushed. The Cheesemore refrigerator is stocked with an assortment of dairy products, including Golly Cheeze Whiz, and the shopping list left on the outside of the fridge hints at this mouse's cheeses of choice. Be sure to check out the cookies on her kitchen table.

As you leave Minnie's House, you'll pass the wishing well in her yard. Don't think you're hearing things: It's been known to share a few parting thoughts.

MICKEY'S HOUSE: A path leads from Minnie's backyard to the front door of Mickey's House. The welcoming yellow dwelling with a tile roof, huge green door, and green shutters is home to the toon who started it all. Not only is Mickey's face on the mailbox out front, but his welcome mat is in the instantly recognizable shape of three circles—his head and ears.

In the living room stands a player piano and a curio cabinet filled with all manner of memorabilia, including Mickey's baby shoes and a picture of him with his friend Walt Disney, as well as some of Pluto's treasures—a huge bone and a half-eaten shoe. In the laundry room, the washing machine chugs merrily away, and laundry supplies, such as Comics Cleanser and Mouse 'n' Glo, are at the ready.

From here, make your way through the greenhouse and into Mickey's backyard, where you'll see Pluto's doghouse and a garden with mysteriously disappearing carrots.

MICKEY'S MOVIE BARN: Ever industrious, Mickey has transformed the old barn in back of his house into a workplace, and guests are welcome to visit him here. The first stop is the Prop Department, where costumes and props from some of his famous cartoons are stored. In the Screening Room, a bumbling Goofy projects clips from remakes in progress,

HOT TIP!

Toontown closes two hours before the rest of Disneyland Park on nights when the park is presenting a fireworks show.

among them *Steamboat Willie* and *The Sorcerer's Apprentice*. Mickey is hard at work on a sound stage, but happy to take a break. Guests enter in small groups for a photo and autograph session with the "famouse" star.

Note: You can't get to Mickey's Movie Barn without going through his house.

CHIP 'N' DALE TREEHOUSE: Just past Mickey's House stands the home of that jolly chipmunk duo, Chip and Dale. Styled to look like a redwood tree, this high-rise can accommodate kids, but not adults. A spiral staircase leads to the lofty perch, whose windows provide a fine view of Mickey's Toontown.

GADGET'S GO COASTER: For the uninitiated, Gadget is the brilliant inventor from the television cartoon *Chip 'n' Dale's Rescue Rangers.* So it's only fitting that some of her handiwork is within view of their treehouse. Gadget, the ultimate recycler, has created this coaster from an assortment of gizmos that once served other purposes. Giant toy blocks are now support beams for the tracks; hollowed-out acorns have become the cars of the train; and bridges have been created from oversize combs, pencils, paper clips, and rubber bands.

The thick red steel tracks give the impression of a tame ride, but Gadget's invention supplies quite a few thrills, right up to the final turn into the station. The entire circuit is visible from the queue area, which snakes under part of the coaster. This experience is exciting but brief (one minute), so if the line is long, save it for later in the day.

Note: Children have to be at least three years old before they can ride Gadget's Go Coaster; those under seven must be accompanied by an adult. The trip is not advised for pregnant women.

MISS DAISY: Donald Duck's houseboat, named for his fair feathered friend, is permanently docked in Toon Lake, adjacent to Gadget's Go Coaster. Parents can relax in a shaded seating area near a waterfall while their children explore the boat, which looks a whole lot like its owner. See if you can recognize Donald's eyes in the large portholes of the pilothouse, his jaunty blue sailor's cap in the roof of the cabin, and his face in the shape of the hull. Would-be

sailors can climb the small rope ladder or the spiral staircase up to the pilothouse to steer the wheel that turns the compass or to toot the boat's whistle.

GOOFY'S BOUNCE HOUSE: Located beside the *Miss Daisy*, this abode is just for kids. Inside, they can literally bounce off the walls, the furniture, and even the fireplace. Since the windows are made of netting, parents get a good view of the goings-on. The

garden outside Goofy's house boasts an odd assortment of delights: stalks of popcorn, spinning flowers, unusually watery watermelons, jack-o'-lanterns, and squished squash. Take a close look at the house itself. Do you see the resemblance to its owner, right up to the green hat on top?

Note: Kids must be at least three years old but no taller than 52 inches. Cubbyholes are provided for their shoes.

HOT TIP!

Mickey's Toontown is a great place to bring young children, but be sure to visit it early in the day, before the area gets too crowded.

TOON PARK: This tiny enclave next to Goofy's Bounce House supplies a safe play area for toddlers. Adjacent seating gives parents and other guests an inviting place to rest and enjoy the youngsters' antics.

TOMORROWLAND

When Walt Disney was alive, the future seemed simple: We would all dress in Mylar and travel in flying saucers. The Tomorrowland he created in the fifties was set in the distant year of 1987, part Buck Rogers and part World's Fair. The latest incarnation of Tomorrowland, rededicated in May 1998, is based on a classic vision of the future, one that looks at it from the perspective of the past. The result is an innocent and hopeful place (imagine, for instance, a planet that renews itself!), one more in keeping with the rest of Disneyland than with the sterile, less-positive future world often depicted in contemporary films.

Visit Tomorrowland today, and you enter a visually engaging terrain, where the palette of colors is not otherworldly but warm and earthy. Futuristic boulders and dreamlike architecture coexist with apple, orange, lemon, and pomegranate trees that line pathways created from gray, mauve, and burgundy bricks. This landscape fires the intellect as much as the imagination.

Galileo Galilei, Leonardo da Vinci, Jules Verne, H. G. Wells, and certainly Walt Disney would have felt at home here. Aldous Huxley probably wouldn't have.

Three of Tomorrowland's most recent additions are also at Walt Disney World, in Florida: Honey, I Shrunk the Audience; Innoventions; and Astro Orbitor (which has an identical twin at Disneyland Paris).

Another attraction, Cosmic Waves, is unique to Disneyland Park. Other well-loved Tomorrowland attractions remain, among them Space Mountain, Star Tours, and Autopia, and all of them have undergone cosmic face-lifts.

A replica of the Moonliner, a Tomorrowland icon from 1955 to 1966, sits on a pedestal near the site of its predecessor. Sleek monorails still glide to and from the Downtown Disney district, while traditional Disneyland Railroad trains continue to chug into the Tomorrowland station, a reminder that the past is, indeed, prologue.

The following attractions are described as you encounter them when proceeding counterclockwise from the Main Street entrance to Tomorrowland.

ASTRO ORBITOR: Towering above the entrance to Tomorrowland, this big whirligig with spinning orbs and speeding starships is a fitting symbol for Tomorrowland. Astro Orbitor, modeled on a drawing made by Leonardo da Vinci almost five centuries ago, is the successor to Rocket Jets, which gave Disneyland guests a lift for 30 years. Each ride vehicle accommodates two passengers (or two adults and one small child), who can maneuver it up and down while spinning clockwise for 1½ minutes, reveling in sweeping views of Tomorrowland, Central Plaza, and Sleeping Beauty Castle.

Note: The minimum age to ride is one year. Young children have to be in the company of an adult.

STAR TOURS: FP Inspired by George
BIRNBAUM'S ★BEST Lucas's blockbuster series of *Star Wars* films, this is one of the most intriguing attractions at Disneyland. It offers guests the opportunity to ride on droid-piloted StarSpeeders, the exact same type of flight simulator used by military and commercial airlines to train pilots. Once aboard the spacecraft, guests embark on a harrowing flight into deep space and encounter giant ice crystals and laser-blasting fighters. It goes without saying that seat belts are definitely required.

The queue area is indoors; it's also air-conditioned. During the pre-show, guests watch as the beloved *Star Wars* characters R2-D2 and C-3PO, here employees of a galactic travel agency, bustle about in a hangar area, servicing the Star Tours fleet of spacecraft.

Riders board the 40-passenger craft for what is intended to be a leisurely trip to the Moon of Endor. The flight is out of control from the start, as the rookie pilot proves that Murphy's Law applies to the entire universe. The sensations are extraordinary and the technology quite advanced. Some interesting trivia: The spacecraft's captain is voiced by Paul Reubens (a.k.a. Pee-wee Herman).

Note: Passengers must be free of back problems, heart conditions, motion sickness, and other physical limitations to ride. Guests

not meeting the minimum height requirement of 40 inches and children under three will not be permitted to board. Pregnant women should not ride. The least bumpy seats are near the center of the compartment; for thrills, sit in the back.

STARCADE: This arcade adjoining Space Mountain is by some accounts one of the best in Orange County. There are easily 200 games—many of them created by Sega, Namco, and Midway—incorporating motorcycles, race cars, skateboards, snowboards, bicycles, jet skis, snow skis, horses, spacecraft, and tanks. Most represent whatever happens to be hottest at the moment. Certainly noteworthy is the R360, a turbulent 360-degree pilot game. A dozen airball machines and a wall of pinball machines are on the upper level. There are also two penny presses.

Cost range from 25 cents to $4 per game. There are $1, $5, and $10 change machines, as well as a cashier, on the premises.

HONEY, I SHRUNK THE AUDIENCE: The
BIRNBAUM'S ★BEST latest in 3-D film techniques link up with state-of-the-art chicanery when Rick Moranis, Marcia Strassman, and the kids reprise their roles from the movie *Honey, I Shrunk the Kids*. In this 18-minute misadventure, Professor Wayne Szalinski manages to unleash all sorts of mayhem.

In the pre-show area, guests watch a movie about the development of the Imagination Institute. Then they are welcomed to the Institute and given an overview of what will happen inside, where Professor Szalinski is to receive the Inventor of the Year Award and demonstrate some of his latest inventions.

On the way into the 575-seat theater, guests receive "protective goggles" (3-D glasses) to shield their eyes in case any flying debris comes their way during the demonstrations. One misguided mishap leads to another when the Shrinking Machine and

then the Dimensional Duplicator go on the fritz. The theater is accidentally shrunk, and when the professor's young son picks it up to show his mom, the audience is left shaken up but screaming for more.

To add to the mix, in-your-face experiences are provided by a gargantuan dog, a menacing viper, an army of mice (don't say we didn't warn you), and a monster cat that morphs into a lynx and then into a lion. Eventually, everyone and everything returns to normal, sort of.

Note: Honey, I Shrunk the Audience is known to frighten small children and more than the occasional grown-up (especially those afraid of snakes or mice).

SPACE MOUNTAIN: FP No longer a spectral white cone on the Tomorrowland-scape, Space Mountain is now covered in metallic greens and copper. Space voyagers board cosmic vehicles and streak at hair-raising speeds through nearly total darkness, spinning stars and whirling galaxies. A sound system built into each car provides riders individual audio, with synchronized music and sound effects. That feature alone makes the ride out of this world.

Between the stars, the Cosmic Vapor Curtain, the Solar Energizer, and the glowing nebula, Space Mountain is incredibly beautiful (and so popular that it behooves queue haters to make a beeline for the mountain

immediately upon arriving in the park). Riders sit in pairs, and—sweaty palms notwithstanding—travel at the relatively moderate speed of about 30 miles per hour. In the pre-show, intergalactic television combines music videos, commercials, and news. If your courage fails you, there are three "chicken exits" in the queue area of Space Mountain—one just past the entrance to the building, another beside the turnstiles, and the last at the loading area.

Walt Disney had the idea for this attraction long before the technology to operate it had been developed. The original sketch, not all that different from the present cone-like structure, was drawn in 1964. The mountain took nearly two years to construct, and the whole thing is sunk 17 feet into the ground so as not to dwarf Sleeping Beauty Castle or the Matterhorn.

Note: Children under three may not ride. Pregnant women and guests who have weak backs, heart conditions, motion sickness, and other physical limitations should sit this one out. Young children must be accompanied by an adult; you must be at least 40 inches tall to ride.

COSMIC WAVES: In front of Redd Rockett's Pizza Port, this hypnotic fountain spews waves and cascades of water in synchronized and surprising patterns, daring anyone to walk through and inviting them to splash at will. More than 300 water jets create a liquid maze, with constantly changing openings; the surface is spongy, not slippery. At its center, a 12,000-pound granite ball balances as if by magic atop a powerful jet of water. It can twirl as fast as 60 miles per hour, and you're welcome to give it a spin. Youngsters find the bait hard to resist, and as wet as this experience can be, it never dampens spirits.

INNOVENTIONS: This two-level pavilion housed in the former Carousel Theater is Tomorrowland's largest attraction, providing a look at a future so near that some of the products showcased are already on the market. Guests hop aboard a slowly rotating base at one of five themed "pods"—home, transportation, work and school, sports and fitness, and entertainment—and enter the foreseeable future as it relates to that particular area.

After receiving a quick introduction from the wisecracking, Audio-Animatronic Tom Morrow (pictured above; voice courtesy of the actor Nathan Lane, who also sings new lyrics to "Great Big Beautiful Tomorrow"), guests are free to explore the world of Innoventions at their own pace, stepping on and off the moving base to visit other areas, watch live demonstrations, and test new products (none of them for sale) at leisure.

A central atrium leads to the second level and The World of Computers, where the exhibits are sponsored by some companies involved in developing new products and technologies: Compaq, Honeywell, Kaiser Permanente, AT&T, General Motors, and the German firm SAP. The second floor of this building, where the exit is located, had not been open to the public since 1974. Now you can walk around almost the entire perimeter, and the views are marvelous.

Note: Parents, hold on to your kids' hands, or the rotating floor might deposit them in a different area from you. There is no time limit at Innoventions; experience it at your own pace.

RADIO DISNEY BOOTH: The "Just Plain Mark & Zippy" show broadcasts live from a glass-enclosed studio under the Observatron, in the heart of Tomorrowland, weekdays from 1 P.M. to 6 P.M. As young fans listen to the antics of the program's namesakes on the radio, Disneyland guests can pause to observe them in person. They might even be invited to participate in a broadcast. The show moved to Disneyland in 1999 from its former home at Walt Disney World in Orlando, Florida.

TOMORROWLAND AUTOPIA: FP The only attraction from the original Tomorrowland, Autopia was coined "The Freeway of the Future" back in 1955. Kids have always loved guiding the small sports cars around the twisting roadways (for them, a top speed of seven miles per hour is thrilling). Now pint-size motorists and their parents encounter a souped-up version of the original ride.

The separate Tomorrowland and Fantasyland roadways were combined into a single attraction recently (yes, there *were* two Autopias; the one in Fantasyland opened in 1959 to accommodate spillover crowds). Guests now enter through a single boarding area in Tomorrowland and watch an entertaining pre-show on a large video screen

that presents the world from a car's point of view. Drivers (and one passenger per vehicle) travel in restyled cars through 21st-century terrain, experiencing a series of roadside surprises along the way. At the ride's end, they receive a commemorative driver's license as a memento.

Note: Kids must be at least 52 inches tall and at least seven years old to drive alone. Pregnant women and guests with back or neck problems should not ride.

DISNEYLAND MONORAIL: America's first daily operating monorail was a novelty when it was introduced at Disneyland in 1959. A decade later it was replaced with four sleek Mark V five-car trains, and it's always a thrill to see them gliding through the park. Straddling a concrete beamway, the monorail has rubber tires, which enable it to glide quietly, as well as braking wheels atop the beam, and guiding and stabilizing wheels on either side.

HOT TIP!

A trip on the monorail yields panoramic views of Disney's California Adventure theme park and its neighbor, the Grand Californian resort.

The 2½-mile-long "highway in the sky" is a distinctive and integral part of Tomorrowland. The nine-minute round-trip ride takes guests around the periphery of Tomorrowland, across the resort to Downtown Disney and its diverting activities, and then back to Tomorrowland.

For a fun experience, tell the cast member on the boarding ramp that you'd like to sit up front in the pilot's cabin. It can usually accommodate up to five passengers; if those seats are taken, you can always wait for the next monorail and try your luck again.

Tomorrowland Icons

MOONLINER: Beside Redd Rockett's Pizza Port, this two-thirds-scale, 53-foot-high replica of an early Tomorrowland icon stands 50 feet from the site of the original rocket. It is set on a 12-foot pedestal that doubles as a refreshment stand, called The Spirit of Refreshment. Water vapor wafts from its nozzles, but the only thing that is "launched" here is bottled beverages (and then only by request).

THE OBSERVATRON: This quirky icon for Tomorrowland towers above the area, constantly beaming electronic messages into space. Every 15 minutes, it comes to life in an orchestrated medley of music and motion. Radio Disney has taken up permanent residence underneath it (see left).

SHOPPING

CRYSTAL ARTS: Gleaming glasses and pitchers, mugs and trays, and other mementos can be engraved (at no added charge) and monogrammed while you wait, or you can purchase them unornamented. The shop also sells glass miniatures, crystal figurines, bells, and paperweights.

DISNEYANA: Collectors and the simply curious alike will discover rare and unusual Disney merchandise here, such as limited-edition art and hand-painted cels inspired by Disney animated classics. Must-have pieces include crystal, bronze, and pewter figurines, and striking porcelain sculptures from the Walt Disney Classics Collection.
   Note: Disney Imagineers and artists often drop by the shop to sign reproduction artwork or recently published books.

DISNEY CLOTHIERS, LTD.: Disney character merchandise has always been popular, as evidenced by the number of T-shirts, sweatshirts, Mickey Mouse ears, and wristwatches sold each year—but if you want something a little more stylish, this is where you'll find it. The spot caters to fashion-conscious shoppers with a love for Disney gear. Almost every item in the vast array of men's, women's, and children's clothing and accessories sold here incorporates Disney characters in some way.

U ntil you get to know Disneyland, you might not expect that anyone would visit just to go shopping. But among Southern Californians, it's a top draw for the quality merchandise and appealing gift items. Mickey Mouse paraphernalia, such as key chains, mugs, T-shirts, hats, and other such souvenirs, is found here in abundance, of course, but there are some surprises, such as character-inspired costumes for kids, Mickey Mouse desk accessories for the office, and upscale items, such as art collectibles, jewelry, and products for the home.

Main Street, U.S.A.

CANDY PALACE: An old-fashioned pageant in pink and white, this shop is alluring at any time of day, but never more than when the candy makers are at work in the glass-walled kitchen confecting candy canes, chocolate-covered strawberries, caramel apples, toffee, fudge, and other temptations for anyone with a sweet tooth. The products made on the premises are for sale, along with a bounty of chocolates, hard candies, and licorice.

CHINA CLOSET: If you're in the market for figurines, picture frames, or snow globes, this is the place to come.

HOT TIP!

Much of the merchandise sold in the Disneyland Resort is not available elsewhere. So if you love it, buy it here. If you regret not making a purchase, call the Disneyland order line at 800-362-4533.

EMPORIUM: Much like an old-time variety store, this large and bustling shop offers an incredible assortment of wares, and it is home to the popular Disneyland logo merchandise. Decorative figurines, clothing, plush toys, character hats, and a wide variety of souvenirs make up the bulk of the stock.

THE MAD HATTER SHOP: This hat shop stocks Mickey Mouse ears in black and various colors, plus a good assortment of other toppers just for fun or to protect tender skin from the sun.

MAIN STREET MAGIC SHOP: Small but well stocked with gags and tricks—and books about how to pull them off—this shop has the wherewithal to inspire budding illusionists.

MAIN STREET PHOTO SUPPLY CO.: If your film gets stuck, or if you encounter other minor mechanical problems, the folks here will give you a hand.

MARKET HOUSE: This Disney version of an old-fashioned general store sells cookies, licorice ropes, jelly beans, chocolates, and hard candy—all goodies you would expect to find in a turn-of-the-century store. Kitchen accessories, dinnerware, and gourmet foods, all loaded with Disney character (and characters), are Market House favorites.

NEW CENTURY JEWELRY: Among the delicate offerings here are 14-karat-gold charms of Tinker Bell, Donald Duck, and Minnie Mouse. The marcasite character jewelry is outstanding—subtle, sophisticated, and highly collectible. Don't overlook the antique pieces.

NEW CENTURY TIMEPIECES: Merchandise in all shapes and sizes, including the ever-popular Mickey Mouse watches and alarm clocks, along with novelty clocks, beckons from polished wood cases at this shop. Designed by such well-known companies as Swiss Army and Seiko, the watches range in price from $22 to $8,500.

PENNY ARCADE: Adjacent to the Gibson Girl Ice Cream Parlor is a virtual Coney Island of food and fun. Jars of "penny"-style candy, available by the piece, fill ornate shelves, and scrumptious saltwater taffy, which you won't find anywhere else in the park, is available by the scoop in

more than a dozen flavors, including licorice, peppermint, and root-beer float. To add to the carnival atmosphere, old-fashioned arcade games that still cost a penny to play and a Welty Orchestrion line the walls.

SILHOUETTE STUDIO: Working at the rate of about 60 seconds per portrait, Disneyland's silhouette artists truly are a wonder to behold.

20TH CENTURY MUSIC COMPANY: This little place carries an extensive selection of classic Disney music. CD on demand stations provide guests the opportunity to create their own ten-track Disneyland CD. There are more than 150 selections to choose from.

New Orleans Square

CRISTAL D'ORLEANS: Glasses and chandeliers, decanters and ashtrays, pitchers and paperweights are typical treasures here. All engraving, and some monogramming, is free.

THE DISNEY GALLERY: Located above the entrance to Pirates of the Caribbean in several rooms originally designed as an elegant apartment for Walt Disney, the gallery displays original drawings and designs for Disneyland, as well as artwork from Disney Art Editions featuring classic Disney animation. Changing exhibits feature the works of Disney Imagineers, long stored in vast archives. Selected pieces of artwork have been reproduced in limited editions and are for sale, along with note cards and postcards, most of which are exclusive to the gallery. Don't overlook the small interior courtyard, a nice escape from the hustle and bustle.

Note: Disney Imagineers and artists often drop by The Disney Gallery to sign reproduction artwork or recently published books.

JEWEL OF ORLEANS: This jewel of a store specializes in one-of-a-kind estate pieces—carefully chosen rings, cameos, watches, broaches, and cufflinks—some date from 1850 to 1990, but most are art deco, from the 1920s and 1930s. Diamonds, rubies, opals, emeralds, sapphires, pearls, and garnets, all in artistic settings, twinkle temptingly from the display counters. Prices range from $125 to $24,000.

LA BOUTIQUE DE NOEL: Filled with the Christmas spirit year-round, this shop is a repository of holiday collectibles. Santa Claus figures, wooden soldiers, Christmas stockings, ornaments, and decorations prove irresistible any time of year.

LA MASCARADE: The elegance and allure of New Orleans have been captured in the intriguing Guissipe Armani sculptures and Disney figurines on display in this charming open-air market. An eclectic mix of both vintage pieces and fine reproductions makes this spot well worth a lingering look or two.

L'ORNEMENT MAGIQUE: The whimsical designs of the artist Christopher Radko fill this tiny shop. Cruella de Vil, Winnie the Pooh, the Seven Dwarfs, and Peter Pan have all inspired ornaments, and each year Radko creates a design exclusively for the Disneyland Resort.

PIECES OF EIGHT: Wares with a pirate theme are purveyed at this shop beside the Pirates of the Caribbean exit. There are pirate rings, T-shirts, ships' lanterns, stocking caps, and fake knives, swords, and skulls in plastic and rubber. For the right price, you can fill up a bag with pirate booty.

PORT D'ORLEANS: For a taste of New Orleans, select from this shop's authentic Cajun and Creole sauces and spices, caramel corn, coffee, chicory, and tasty pralines. There's also a selection of Mardi Gras merchandise, including authentic masks and beaded necklaces.

Frontierland

BONANZA OUTFITTERS: Mosey in and try on something fit for living legends. You'll find everything from apparel to western-inspired household and gift items. With Pioneer Mercantile right next door, this is truly one-stop shopping for western gear and getups for the whole family.

PIONEER MERCANTILE: This spacious shop carries all manner of paraphernalia inspired by the pioneer period in American history and this country's folk heroes. Young buckeroos will be delighted with the videos and books about the Wild West, and every budding Pocahontas or Pecos Bill will find authentically styled costumes, along with western Mickey and Minnie plush toys to be their sidekicks.

WESTWARD HO TRADING COMPANY: It's on the right as you enter Frontierland from Central Plaza, directly behind the wooden Indian. Hitch up your wagon and come on in. A huge assortment of candies awaits you: tempting candy bars, yummy fudge sold by the piece or the pound, and "scoop your own" jellybeans. The Mickey, Minnie, Donald, and Goofy cookie tins make great souvenirs long after the last morsel has been savored.

Critter Country

BRIAR PATCH: Inside this small shop, all is soft and cuddly. Its specialty is plush toys in all shapes and sizes.

POOH CORNER: All manner of Pooh merchandise awaits, including plush toys, note cards, photo albums, cookie jars, bookends, watches, infants' apparel, children's clothing, sleep shirts, and bedroom slippers.

POOH & YOU PHOTOS: Pooh and his pals can be found by the exit of Country Bear Playhouse. You can take as many photos as you like with your own camera or indulge in a five-by-seven ($10) or an eight-by-ten ($15) taken by a Disneyland photographer.

Adventureland

ADVENTURELAND BAZAAR: The plush jungle animals corralled here include lions, tigers, and panda bears (oh my!).

INDIANA JONES ADVENTURE OUTPOST: This outfitter can supply the most daring expeditions with all manner of safari apparel, notably Indy's trademark headgear, as well as other rough-and-ready wear and "artifacts" related to Indiana Jones.

SOUTH SEAS TRADERS: This is *the* spot to browse for safari- and resortwear, such as T-shirts, shorts, jackets, windbreakers, bags, belts, and a selection of straw and safari hats.

TROPICAL IMPORTS: This emporium is almost always irresistible to youngsters. The reason: rubber snakes, spiders, lizards, frogs, and bugs by the barrel- or basketful. The squeamish will prefer the large selection of plush jungle animals.

Fantasyland

CASTLE PRINCESS SHOP: Gowns and crowns dazzle the eyes of every young princess who enters this royal boutique, tucked inside Sleeping Beauty Castle, just to the left of the entrance to Fantasyland. From wish-upon-a-star-perfect costumes to jewelry and other courtly keepsakes, this little shop has made more than a few special dreams come true.

FANTASY FAIRE GIFTS: On Disneyland's parade route, near the entrance to the Fantasyland Theatre, this open-air stand stocks special souvenirs spun from the tales and sights in Fantasyland.

GEPPETTO'S TOYS AND GIFTS: Situated alongside Pinocchio's Daring Journey, this is the place to find Disney fairy-tale figures, Marie Osmond dolls, Bob Baker Marionettes, and teddy bears from Boyd's Bear Collection, as well as Annette Funicello Bears, created by the former Mouseketeer. The popular Engel-Puppen dolls (Snow White and Belle among them) are custom-made to your specifications; their creator, the German doll maker Helmut Engel, often stops by to chat with guests and sign certificates for the dolls they have chosen. Each one comes with its own dress; three additional costumes made famous by Disney leading ladies are available for separate purchase.

HERALDRY SHOPPE: At this tiny shop in Sleeping Beauty Castle, you can trace your family name through centuries and continents and have its history printed up (a great gift idea). Or choose from hand-painted marble or bronze shields, coat-of-arms certificates, rings, T-shirts, and hats emblazoned with your family crest.

PHOTO BY ALICE GARRARD

IT'S A SMALL WORLD TOY SHOP: The whimsical structure near the entrance to It's a Small World stocks an assortment of Barbie dolls and accessories, Hot Wheels, and Disney-licensed Mattel toys, dolls, and plush toys featuring the Disney characters.

LE PETIT CHALET GIFTS: As cozy as a warm cup of cocoa on a winter evening, this small Swiss shop, nestled at the base of the Matterhorn, is the repository of traditional Disneyland gifts and souvenirs.

HOT TIP!

The best places to find character costumes are in Fantasyland, at the Castle Princess Shop and the Tinker Bell Toy Shoppe. Disney Clothiers, Ltd., on Main Street, U.S.A., carries character clothing for infants and toddlers.

MAD HATTER: Always a great place for hats and plush character caps—and Mouse ears, of course (they'll embroider them for you). The large selection of novelty headgear includes Donald's sailor cap, a hat sporting Goofy's ears, Jiminy Cricket's and Uncle Sam's top hats, and floppy jester caps.

PRINCESS PHOTOS: Capture a magic moment with Belle, Cinderella, Snow White, or Sleeping Beauty outside the queue area for Pinocchio's Daring Journey. You can snap as many photos as you like with your own camera or indulge in a five-by-seven ($10) or an eight-by-ten ($15) photo taken by a Disneyland photographer.

STROMBOLI'S WAGON: Located near the Village Haus, this stand offers sundry souvenirs—everything from Disney plush toys to Mickey Mouse sunglasses. Some of the smaller items available here include character key chains, pens, buttons, and candy. The shop is named after the villain in *Pinocchio*.

Get Your Ears Done Here

Since Disneyland first opened in 1955, there has been no more coveted souvenir of the park than a pair of Mickey Mouse ears personalized with the lucky owner's name—or that of a family member. They can be embroidered for no additional charge at both locations of the Mad Hatter, in Fantasyland and in Main Street, U.S.A., as well as at the Gag Factory in Toontown and at The Star Trader and The Hatmosphere in Tomorrowland. The shops do not embroider company names on hats.

TINKER BELL TOY SHOPPE: At the western end of Sleeping Beauty Castle, this is the main stop at Disneyland for serious toy and costume shopping. Youngsters will go for the inexpensive souvenirs and perhaps cajole parents or grandparents into springing for one of the fantasy costumes. These outfits can transform young guests into Minnie Mouse, Peter Pan, Alice in Wonderland, Buzz Lightyear, or even the nasty Captain Hook. Children's books, videos, games, dolls (including Madame Alexander) and the like complete the offerings.

HOT TIP!

Each afternoon a Disney princess reads stories to children at the Tinker Bell Toy Shoppe.

VILLAINS LAIR: This wickedly tempting den, across the castle courtyard from the Tinker Bell Toy Shoppe, is dedicated to well-known doers of dastardly deeds—Maleficent, Ursula, Cruella de Vil, and other beloved Disney baddies.

Mickey's Toontown

GAG FACTORY: A Laugh-O-Meter outside this shop gives some indication of the fun to be found inside, along with an assortment of character merchandise—plush toys, stationery, souvenirs, T-shirts, novelty headwear, and candy—all featuring the Fab Five (Mickey, Minnie, Donald, Pluto, and Goofy) and their friends. Take a moment to admire the toon architecture, especially the pillars at the back of the store.

MICKEY & ME PHOTOS: Trying to get your photo taken with Mickey on busy days can be challenging, but if you follow this insider tip, it's a piece of cake: Mickey can often be found working in the Movie Barn behind his house in Toontown, and he's always happy to stop what he's doing to greet his guests and pose for pictures. You can take as many photos as you like with your own camera or opt for a five-by-seven ($10) or eight-by-ten ($15) shot taken by the Disneyland photographer who works on the set with the star.

TOON UP TREATS: The enterprising Goofy has added a seasonal convenience counter to his Toontown Gas Station to supply sweet treats to toons and toon-wannabes. Be forewarned, though: While you satisfy that sugar craving, Goofy might just goof up your car.

Tomorrowland

THE HATMOSPHERE: Caps, hats, visors, Mouse ears, and headbands with ears—the headgear here ranges from the rudimentary to the ridiculous. Mouse ears make lasting Disneyland souvenirs, especially if your name is embroidered on them.

PREMIERE SHOP: Create a custom ten-track CD from 150 selections of Disney and Disneyland music at the CD on Demand stations, or stock up on Tomorrowland souvenirs, including candy in futuristic metallic wrappers. Old vehicles from PeopleMover and Rocket Jets are part of the decor.

THE STAR TRADER: The Star Trader is the repository of T-shirts and sweatshirts, pens and rulers, back scratchers, shoehorns, jewelry, mugs, figurines, key chains, watches, pewter charms, candy, and much more—all emblazoned with the names and likenesses of the Disney characters.

Buzz Lightyear, Woody, and the gang from *Toy Story* can usually be found here, along with hundreds of stuffed animals. In the section beside the Star Tours exit, the *Star Wars* legends have come to collectible life: small mementos like magnets, fiber-optic models, or authentically reproduced limited-edition figures priced in the thousands.

Walk of Magical Memories

Now you can own a little piece of Disneyland—10 inches of it, to be exact. For $150 you can purchase and personalize one of the hexagonal bricks that line the esplanade between Disneyland and California Adventure. Inscriptions and Disney logos mark special occasions or salute family names and hometowns. For more information, or to purchase a brick, call 800-760-3566.

ENTERTAINMENT

Together with Walt Disney World, Disneyland books more entertainment than any other organization in the world. While no two years provide quite the same mix of shows, what follows is typical of the variety you can expect. Check your guidemap's entertainment schedule or the Information Board for daily offerings.

Performers & Live Shows

Performers stroll, march, croon, and pluck their way through Disneyland every day—so frequently that all you usually have to do to find them is follow your ears.

Main Street, U.S.A.

CORNER CAFE PIANIST: Someone is almost always on hand to tickle the ivories on the snow-white upright piano at this centrally located eatery. Daily.

DAPPER DANS: The official greeters of Main Street, U.S.A., this classic singing quartet performs standards such as "In the Good Old Summertime" and "Coney Island Baby" in perfect four-part harmony. They may be found strolling on the sidewalk or pedaling their bicycle built for four. Five days a week.

DISNEYLAND BAND: A presence in the park since opening day in 1955, Disneyland's signature musical group specializes in turn-of-the-century band music, but it can play just about anything. The band performs inside the main entrance when the park opens, in Town Square (at the south end of Main Street), and at other locations. Check at City Hall for a schedule. Five days a week.

FLAG RETREAT: The flag at Town Square is lowered just before sunset each day (check at City Hall for the exact time). It's best in summer, when the Disneyland Collegiate All-Star Band plays rousing marches and "The Star-Spangled Banner" as the finale, bringing guests to their feet, hands over hearts, in a moving patriotic moment. Other times of the year, the music is a soundtrack. Daily.

Adventureland

ALADDIN & JASMINE'S STORYTALE ADVENTURES: The story of Aladdin is re-created by Aladdin and Jasmine themselves, with the help of a few "guest stars" picked from the audience. Hosted by two storytellers, Barker Bob and Kazoo, the tale unfolds in front of Aladdin's Oasis. Fridays, Saturdays, and Sundays year-round; daily in summer.

TRINIDAD TROPICAL STEEL DRUM BAND: Enjoy the calypso beat of this colorful group that performs near the entrance to the Jungle Cruise. You can catch them on selected weekends and four days a week during the summer months.

New Orleans Square

BAYOU BRASS BAND: The hip, funky sounds of contemporary New Orleans brass bands have arrived at Disneyland, courtesy of this lively six-piece band. Five days a week.

GLORYLAND BRASS BAND: New Orleans funeral processions are unique experiences—soulful, energetic, and always musical. The Gloryland Brass Band embodies the spirit of this tradition. Five days a week.

Dancing

Bands play several sets at the Tomorrowland Terrace on Saturdays year-round and nightly during peak seasons. In addition, Plaza Gardens Stage, adjacent to Central Plaza, hosts the "Jump, Jive, Boogie Swing Party" on Friday evenings in summer, and "Big Band Bonanza" on Saturdays. Delighted guests spin like teacups around the dance floor.

ORLEANS STREET BAND: The "second line" tradition comes to life each time this upbeat group hits the Square. The talented collection of musicians performs a classic New Orleans street-band repertoire with exuberance and style. Five days a week.

ROYAL STREET BACHELORS: Their style is early traditional Jazz and Blues, with a mellow four-beat sound similar to those once commonly heard in the Storyville section of the Crescent City. Five days a week.

VARIETY ACTS: In New Orleans Square, street performers, and personalities of every kind serve up a mix of sights and sounds inspired by blues, jazz, cajun, and zydeco traditions. Specialty acts include mimes, tap dancers, and street-corner musicians. Daily.

Frontierland

BILLY HILL & THE HILLBILLIES: Dishing up a lively mix of bluegrass and comedy on the Golden Horseshoe Stage, these four brothers, all named Billy and all first-rate musicians, never take themselves—or their guests—too seriously. Daily.

LAUGHING STOCK CO.: Sheriff Clem Clodhopper has no desire to marry Mayor McGillicuddy's "comely" daughter, Sallie Mae, but neither of them will take "no" for an answer. An old-time serial in three parts is played out as the dysfunctional trio finagles to get Sallie Mae hitched to someone (anyone), even an unsuspecting park guest. Four days a week.

Fantasyland

ANIMAZEMENT—THE MUSICAL: Stars of Disney's animated classics *The Lion King, Beauty and the Beast, The Little Mermaid, Aladdin, Pocahontas, The Hunchback of Notre Dame,* and *Hercules* come to life in this 25-minute musical stage show. One story (and song) evolves into the next, as animation moves from page to stage. The show takes place in the Fantasyland

Theatre, where the open-air seating accommodates 1,200 guests under a big-top-style covering. Daily in summer (usually five shows a day); weekends and selected weekdays during the remainder of the year.

SWORD IN THE STONE CEREMONY: A lucky child is appointed king or queen of the realm by pulling a magic sword named Excalibur from the stone in front of King Arthur Carrousel. Merlin the Magician presides over the proceedings. Weekends year-round; daily in summer.

Tomorrowland

TOMORROWLAND TERRACE: Pop, rock, Top 40, and a variety of other high-energy bands serve up contemporary sounds from the Tomorrowland Terrace Stage, which rises dramatically at showtimes. Weekends.

TRASH CAN TRIO: Custodians or musicians? They're both. This surprising group of percussionists have the wonderful ability to turn trash cans into musical instruments. Weekends, holidays, and daily in summer.

Parades

No Main Street is complete without a parade, and Disneyland has plenty. The usual route runs between Town Square and the promenade in front of It's a Small World—or vice versa. The direction, and sometimes the route, can vary, so it's wise to inquire at the Information Center at City Hall or Central Plaza.

DISNEYLAND PARADE OF THE STARS: Mickey Mouse, Donald Duck, Snow White, and other classic stars shine in this tribute to Disney's greatest celluloid hits. Golden floats themed around vignettes from the original *Fantasia* film carry clusters of waving characters effortlessly down Main Street (pictured above). Twirling ostriches, hippos on pointed toe, and other familiar *Fantasia* characters dance with guests along the parade route. The parade lasts about 20 minutes, and takes place daily in summer—usually once during the day and again in the evening—as well as on weekends year-round and on selected holidays. This parade may have changed in format by the time you visit; check your guidemap's entertainment schedule for details.

A CHRISTMAS FANTASY PARADE: Rows of toy soldiers right out of *Babes in Toyland* march down Main Street, accompanied by dancing gingerbread men, skating snowflakes, and whirling snowmen and women. Mrs. Claus and the Seven Dwarfs, Pinocchio and Geppetto, Buzz and Woody, the Little Mermaid, Daisy Duck and Clarabelle, and even Scrooge McDuck and Cinderella's wicked stepfamily are all part of the fun. Mickey and Minnie, in a horse-drawn carriage, and Santa Claus himself, with Pluto filling in for Rudolph, put in an appearance at the end of the parade. It takes place daily from Thanksgiving Day through New Year's Day.

Where to Watch the Parades: The best vantage points from which to see the parades are the platform of the Disneyland Railroad's Main Street depot, Town Square near the flagpole, and the curb on either side of Main Street. If you hate crowds, any park location *other than* Main Street will be better.

Two other options are the terrace outside the Plaza Inn (but be aware that the seating is limited here) and the tables in the courtyard of the Carnation Cafe, where the view may be partially obstructed. Better still, plan to catch a later parade on nights when more than one is scheduled.

You can also stand on either side of the promenade area in front of It's a Small World, whose multicolored facade provides a whimsical only-at-Disneyland backdrop. Wherever you station yourself, plan to arrive about an hour beforehand to claim your piece of curb.

Fireworks

BELIEVE: THERE'S MAGIC IN THE STARS: This magnificent show, presented nightly in summer and on New Year's Eve, ignites the sky with a kaleidoscope of colors over Sleeping Beauty Castle. At about 9:30 P.M., Tinker Bell waves her magic wand to start the spectacular light show, to the accompaniment of a medley of Disney tunes and traditional patriotic favorites. More than 200 pyrotechnic shells are fired, one every couple of seconds, in time to the music. As the show's dramatic finale, Tinker Bell takes flight from the Matterhorn's snowy apex.

Where to Watch: The best area is midway down Main Street, U.S.A., near the Main Street Photo Supply Co.

Special Occasions

Though plenty of special events take place in the park year-round (some require special-admission tickets), Disneyland does not celebrate specific holidays in a major way, except for the period between Thanksgiving and New Year's, when the entire park glows with a Home for the Holidays theme.

A Christmas Fantasy Parade, a Disney yuletide favorite, takes place throughout this season. Live music and hundreds of performers bring to life beloved holiday traditions of the past. **It's a Small World Holiday** celebrates yuletide customs around the world. The singing dolls add "Jingle Bells" to their repertoire in numerous languages, and the ticktock clock in the whimsical facade dons a Santa hat. **Main Street, U.S.A.**, is decked out in traditional red and green, including hundreds of poinsettias and a huge white fir decorated with several thousand lights and ornaments, and surrounded by oversize holiday packages. Carolers hold forth at the **Fantasyland Theatre**. On two nights at the beginning of the season, a candlelight procession ending at the theater takes place. Special music is provided by a large choir and a holiday story is read by a well-known entertainer. Live entertainment and a fireworks show on **New Year's Eve** (a special ticket is required) provide the grand finale for this festive and fun holiday season.

For more information about seasonal happenings in the park, see the *Getting Ready to Go* chapter; for specifics on upcoming special events, call the Guest Relations office (714-781-4560).

Where to Find *the Characters*

Look for the Disney characters in Town Square and in front of The Walt Disney Story, both on Main Street, U.S.A., as well as in Mickey's Toontown, where they live. The Little Mermaid greets guests at Ariel's Grotto, just north of Triton Garden. Pooh and his pals congregate in Critter Country. Belle, Cinderella, and Snow White drop by Tinker Bell Toy Shoppe in Fantasyland. In Adventureland, Jane and Terk hang out at Tarzan's Treehouse, while Aladdin and Jasmine stop to chat outside Aladdin's Oasis.

Also see "Where to Dine with the Characters" in the *Good Meals, Great Times* chapter, and your Disneyland guidemap.

Imagination Runs Wild in Fantasmic!

This spectacular 22 minutes of magic, music, live performances, and sensational special effects light up the Rivers of America nightly on weekends, holidays, and throughout the summer season. More than 50 performers put on an unforgettable show in an unprecedented display of pyrotechnics, lasers, fog, fiber optics, and giant props.

In this tale of good versus evil, it's up to Mickey to overcome a vast array of villains. He first appears in cartoon form at the tip of Tom Sawyer Island and uses his imagination to make comets shoot across the sky while the river waters dance. A live Mickey materializes in a cone of specially programmed lights, and a shower of sparks seems to shoot from his fingers.

Spectacular technology makes Fantasmic! all the more fantastic. Mickey works his magic, and a specially prepared film sequence appears, seemingly in midair above the river. This effect is

Mickey's fantasy. Fearsome creatures all have an opportunity—a 20-foot-tall Ursula, the scary sea witch from *The Little Mermaid*; an animated Chernabog demon; and the evil Maleficent, who morphs into the 45-foot-tall fire-breathing dragon from *Sleeping Beauty*.

The villains turn Mickey's dreams into nightmares, and he must overcome them with his own powers of goodness, plus a little help from his friends. The *Columbia* sailing ship glides through the show with the swashbuckling cast of *Peter Pan* on board, and the *Mark Twain* riverboat brings along a host of favorite Disney characters.

Where to Watch: The best spots are in front of Pirates of the Caribbean (be sure you can see the water and Tom Sawyer Island, and get there at least one hour early) and on the balcony of The Disney Gallery, where a reservations-only

achieved by projecting 70mm film onto three giant mist screens, each one 30-feet tall by 50-feet wide. The screens are transparent, so that the live performers behind and in front of them appear to be interacting with the filmed images.

In one scene, Monstro the Whale from *Pinocchio* makes waves in the real water of the Rivers of America. In the "Pink Elephants on Parade" scene, the animated pachyderms from *Dumbo* interact with live performers in flexible, glow-in-the-dark elephant costumes. The illusions build toward a breathtaking confrontation of good and evil, in which Disney villains attempt to disrupt

dessert buffet costs $41 (if you decide to splurge, book a seat *early* at the Guest Relations window at the park entrance). Late arrivals can usually find a good place to watch below the Haunted Mansion, near the river's edge.

Note: Fantasmic! is shown twice nightly during busy seasons, and there can be a crush of people trying to leave after the show. Try exiting via the Big Thunder Trail, or hang out in New Orleans Square until the crunch eases. The later show is always less crowded. Parents, be aware that some of the effects are quite realistic and may be intense for very young viewers.

• Study a map of the park before you arrive to familiarize yourself with the layout.

• Tuesday, Wednesday, and Thursday are the least crowded days to visit year-round. If you should come on a weekend, choose Sunday over Saturday.

• Measure your child's height before your visit so you'll know ahead of time which attractions he or she may be too short to ride. This can prevent intense disappointment later. (Notes at the end of individual listings in this chapter give any height, age, or health restrictions.)

• Wear your most comfortable shoes. Blisters are the most common malady reported to First Aid.

• Main Street, U.S.A., usually opens half an hour before the rest of the park, unless the park has an early-entry opening. Take advantage of this to grab a quick snack, shop, or pose for photos with the characters.

• Check the daily entertainment schedule in your Disneyland guidemap and plan your day accordingly.

• Wait times posted at the attractions and on the Information Board at the north end of Main Street, U.S.A., are updated every hour.

• Break up your time in the park (unless you have only one day). Arrive early, see the major attractions until things get congested, return to your hotel for a swim or a nap, then go back to the park in the evening. Remember, you must have your hand stamped and keep your ticket to re-enter Disneyland Park.

• An attraction may reach its Fastpass limit before the end of the day, especially if the park is packed. Be sure to get yours early if you don't want to wait in the stand-by line.

• Try to have lunch before 11 A.M. or after 2 P.M., and dinner before 5 P.M. or after 8 P.M. to avoid lines (which tend to be shorter on the left side of the fast food counters).

• For a change of pace foodwise, head to Downtown Disney or one of the three hotels on property. They have something for every budget and taste—from simple to sublime, sandwiches to sushi—as well as buffet meals with some of the characters, and tea with a very special hostess.

• Avoid rides such as Star Tours, Space Mountain, Splash Mountain, the Matterhorn Bobsleds, and the Mad Tea Party immediately after meals.

• On crowded days, you can make your way between the east and west sides of the park most quickly via the Big Thunder Trail.

• Lines for the Disneyland Railroad move more quickly at the Main Street station.

• Try to visit the major attractions—Honey, I Shrunk the Audience, Space Mountain, Star Tours, the Indiana Jones Adventure, Big Thunder Mountain Railroad, Jungle Cruise, the Haunted Mansion, the Matterhorn Bobsleds, and Splash Mountain—early in the day or during parades. The lines move faster then.

• During the busy afternoon hours, go to the smaller attractions where the wait times are comparatively shorter; the *Mark Twain* riverboat is always a good choice. The afternoon is also prime time for shopping, enjoying outdoor musical performances, or taking in a show at the Golden Horseshoe Stage.

• Shops are a good place to escape the midday heat, but steer clear of them in late afternoon and at the end of the park's operating hours, when they tend to be crowded.

• For most rides, if you're in line *even one minute* before the park closes, you'll still be allowed on. This is a great tactic for Space Mountain, Splash Mountain, and the Indiana Jones Adventure.

Disney's California Adventure

F ame, fortune, and fun in the sun have lured adventurous spirits to California for centuries. But now, visitors have a whole new way to enjoy the glories of the Golden State: through Disney's eyes. In February 2001, the company officially unveiled Disney's California Adventure theme park, the largest addition to the Disneyland Resort since Disneyland Park itself opened in 1955 (and premiering with just about as much anticipation and hoopla).

California Adventure sits snugly in the heart of the Disneyland Resort, sharing an entrance esplanade with Disneyland and neighboring Downtown Disney and the three Disney hotels. But once you set foot inside the park, you're in a world all its own — a kaleidoscope view of California. Unlike Disneyland, where each land's theming is kept separate from the next, the lines here are blurred. Districts blend into each other, and no matter where you stand inside the park, you're sure to see (or hear whoops and hollers coming from) one of the park's towering icons — the Golden State's sierra-inspired Grizzly Peak mountain, or Paradise Pier's gleaming white roller coaster, California Screamin'.

With a working vineyard and winery, educational micro-factories, upscale restaurants, and scream-inducing thrill rides, the 55-acre theme park is clearly geared toward grown-ups. But there's something here for everyone to enjoy, and that includes tots and teens, and all kids in between. California, here we come!

HOLLYWOOD PICTURES BACKLOT

1. Disney Animation
2. Hyperion Theater
3. Jim Henson's Muppet*Vision 3-D
4. Superstar Limo
5. The Hollywood Backlot Stage

GOLDEN STATE

6. Bountiful Valley Farm
7. Golden Dreams
8. Golden Vine Winery
9. Grizzly River Run
10. It's Tough to Be a Bug!
11. Mission Tortilla Factory
12. Redwood Creek Challenge Trail
13. Soarin' Over California
14. The Boudin Bakery

PARADISE PIER

15. California Screamin'
16. Golden Zephyr
17. Jumpin' Jellyfish
18. King Triton's Carousel
19. Maliboomer
20. Mulholland Madness
21. Orange Stinger
22. S.S. Rustworthy
23. Sun Wheel

GETTING ORIENTED

HOT TIP!

When you enter Disney's California Adventure through the Entry Plaza, east is to your left and west is to your right.

Disney's California Adventure is smaller in area than Disneyland, its sister park next door. So guests should have no trouble covering all of the new park on foot, as long as they wear comfortable walking shoes.

In the esplanade directly outside the park, guests find themselves facing a giant three-dimensional picture postcard of California, where huge letters spell CALIFORNIA and a stylized Golden Gate Bridge soars overhead, a conduit for monorails instead of automobiles. Guests are quickly enveloped in the postcard mural of landscapes and seascapes.

In the hub of the park's Sunshine Plaza gleams a huge sun icon. A high-tech mirror system bounces rays from the real sun onto the reflective surfaces of the icon to create a welcome for park guests. It may also conjure up a romantic image of the sun setting over the Pacific Ocean, while a fountain at the base celebrates the dynamic energy of that body of water.

Three vastly different districts compose Disney's California Adventure. East of the Sunshine Plaza lies the Hollywood Pictures Backlot, a mock production studio and backlot where guests learn about moviemaking by joining in on the action. Southwest of the Gateway Plaza is the Golden State, a district dedicated to the cultures, industries, and natural beauty that have shaped California over the years, complete with a winery and microfactories. Paradise Pier, the third California Adventure district, is located southwest of the Golden State and can be accessed through the Bay Area. A tribute to early 1900s amusement parks, Paradise Pier features a string of nostalgic thrill rides with a modern twist, located around a lagoon.

PARKING

Guests park in the six-level parking structure on Disneyland Drive, which can be accessed from the I-5 freeway. There are also some ground lots that guests may be guided to park in if the parking structure is full or overly congested.

Parking Fees: Guests arriving in passenger vehicles generally pay $7 to park. (The fee for vans and RVs is $8; for buses, $9.) You may leave the lot during the day and return later the same day at no extra fee. Just hold on to your parking stub as proof of earlier payment.

Lost Cars: Even if you take careful note of where you parked your car, you might have trouble remembering or recognizing the exact spot when you return hours later. Hundreds more vehicles will likely be parked around yours. If this happens, contact a cast member and tell him or her approximately when you arrived. With that little bit of information, parking lot personnel can usually figure out the car's general location, and someone will then comb the lanes for it on a scooter.

GETTING AROUND

You'll have to depend on your own two feet. There's no transportation within this easily traversed park. However, wheelchairs and Electric Convenience Vehicles are available.

Guests staying at Disney's Grand Californian and Paradise Pier hotels have their own private entries into the park (Grand Californian guests enter through the Golden State; Paradise Pier guests through the Paradise Pier area). All other visitors enter and exit the park through the main entrance, just across the esplanade from Disneyland's front gate. From here, trams transport guests to the Mickey & Friends tram station and the Timon parking lot. Since the area is pedestrian-friendly, guests may also opt to walk from the park along the esplanade to the hotel and Downtown Disney part of the property.

DISNEY'S CALIFORNIA ADVENTURE

PARK PRIMER

BABY FACILITIES

Changing tables, baby-care products, and facilities for nursing mothers can be found at the Baby Care Center by the Pacific Wharf's Cocina Cucamonga.

DISABILITY INFORMATION

Many park attractions and nearly all shops and restaurants are accessible to guests using wheelchairs. Services are also available for those with visual or hearing disabilities. (To find out more, read *Getting Ready to Go*.)

FIRST AID

Minor medical problems can be handled at the First Aid Center, located by the Pacific Wharf's Mission Tortilla Factory.

INFORMATION

Guest Relations, located on the east side of the Entry Plaza, is equipped with guidemaps and a helpful staff. Free guidemaps are also available at most shops throughout the park.

Information Boards: Updated on the hour, these important resources for attraction wait times and show schedules are located in the Entry Plaza next to Engine-Ear Toys and on the bridge leading to Paradise Pier.

HOURS

Disney's California Adventure is generally open from 8 A.M. to 10 P.M. Monday through Thursday and 8 A.M. to midnight Friday, Saturday, and Sunday. For the exact times, visit *www.disneyland.com,* or call 714-781-4565.

LOCKERS

Various-sized lockers are located just inside the main entrance and at Golden Gateway near the Golden Gate Bridge. Rental fees range from $3 to $6 per day, depending on size.

LOST & FOUND

The department is located next to Guest Relations in the Entry Plaza.

LOST CHILDREN

Report lost children at Child Services near Mission Tortilla Factory in the Golden State, or alert the closest Disney employee to the problem.

MONEY MATTERS

There are several ATMs in the park: one each near Guest Relations, Disney Animation, Golden Dreams, and Cocina Cucamonga, and two by the eateries of Paradise Pier. Currency exchange and Disney Dollar sales are handled at Guest Relations. Cash, credit cards, traveler's checks, and Disneyland Resort Hotel IDs are accepted for most purchases.

PACKAGE EXPRESS

Shops at Disney's California Adventure can arrange for guests' purchases to be transported to Package Express by the park's entrance for later pickup (packages will be ready for pickup two hours after purchase). The service is free. Disneyland Resort hotel guests can arrange for packages to be delivered to their resort at no additional charge.

SAME-DAY RE-ENTRY

Be sure to have your hand stamped upon exiting the park and hold on to your ticket if you plan to return later the same day.

STROLLERS & WHEELCHAIRS

Strollers, wheelchairs, and Electric Convenience Vehicles (ECVs) can be rented across from Guest Relations on the west side of the Entry Plaza and in Condor Flats at Fly 'n' Buy.

Ticket Prices

Although ticket prices are subject to change, the following will give you an idea of what you can expect to pay. Note that prices are likely to increase in 2002. For current prices, call 714-781-4565 or visit *www.disneyland.com*. Refer to page 18 for complete details on ticket options and benefits, including annual passports and Resort Park Hopper Tickets.

	Adults	Children*
One-Day Ticket	$43	$33
Three-Day Ticket	$111	$87
Four-Day Ticket	$137	$107

*3 through 9 years of age; children under 3 free

HOLLYWOOD PICTURES BACKLOT

Lights! Camera! Action! The spotlight is on *you* in the glitzy Hollywood district of Disney's California Adventure, where the action unfolds all around you. Motion picture soundstages and backlot scenery provide the setting for the numerous movie-making antics and entertaining demonstrations that reveal the secrets behind a few tricks of the trade. No movies are actually filmed here, so you'll have to keep waiting for your big break. But you can think of this area as the "Hollywood that never was and always will be."

Classic Los Angeles architecture was the inspiration for the buildings that line Disney's Hollywood Boulevard and Backlot area. The entertainment here comes in many surprising forms, and everyone gets in on the act—from actor Robin Williams as one of Peter Pan's Lost Boys to Miss Piggy as a singing Statue of Liberty. Hurray for Hollywood!

Hollywood Boulevard

Pass through the studio gates and you enter into Disney's version of the legendary Hollywood Boulevard. And it all fits neatly into a two block strip.

JIM HENSON'S MUPPET*VISION 3-D: FP

BIRNBAUM'S **BEST** One of the most entertaining shows at the Disneyland Resort, much of the appeal of this 3-D movie is in the details. A funny song-and-dance pre-show, hosted by Gonzo and viewed on TV monitors, gives clues about what's to come. The theater (set inside a soundstage) looks just like the one from the classic television series *The Muppet Show*, and comes complete with an orchestra of penguins. Even the two curmudgeonly fellows, Statler and Waldorf, are sitting in the balcony, bantering with each other and flinging barbs at the performers and the audience.

The production comes directly from Muppet Labs, presided over by Dr. Bunsen Honeydew—and his long-suffering assistant Beaker—and introduces a new character, Waldo, the "spirit of 3-D." Among the highlights is Miss Piggy's solo, which Bean Bunny turns into quite a fiasco. Sam Eagle's patriotic grand finale leads to trouble as a veritable war breaks out, culminating with a cannon blast to the screen from the rear of the balcony, courtesy of everybody's favorite Swedish Chef.

HOT TIP!

Spend some time admiring the props displayed in the pre-show of Jim Henson's Muppet*Vision 3-D. They were all inspired by Muppet television and movie moments.

The 3-D effects, spectacular as they may be, are only part of the show: There are appearances by live Muppet characters, fireworks, and lots of funny details built into the walls of the huge theater. Including the pre-show, expect to spend about 25 minutes with Kermit and company. Shows run continuously.

DISNEY ANIMATION: When you look around at all the thrilling attractions, themed hotels, and dozens of familiar animated faces that Disney has become famous for, it's almost impossible to believe it all started with a simple sketch of a mouse. This fascinating behind-the-scenes exploration invites guests to step into Disney's wonderful world of animation. Here visitors are given a true insider's look at the entire process, the heritage, and, above all, the artistry of this world-renowned art

BIRNBAUM'S **BEST**

form, along with a sneak preview of a few Disney animation feature works that are currently in progress.

Animation Courtyard: This central area makes visitors feel as if they are literally stepping into an animated film. Larger-than-life backgrounds from Disney film classics surround the area, as full-scale sketches of famous characters are projected into the scene. Within moments, the sketches are transformed before guests' eyes into full-color animation. It's just one sample of the Disney animation magic that awaits at the attractions inside.

Drawn to Animation: Mushu, that wisecracking dragon from *Mulan,* doesn't quite get the idea that he's a product of an animator's imagination. This presentation, performed in a 230-seat theater, proves it to him by revealing the secrets of animated character development, from concept through constant change all the way to finished personality. The presentation is illustrated on an oversized television screen at a mammoth animator's desk.

Sorcerer's Workshop: Budding animators and artists particularly get a kick out of these three rooms. They are built around interactive exhibits featuring animation special effects. At Ursula's Grotto, for example, you can supply the voice of a favorite character from *The Little Mermaid,* and then see and hear the completed scene containing your own vocals. At Enchanted Books, you can take a personality survey (hosted by *Beauty and the Beast*'s Lumière and Cogsworth) to determine which Disney animated character or villain you most resemble.

Latest Attraction

Ready for your turn in the "hot seat"? Then you'll be glad to hear that an all-new version of the ABC game show *Who Wants to Be a Millionaire* is one of the latest additions to the list of Disney's California Adventure attractions. A fairly faithful recreation (minus host Regis Philbin, of course), Who Wants to Be a Millionaire—Play It! features the popular TV show's high tech set and lighting, distinctive music, and 50/50, Ask the Audience, and Phone-a-Friend (or in this case, Phone-a-Complete-Stranger) lifelines. Players chosen from the audience answer trivia questions to win points that can be redeemed for T-shirts, hats, and other prizes. The attraction runs throughout the day.

Back to Neverland: A short, funny film starring Walter Cronkite and Robin Williams, *Back to Neverland* takes viewers through the entire animation process, from first sketch to finished product. The comedic spin makes this fun and educational film a Disney Animation highlight. Shows run continuously.

HYPERION THEATER: FP Disney brings Broadway to its backyard with the grand stage of the 2,000-seat Hyperion Theater. Reminiscent of Hollywood's lavish Art

DID YOU KNOW...

The "Hyperion" name has a special Disney heritage. The Walt Disney Studios moved to 2719 Hyperion Street, Los Angeles, in 1926. It was there that Mickey Mouse was born. In 1940 Walt moved his studios to a bigger lot in Burbank, but he took some of the original Hyperion buildings with him.

Deco movie palaces, and patterned after a vaudeville performing house in Los Angeles, Disney's theater invites guests to experience musical productions based on classic Disney films.

Note: Show schedules vary; check a park guidemap for performance times, and arrive about 30 minutes before the curtain rises to be sure you'll get a seat.

The Backlot

In contrast to starstruck Hollywood Boulevard, the Backlot peels away the facade and takes a backstage look at Hollywood without its makeup. Alongside soundstage buildings, behind-the-scenes support departments do their unseen, essential work: props are put into position (even the trees here are on wheels), Klieg lights are set to shine on the scene, and the crew is busy making sure every performer is on his or her mark before the director yells *Action!*

More than anywhere else in Hollywood, the Backlot shows how—with the right paint, props, and portable greenery—anyone (yes, even you!) can create some real movie magic.

SUPERSTAR LIMO: Ever wonder what life is like for a movie star? The lights . . . the cameras . . . the crowds of adoring fans begging for an autograph! Unfortunately, Superstar Limo won't deliver that experience; instead, it is designed to give a taste of the celebrity lifestyle to everyone whose 15 minutes of fame hasn't arrived yet. Guests are swept into a silly pop-up book of Los Angeles and whisked through the star-studded streets of Hollywood on a limo ride that attempts to poke fun at the movie-making capital of the world and shows you that looks in La La Land can be a bit deceiving.

The journey begins at Los Angeles Airport, as a chauffeured limousine takes guests through simple re-creations of Rodeo Drive, Malibu, Bel Air, the Sunset Strip, and other legendary Los Angeles locales. Along the way, there are encounters with odd caricatures of celebrities and some takeoffs on the Hollywood lifestyle. By the end of the ride, you'll have made your big debut as a Hollywood star—though you may choose not to use that limo driver in the future.

Note: Superstar Limo may be closed for a tune-up during your visit, or may have a whole new look by the time you ride. Check a guidemap when you arrive at the park.

HOT TIP!

Ready for your close-up? Better smile—the flash of paparazzi lights at the end of Superstar Limo is the real deal. You'll get a glimpse of the shot just before you make your grand exit.

GOLDEN STATE

From pristine forests to fertile farmlands, the colorful valleys of wine country to the cultural hills of San Francisco, this district celebrates California's diverse geography, culture, and lifestyles. Whether it's through a bird's-eye view of the state or a bug's-eye view of the world, the Golden State's attractions offer guests a whole new perspective.

HOT TIP!

For a really soaring experience, sit in the first row—it flies the highest, while the third stays closest to the ground.

Condor Flats

Inspired by California's Vandenburg Air Force Base, home to some of aviation's most prominent pioneers, this airfield and its display area pay tribute to famous flyers and their trusty aircraft. While you're here, take time to explore the aviation memorabilia and tour period buildings. A huge aircraft hangar, the focus of this site, houses the Soarin' Over California attraction. As you enter the attraction, don't miss the Wings of Fame gallery. (It's also a great way to pass the time while the rest of your group rides, if you'd rather keep your feet firmly planted on the ground.)

SOARIN' OVER CALIFORNIA: **FP** It's no wonder California has an ongoing romance with aviation—how better to experience its breathtaking landscapes than soaring through the skies above them. On this high-flying attraction, you're suspended up to 45 feet in the air, above a giant Omnimax projection dome that showcases some of the state's most glorious sights. With the wind in your hair and your legs dangling in the breeze, the hang glider feels so convincingly real that you may even be tempted to pull up your feet for fear of tripping over a treetop as you dip down toward the ground. During the journey, flyers glide toward the Upper Yosemite Falls of Yosemite Valley, past an active naval aircraft carrier in San Diego Bay, by San Francisco's Golden Gate Bridge, and then down over the vast deserts in Death Valley and the lush wine country of Napa Valley, and up past skiers swooshing down the slopes in Lake Tahoe. In all, the airborne trip takes about four minutes and employs synchronized wind currents, scent machines, and a moving musical score set to a film that wraps 180 degrees around you, making this a thoroughly enveloping experience.

Note: You must be 42 inches tall and free of back problems, heart conditions, motion sickness, and other physical limitations to ride. If you're afraid of heights, skip this one.

Grizzly Peak Recreation Area

Just north of Condor Flats lies Grizzly Peak Recreation Area. Its centerpiece is the unmistakable grizzly-bear-shaped mountain peak that juts 110 feet into the California Adventure skyline. The eight-acre mini-wilderness surrounding Grizzly Peak pays tribute to California's spectacular rural areas, such as Yosemite Valley and the California Redwoods. Tall trees dot the rustic landscape, and there are hiking trails, challenges to test your climbing abilities, an interactive ranger's station play area, and a white-water rafting experience that's sure to set your heart racing.

DISNEY'S CALIFORNIA ADVENTURE

GRIZZLY RIVER RUN: [FP] Disney legend says that Grizzly Peak was once chock-full of gold—which made it a magnet for miners in search of riches, as is evidenced by the mining relics scattered about the mount. But the gold rush has come and gone, and the peak has since been taken over by another enterprising group—the Grizzly Peak Rafting Company. They recently converted the area into an adventurous white-water rafting expedition known as Grizzly River Run.

Each circular raft whisks six passengers on a drenching tour of Grizzly Peak. The trip begins with a 45-foot climb, and it's all gloriously downhill from there. Fast-moving currents send adventurers spinning and splashing along the river, bumping off boulders and through an erupting geyser field. Because the raft is constantly spinning as it moves through the water, each rider's experience is slightly different, but one thing's for sure—*everyone* gets wet. During the expedition, rafters encounter two major drops, the bigger of which is a breathtaking 21-foot fall. It's the dizzying drop that earns Grizzly River Run the distinction of being the tallest, fastest raft ride in the world.

Note: Passengers must be free of back problems, heart conditions, motion sickness, and other physical limitations to ride. Pregnant women, guests not meeting the 42-inch height requirement, and children under three will not be permitted to board.

HOT TIP!

Don't bring cameras or other valuables that must stay dry onto Grizzly River Run. They will get drenched!

REDWOOD CREEK CHALLENGE TRAIL: Lace up your sneakers and test your skills on this simple obstacle course set adjacent to the eastern slope of Grizzly Peak. The campsite features cable slides, rocks to scale, bouncy rope bridges, "floating" logs, and climbable cargo netting connecting treetops, to keep young mountaineers on their toes. Need a helping hand to assist you through the course? Just whistle for one of the cast members outfitted in ranger gear. He or she will be happy to help.

The ranger's station has towers to climb (perfect for burning off excess energy) and an adjoining stage, the Ahwahnee Camp Fire Circle Story Theater (for when a rest is needed). Here, performers share animal folklore and tales of the land through storytelling and song. Keep an eye out for creature tracks along the trail; they lead to interesting information on each type of species.

Bountiful Valley

This area celebrates California's rich agricultural heritage. Fruits and veggies that thrive under the warm California sun are showcased here, and some of them—avocados, artichokes, and citrus fruits, all indigenous to the state—are actually harvested on site year-round. Check out the farm-related exhibits; and when you get antsy for some thrills, make a beeline to It's Tough to Be a Bug!

BOUNTIFUL VALLEY FARM: The Farmer's Expo hosts its own farmer's market here each day; it resembles a cluster of rural roadside stands. California's culinary staples are integrated into healthy snacks and meals (for dining details, see page 120 of *Good Meals, Great Times*).

While fruit smoothies and shaded picnic benches appeal to the grown-ups in the group, small children enjoy the area's interactive water course. Kids of all ages can splash through a simple maze made up of sprinklers and water gates that open and close when triggered. Budding horticulturalists are treated to an up-close view of gardens filled with avocados, artichokes, citrus fruits, and other crops native to California, all grown and harvested on site.

IT'S TOUGH TO BE A BUG!: [FP] The underground Bug's Life Theater, by the entrance to the Bountiful Valley Farm, features an eight-minute, animated 3-D movie augmented by some surprising "4-D" effects. The stars of the show are the world's most abundant inhabitants—insects. They creep, crawl, and demonstrate why, someday, they just might inherit the earth. It's a bug's-eye view of the trials and tribulations of their multi-legged world.

As guests enter the auditorium, the orchestra can be heard warming up amid the chirps of crickets. When Flik, the emcee (and star of *A Bug's Life*), makes his first appearance, he dubs audience members honorary bugs and instructs them to don their "bug eyes" (or 3-D glasses). Then our oh-so-mild-mannered hero introduces some of his not-so-mild-mannered pals, including the black widow spider, a duo of dung beetles, and "the silent but deadly member of the bug world"—the stink bug. Hopper, Flik's nemesis and the leader of the evil grasshopper pack, crashes the show and adds to the antics. What follows is a manic, often hilarious, not-to-be-missed revue.

Note: The combination of intense special effects and frequent darkness tends to frighten toddlers and young children. In addition, anyone leery of spiders, roaches, and their ilk is advised to skip the performance, or risk being seriously bugged.

Pacific Wharf

Inspired by Monterey, California's Cannery Row, this industrial waterfront salutes the diverse cultures, products, and industries that make California so international in nature. Guests can tour working micro-factories and watch local products, such as San Francisco sourdough bread and Mission tortillas, being prepared.

Especially lively in the evening hours, the section of this district that overlooks the water is speckled with small tables that provide the perfect spot for sampling a snack or stopping to people-watch as the crowds pass by.

THE BOUDIN BAKERY: Soft sourdough bread is featured at this working bakery. While baking tips are shared in the walk-through corridor tour (courtesy of a short video starring Rosie O'Donnell and *Whose Line Is It Anyway*'s Colin Mochrie), the famous Boudin-family recipe remains a well-kept secret.

MISSION TORTILLA FACTORY: Flour and corn tortillas are rolled flat and baked to perfection at Mission's display factory. Sample a warm tortilla once you're in the open kitchen, where chefs demonstrate simple ways to cook with the versatile wrap.

Golden Vine Winery

Northern California's fruitful Napa Valley provides inspiration for the Golden Vine Winery, presented by one of the state's (and the world's) most notable winemakers, the Robert Mondavi family. Both an active micro-vineyard and a wine-tasting facility, the courtyard complex, nestled against the base of Grizzly Peak, is designed as a contemporary version of a classic Mission-style estate.

SEASONS OF THE VINE: Set in a 50-seat wine-aging room, this show provides a window on the world of wine-making. As the smell of aged wine fills the air, the show's host reveals the scientific nature of wine production by narrating a seven-minute presentation on the vineyard's seasonal cycles. At show's end, guests can put their newly acquired knowledge to use by heading to the Golden Vine Winery's regularly-held wine tasting.

The Bay Area

A rotunda suggesting San Francisco's Palace of Fine Arts defines this section of the Golden State, which re-creates the enchanting "City by the Bay." The palace's grand rotunda is the entrance to Golden Dreams, a cinematic look at the people and events that have shaped California.

GOLDEN DREAMS: Most tourists (and residents, for that matter) don't know that the name California was inspired by a 16th-century Portuguese myth. In it, a sun-kissed paradise, where ripe fruits drop from the trees and sparkling gold springs bubble up from the ground, is presided over by the Goddess Califia. This 20-minute movie about the history of the Golden State is hosted by an irreverent Califia, the spirit of California (embodied by Whoopi Goldberg). She takes the audience on an educational journey through time to find out why so many generations of immigrants have been drawn to this land of plenty. From the Sutter's Mill rush for gold in the 1800s to Silicon Valley's push for Web dominance, folks will forever dream of striking it rich in the Golden State. But, as Califia discovers, the Midas touch is more elusive than it seems.

PARADISE PIER

Just south of The Bay Area, it's all about fun in the sun at Paradise Pier, a throwback to such California seaside boardwalks of yesteryear as the Pacific Ocean Park, the Pike, and the Playland of the Pacific. Like most classic amusement zones, the rides here are designed to offer simple thrills of speed and weightlessness—but don't let the nostalgic look fool you: The technology is cutting-edge.

At night, the district undergoes a dazzling transformation. Thousands of tiny lights illuminate the rides and building facades, creating a magical display—especially as you soar past them on one of the thrilling attractions.

CALIFORNIA SCREAMIN': FP Like many classic boardwalks, the center-piece of Paradise Pier is a gleaming white roller coaster. A steel coaster, California Screamin' is designed to look (and sound) like an old-fashioned wooden roller coaster, but the thrills are as modern as they get. The ride starts at lagoon level, where the long car bursts up the track, as if catapulted up by a crashing wave. The car goes from zero to 55 m.p.h. in 4.7 seconds—*before* reaching the first hill. Several long drops are combined with an upside-down loop around the giant Mickey head that adorns the coaster, as well as a blasting soundtrack. The result is the longest, fastest, and scariest thrill ride at the Disneyland Resort.

BIRNBAUM'S **BEST**

Along the way, vehicles travel through blue "scream" tubes that trap guests' yells as they test their vocal chords on the big drops, magnifying the hoots and hollers, and adding to the excitement. Every time you approach a tube, you know you're in for a big thrill, so brace yourself and prepare to scream!

Daredevils should save this ride for after the sun goes down, when the night sky is speckled with the pier's glowing lights, and the topsy-turvy twists and turns on the roller coaster will prove even more disorientingly thrilling.

Note: Passengers must be at least 48 inches tall and free of back problems, heart conditions, motion sickness, and other physical limitations to ride.

DID YOU KNOW...

The origin of the roller coaster can be traced back to the 1400s in Russia, where thrill-seekers took turns riding chairs down a series of icy wooden slides.

SUN WHEEL: FP A modern loop-de-loop, this beaming Ferris wheel, centered by a huge sunburst, takes guests on a head-spinning trip. If you think this is a run-of-the-mill Ferris wheel, you're in for quite a surprise: While the wheel turns, most of its cabins rotate in and out along the interior edges of the wheel's giant frame—which creates a dizzying and sometimes disorienting effect. At 150 feet, this is one of California Adventure's tallest attractions, and while it may wreak havoc on sensitive stomachs, thrill-seekers rave over its ride within a ride.

HOT TIP!

A few Sun Wheel cars remain fixed on the edge as the wheel spins. Request to sit in one of these if you'd prefer to take a more tranquil trip.

Note: Passengers must be free of back problems, heart conditions, motion sickness, and other physical limitations to ride. Afraid of heights? Better skip this one!

ORANGE STINGER: This ride, set inside the giant swirl of a California orange peel, is sure to leave your brain buzzing. Riders take flight in swings resembling yellow-and-black-striped bumblebees. As the attraction's momentum picks up, buzzing sounds fill the air, and the bees swarm into a frenzy inside the peel.

Note: Riders must meet the Orange Stinger's height requirement of 48 inches, plus be free of back problems, heart conditions, motion sickness, and other physical limitations to follow this flight of the bumblebee.

MULHOLLAND MADNESS: FP No license? No problem. This compact (though jarring) coaster, inspired by the famous road that winds its way from Hollywood to the Malibu coast, invites "drivers" of all ages to jump into a vehicle and experience the hectic and harrowing nature of California's congested freeways. Small police cars, red fire engines, and old vans follow a winding freeway map while careening over a maze of roundabout roadways and interchanges. Unlike the real thing, riders of this attraction won't be stuck in the infamous southern California traffic—unless, of course, you count the line for the ride.

Note: Although it's billed as a junior-varsity roller coaster, the ride's sudden stops and herky-jerky motion during turns may prove too scary for riders not used to more strenuous coasters.

Riders must be at least 42 inches tall and free of back problems, neck problems, heart conditions, motion sickness, and any other physical limitations to take this jolting ride. This attraction may not be operating during your visit.

JUMPIN' JELLYFISH: A dense kelp bed tops this sea-themed attraction, from which riders sitting in brightly colored jellyfish seats are lifted straight up in the air. When you reach the top, hang on to your tentacles! A parachute unfolds, and fish and friend float safely back down to the ground. While the trip is a gentle one with special appeal to younger riders, it might take a few minutes for guests with the most sensitive of stomachs to get their land legs back.

Note: Guests must be at least 40 inches tall and be free of back problems, heart conditions, motion sickness, and other physical limitations to ride.

SS RUSTWORTHY: This fireboat has seen better days—it has run aground and is full of leaks. While the captain of the ship might despair at the sad sight, young guests rejoice. They love getting showered by the water that spurts from the holes in the old rustbucket. There's plenty for them to explore aboard the

HOT TIP!

Even the hardiest stomachs may start to suffer if the thrilling Paradise Pier rides are tackled back to back. Spend time at the Midway when you need to take a short break.

old boat, too. Children can squirt firehoses and take a turn at spinning the big, wooden captain's wheel. A soft, fountain-laden play area surrounds the vessel. It keeps even the youngest guests entertained.

The *SS Rustworthy* is a nice place for children to cool down and burn off some excess energy, so pack kids' bathing suits or a change of clothes (and waterproof diapers for toddlers), and remember to reapply kids' sunscreen after they're finished romping through the water.

MALIBOOMER: **FP** Along the boardwalks of yesteryear, strollers were sure to hear the resounding ring of the high bell on a slam machine, followed by uproarious cheers for the sledgehammer-wielding contestant, who had just won the game of strength. This rocketing ride represents Disney's twist on that old game. Only this version is more a test of *endurance* than strength. Guests challenge their nerves as they become the high-flying projectiles on this extra-large, ultra-modern

slam machine. Riders are strapped into the vehicle, enveloped by a plastic shield, where they wait on pins and needles for the gong to sound. That's the cue to launch them skyward toward the target, 180 feet into the air, in 2 seconds. A string of bells and flashing lights erupt when the goal is hit, sending the vehicle dropping to the ground (we can't promise your stomach will fall quite as quickly).

Note: Guests must be at least 52 inches tall and be free of back problems, heart conditions, claustrophobia, motion sickness, and other physical limitations to ride.

KING TRITON'S CAROUSEL: Take a spin under the sea on this majestic merry-go-round inspired by *The Little Mermaid*, and presided over by Ariel's father, King Triton. The deep-sea theme is carried out in aquatic detail right down to the ride vehicles themselves. The only horses you'll find here are golden sea horses. They're joined by dolphins, sea otters, seals, and fish, which rise up and down to classic organ tunes as the elegant carousel revolves. Be sure to notice all of the marine mammals as they float by—each one was hand-carved, and no two creatures are exactly alike.

GOLDEN ZEPHYR: Disney Imagineers took the rocket ride to new heights with the launch of Astro Orbiter in Disneyland. But long before those space-age ships took off, riders were taking flights in rocket-shaped swings on boardwalks and amusement piers across America. Disney pays homage to these old-fashioned attractions with the nostalgic Buck Rogers rocket ships that take guests on a scenic spin beneath the shining Golden Zephyr tower. As speed picks up, the rockets lift into the air and fly over the Paradise Pier lagoon several times before touching down for a safe landing.

Note: Passengers must be free of back problems, heart conditions, motion sickness, and other physical limitations to ride. This attraction may not be operating during your visit.

MIDWAY: The games of skill and chance that make up Paradise Pier's classically inspired Midway are themed to Southern California locales and sea creatures. Guests can try their hand at amusements like Reboundo Beach (a basketball toss) and Dolphin Derby (a wooden ball-propelled porpoise race). Other games include Angels in the Outfield, Boardwalk Bowl, Cowhuenga Pass, New Haul Fishery, San Joaquin Volley, and Short Shot.

Note: The games here are pay per play, but winners are rewarded with a prize, possibly in the form of a plush toy.

SHOPPING

The shops in Disney's California Adventure are as diverse as the cultures that make up the state itself. While Mickey Mouse and his cartoon cohorts adorn much of the merchandise sold at Disneyland, the wares here are somewhat less recognizably Disney. When characters do crop up on merchandise, they appear in a much more subtle form. That said, a Disney theme park would not be complete without at least a few shelves of plush toys.

Entry Plaza

ENGINE-EARS TOYS: Located in an oversized model train, this store sells innovative interactive toys, mini train sets and related railroad items, small versions of theme park rides, plush toys, and character merchandise.

GREETINGS FROM CALIFORNIA: The counterpart to the Emporium in Disneyland, this well-stocked shop is the place to head for nearly everything under the sun at Disney's California Adventure—souvenirs, books, toys, clothing, and character plush toys. Merchandise themed to all the major attractions in the park can be found here, along with a selection of items specific to each district.

Hollywood Pictures Backlot

ABC SOAPLINK: Shop for merchandise inspired by ABC's daytime dramas, and catch up on the escapades of your favorite divas and villains—TV screens show recaps of recent episodes—at this shop adjacent to the Soap Opera Bistro.

GONE HOLLYWOOD: "Kitsch" is the key word in this larger-than-life boutique, which parodies the shopping styles of Hollywood's rich and famous. Here you'll find what is hot and current in Hollywood merchandise: at-home spa and sleepover kits, dress-up costumes, and over-the-top cosmetics and accessories.

HOT TIP!

Looking for more traditional (i.e., character-adorned) Disney souvenirs? Greetings from California and Engine-Ear Toys are your best bets.

OFF THE PAGE: The magic of Disney animation leaps off the page at this special shop that showcases collectible Disneyana pieces. Cels, limited-edition prints, and figurines are sold here, as well as attraction-inspired items. A selection of books about Disney history, art, and animation is also available.

RIZZO'S PROP & PAWN SHOP: The wares at this wacky gift stop reflect the Muppets' irreverent sense of humor. Clothes, toys, and souvenirs featuring Kermit, Miss Piggy, Gonzo, Fozzie, and other familiar Muppet faces are for sale here. The stand is worth a browse for the clever Prop Shop theming, which feels like an extension of the nearby Muppet*Vision 3-D attraction.

Golden State

FLY 'N' BUY: When you see the large selection here, you know this is no fly-by-night operation. The aviation-inspired merchandise includes model airplanes, pilot patches, decals, and other accessories. To enhance the wardrobe of aspiring pilots, there are also authentic flight jackets, T-shirts, hats, ties, and watches. Merchandise from Soarin' Over California—postcards, music, videos, books, and T-shirts—is showcased here as well.

GOLDEN VINE WINERY: Countless bottles of fine wine line the shelves of this spot catering to wine connoisseurs. Past and present vintages are available, as well as corkscrews, bottle stoppers, souvenir wine glasses, and wine-inspired books, art, and clothing.

RUSHIN' RIVER OUTFITTERS: This outpost is the perfect place to gear up for an adventure in the wilderness. You'll find hiking wear, gear, and supplies—backpacks, sport bottles, polar fleece pullovers, multi-pocket jackets, and compass watches. California wildlife is represented in animal wood carvings, patches, plush hats, and jackets. And don't overlook the great Grizzly Bear icon of Disney's California Adventure, represented in an assortment of goods themed to the great outdoors.

SANTA ROSA SEED & SUPPLY: The Golden State's rich agricultural heritage is celebrated at this roadside stand, laden with gardening supplies, tools, and packets of seeds, plus T-shirts and souvenirs.

Paradise Pier

DINOSAUR JACK'S SUNGLASS SHACK: The California look is not complete without a pair of shades. Head here for the ultimate selection in eyewear—sun specs in both classic and wacky styles.

MAN, HAT 'N' BEACH: Trendy duds for surfer dudes and dudettes are for sale at this beachside hangout, well-stocked with surf-inspired T-shirts, sweatshirts, and shorts for men, women, and children (despite the shop's name). Beach towels, swimwear, flip-flops, surfboards, and headgear line the shelves and vie for space with beach-themed souvenirs, such as key chains, magnets, and decals.

POINT MUGU: Fashion accessories are the stock in trade at this look-good, feel-good shop. Point Mugu has watches, earrings, necklaces, bracelets, and a large selection of hair accessories (barrettes, combs, headbands, and hair twisters), along with sunglasses, purses, and bags. To add a little sparkle, there's also a selection of lip gloss, glitter, nail polish, and temporary tattoos.

HOT TIP!

Can't find the particular Pooh you're looking for? Head to the World of Disney shop in nearby Downtown Disney. It's teeming with character merchandise and Disney souvenirs.

SIDESHOW SHIRTS: The spotlight here is on shirts of all sorts—tanks, tees, and sweatshirts representing every attraction on Paradise Pier. To complete the look, hats and caps with similar logos or patterns are also available.

SOUVENIR 66: The well-traveled road, Route 66, provides the inspiration for this roadside souvenir shop. The mementos here come in the form of Paradise Pier-themed key chains, magnets, pins, iron-on patches, and postcards. Many of the items for sale, such as mugs, beaded necklaces, and T-shirts, can be personalized.

TREASURES IN PARADISE: Here you'll find troves of Paradise Pier-themed merchandise, such as plush sea creatures and candy containers inspired by King Triton's Carousel, and souvenir music boxes, picture frames, snow globes, and figurines. The California Screamin' memorabilia—toys, earrings, necklaces, and wristwatches—are as dazzling as the ride itself. Containers of candy, such as saltwater taffy, pay tribute to the seaside amusement parks that once populated the California coast.

Pin Trading

It's the latest collectibles craze to sweep through Disney's land—pin trading. These small enamel pins (there are hundreds of different styles) can be purchased all over property, but buying them is only half the fun. The real joy comes when you encounter another pin trader with a worthy swap. To get a head start, bring pins from home (the Disney Store carries its own line). Once on-property, keep an eye out for cast members sporting a good selection of pins—they tend to be agreeable to almost any trade. And when negotiating with a cast member, always remember these rules: (1) only Disney pins may be traded, and (2) every trade must be an even pin-for-pin exchange.

DISNEY'S CALIFORNIA ADVENTURE

ENTERTAINMENT

EUREKA! DISNEY'S CALIFORNIA ADVENTURE PARADE: To celebrate the rich diversity California, Disney created a parade that's a virtual postcard collage of the state: Old Town fiestas in San Diego, the culture of Los Angeles, the laid-back style of the Pacific, and Chinatown street parties in San Francisco. Featuring several variations of Eureka, a character representing the spirit of the state, the parade travels around the park's sun icon, weaves its way through the Golden State, and ends at the far end of Paradise Pier. Check a park guidemap for schedules.

DISNEY'S ELECTRICAL PARADE: A sequel of sorts to the Main Street Electrical Parade, the classic processional first performed at Disneyland Park in 1972, this updated version made its California Adventure debut in the summer of 2001. It features 30 floats aglow with over half a million twinkling lights, as well as a cast of 100 performers and a score of electronically synthesized Disney favorites. Performed most nights; check a park guidemap for schedules, and grab a spot curbside at least 30 minutes before it starts.

HOLLYWOOD PICTURES BACKLOT: Live productions such as Steps in Time, a salute to Disney's musical storytelling, are staged often at the elegant, 2,000-seat Hyperion Theater. Check a guidemap for showtimes.

GOLDEN STATE: At the Ahwahnee Camp Fire Circle, located along the Redwood Creek Challenge Trail, camp leaders host sing-alongs, share animal folklore, and tell tales inspired by the great outdoors. Refer to a park guidemap for performance times.

PARADISE PIER: Music emanates from every attraction at this classic pier, creating a medley of sounds. A stylized organ track, updated through a synthesizer, is incorporated into each ride's soundtrack. The heart of the sound comes from King Triton's Carousel, and individualized versions from other attractions around the lagoon add to the blended tune.

HOT TIPS

- Plan to visit this park when Disneyland Park offers early-entry days.
- Check the Information Boards often to get an idea of showtimes and crowds.
- Stay at a Disneyland Resort hotel to take advantage of guaranteed admission (you'll get in, even when the park is closed to others).
- The standby line for Soarin' Over California tends to dwindle a bit by midday. Ride it then if you choose to forgo the Fastpass option (the experience is enjoyable any time of day).
- Shops in the Entry Plaza stay open a half hour after the park closes.
- On a sweltering day, head to Grizzly River Run, the *S.S. Rustworthy*, or the water maze at the Bountiful Valley Farm, splashy attractions that provide relief from the heat.
- Need a break from the park? Head to neighboring Downtown Disney for a shopping spree or to grab a bite to eat.
- Some of the park's entertainment may take you by surprise—be on the lookout for performers such as mountain climbers on Grizzly Peak and starlets in Hollywood.

Good Meals, Great Times

Dining at the Disneyland Resort is definitely an adventure—and not just in Adventureland. There's more to any meal in a theme park, Downtown Disney, or Disneyland Resort hotel than just food. Goofy, Tigger and Pooh, Merlin and Minnie, or Chip and Dale might drop by your table to say hello. A colorful parade or a romantic paddle wheeler could drift by. Or you might find yourself surrounded by twinkling stars and fireflies (in the middle of the day!) as you savor Cajun cooking in a bayou setting.

In this chapter, the Disneyland Resort restaurant section is divided by location (Disneyland Park, Disney's California Adventure, the three Disney hotels, and Downtown Disney), within the theme parks arranged by area, and then by category—table service or fast-food and snack facilities, including food courts; individual eateries are alphabetized within each category.

If you're hankering for something to do after dinner, or you just need to take a break from the theme parks, you'll find plenty of suggestions at the end of the chapter. Downtown Disney, the property's new dining and entertainment district, is party central. For a more relaxed atmosphere, select a lounge at one of the Disneyland Resort hotels. If it's a particular concert or dinner show in Orange County that interests you, spend the evening at that locale or venue.

DINING

In Disneyland Park

The most popular food in Disneyland is the hamburger, followed closely by ice cream and *churros* (sticks of deep-fried dough rolled in cinnamon and sugar). But health-conscious eaters will also find salads, grilled chicken, and vegetable stew, plus fresh fruit and fruit juices. Disneyland's two popular table-service restaurants, the Blue Bayou and the Carnation Cafe, provide full-course meals and lighter fare, respectively, plus a welcome break from long lines and the California sun.

Main Street, U.S.A.

TABLE SERVICE

CARNATION CAFE: On the west side of Main Street, near Town Square, this outdoor cafe is exceptionally pleasant, especially in springtime, when its planters are bursting with seasonal flowers. Stroll through a gazebo to enter the courtyard dining area, filled with umbrella-shaded tables and surrounded by a cast-iron fence; from your table you'll get glimpses of any passing parade. Breakfast choices include Mickey Mouse waffles, cinnamon-roll french toast, sticky buns, "croissantwiches" (egg, cheese, and ham grilled in a flaky croissant), cereal, or continental breakfast, along with coffee or tea and fresh-squeezed orange juice.

For lunch and dinner, deli-style sandwich plates are the big draw, with thick potato chips and either potato salad, pasta salad, or coleslaw. The sandwiches include smoked ham and cheddar cheese, peppered turkey, tuna salad, and a veggie medley. Beef Stroganoff, chicken puff pastry, Caesar salad (with or without chicken), soup, and kids' specials are also on the menu, along with dessert items such as pecan tort, caramel nougat cheesecake, strawberry shortcake, fruit pies, and a variety of coffees. This cafe is one of only two restaurants at Disneyland that offer table service for lunch and dinner (Blue Bayou, in New Orleans Square, is the other). B, L, D.   **$-$$**

Restaurant Primer

Eateries in this chapter have been designated inexpensive (lunch or dinner under $10), moderate ($11 to $20), expensive ($21 to $45), and very expensive ($46 and up). Prices are for an entrée, a soft drink, and either soup, salad, or dessert for one person, excluding tax and tip.

The letters at the end of each entry refer to the meals offered: breakfast (B), lunch (L), dinner (D), and snacks (S). An asterisk (*) after a letter means that the meal is served only during the park's busy seasons.

Cash, credit cards, traveler's checks, or personal checks with proper ID can be used as payment at all of the following full-service restaurants and fast-food spots. Disneyland Resort hotel guests can charge meals from most theme park eateries to their rooms. Only cash is accepted at snack carts.

While only a few theme park restaurants (Blue Bayou, in Disneyland; and Avalon Cove, the Vineyard Room, and ABC Soap Opera Bistro, in California Adventure) take reservations, you can book a table at most dining spots in Downtown Disney and at the Disney hotels. Unless otherwise noted, make arrangements by calling 714-956-6755.

B breakfast   **L** lunch   **D** dinner   **S** snacks   **$**   under $10   **$ $** $10–$20   **$ $ $** $21–$45   **$ $ $ $** $46 and up

FAST FOOD & SNACKS

BLUE RIBBON BAKERY: Pungent aromas emanate from the espresso machines; fresh-baked cinnamon rolls, muffins, scones, chocolate-filled croissants, giant sticky buns, mini-Bundt cakes, biscotti, jumbo cookies, and demi-baguettes beckon from the display counter; and a chef adds the finishing touches to freshly baked cakes and pastries in an open preparation area. Among the less caloric choices: containers of yogurt; vegetable, tuna fish, peppered turkey, or smoked-ham sandwiches in bread pouches; and hot chocolate, soft drinks, orange juice, lemonade, fresh-brewed coffee, cappuccino, caffé latte, and café mocha (the coffees are served iced or hot). It's hosted by Nestlé Toll House. B, L, S. $

HOT TIP!

For a jolt of java, head to the Blue Ribbon Bakery on Main Street, Bengal Barbecue in Adventureland, or Royal Street Veranda in New Orleans Square. Their iced and hot specialty coffees are sure to please.

GIBSON GIRL ICE CREAM PARLOR: Next door to the Blue Ribbon Bakery, this perennially popular place, with a polished-wood soda fountain, marble countertop, and black-and-white-checkered floor, serves up a delightful array of scoops and toppings in cups, sugar cones, or handmade waffle cones, plain or dipped in chocolate. Fantasia is the most interesting flavor on the menu. There is also frozen yogurt, including low-fat, nonfat, and no-sugar-added selections.

Don't be daunted by the long line; it moves fast. The ice cream parlor is hosted by Nestlé Ice Cream. S. $

LITTLE RED WAGON: Between the Main Street Photo Supply Co. and the Plaza Inn, it's a throwback to the delivery trucks of the early 1900s, with ornate beveled and gilded glass panels. Step right up and get your hand-dipped corn dogs, available nowhere else in the park. Lemonade and soft drinks are also served. L, D, S. $

MAIN STREET CONE SHOP: Located between Disney Clothiers, Ltd., and Market House, behind the fruit cart, this busy window dispenses single or double cones with vanilla, strawberry, chocolate, mocha almond fudge, chocolate chip, and chocolate mint ice cream, and orange sherbet. Two-scoop sundaes are smothered in hot fudge or caramel and topped with whipped cream and a cherry. Mickey Mouse Ice Cream Bars, Nestlé ice cream bars, apple slices covered with caramel, and soft drinks are also available. Tables with umbrellas provide a pleasant resting spot. It's hosted by Nestlé Ice Cream. S. $

Where to Dine with the Characters

Character breakfasts take place at Disneyland's Plaza Inn and at Storyteller's Cafe in Disney's Grand Californian Hotel. You can share breakfast, lunch, or dinner with the characters at Goofy's Kitchen in the Disneyland Hotel. Or go next door to Disney's Paradise Pier Hotel for breakfast with Minnie & Friends or tea in high style with Mary Poppins.

B breakfast **L** lunch **D** dinner **S** snacks $ under $10 $ $ $10–$20 $ $ $ $21–$45 $ $ $ $ $46 and up

MAIN STREET FRUIT CART: Parked between Disney Clothiers, Ltd., and Market House, this old-fashioned cart is stocked with fresh fruit and chilled juices, bottled water, and soft drinks. It's the perfect pit stop for a healthy snack. S. `$`

MARKET HOUSE: This quaint Victorian-style market offers a generous selection of cookies in tins, tangy dill pickles plucked right from a barrel, dried fruit, and various candies. Hot coffee and ice-cold apple cider are also available. The market is hosted by Hills Bros. S. `$`

> **HOT TIP!**
>
> Gratuity is automatically added to the bill at some Disney restaurants. Examine the bill and tip accordingly.

PLAZA INN: On the east side of Central Plaza, this fast food restaurant (though it certainly doesn't look like one) is the one Walt Disney was most proud of, and with good reason. Tufted velvet upholstery, gleaming mirrors, and a fine, ornate floral carpet elevate this cafeteria well above similar eateries. Two ceilings are stained glass, framed by elaborate painted moldings. Sconces of Parisian bronze and Baccarat crystal are mounted on the walls, and two dozen basket chandeliers hang from the ceiling.

This setting, including front-porch and terrace dining (with heat lamps at night), creates a lovely backdrop for the food—roast chicken; choice of pasta with either

marinara, Bolognese, or Alfredo-pesto sauce with chicken; puff pastry topped with vegetable stew, pot roast, or turkey; Cobb salad; and specialty desserts.

An extremely popular character breakfast is held here daily, from park opening until 11 A.M. Pooh, Tigger, Eeyore, and Piglet make the rounds, signing autographs and posing for pictures with guests. A fixed-price buffet ($17.99 for adults, $9.99 for children 4 through 12) features made-to-order omelettes, scrambled eggs, french toast, Mickey waffles, cheese blintzes, sausage and bacon, fresh fruit, pastries, and more. B, L, D, S. `$ - $$`

REFRESHMENT CORNER: Better known as Coke Corner, this lively eatery at the northern end of Main Street opposite Main Street Photo Supply Co. is presided over by a talented ragtime pianist who tickles the ivories periodically throughout the day while visitors nibble foot-long beef hot dogs, Mickey Mouse pretzels (cheese optional), and cookies. Soft drinks, lemonade, and coffee are sold. It's hosted by the Coca-Cola Company. L, D, S. `$`

Adventureland

FAST FOOD & SNACKS

BENGAL BARBECUE: Opposite the entrance to the Jungle Cruise, this is a great place to listen to the rhythms of Alturas while munching on a skewered snack of bacon-wrapped asparagus (a local favorite), chicken, beef, or veggies. Other menu items include fresh fruit with yogurt dressing, Mickey Mouse pretzels, leopard tails (breadsticks), and cinnamon snake twists (pastries). A variety of specialty coffees is also available. L, D, S. `$`

TIKI JUICE BAR: Located at the entrance to the Enchanted Tiki Room, this thatched-roof kiosk sells fresh Hawaiian pineapple spears and pineapple juice, but the biggest draw here is the Dole Whip soft serve—an extremely refreshing pineapple sorbet (it's nondairy). Coffee is also offered. It's presented by Dole Pineapple. S. `$`

Critter Country

FAST FOOD & SNACKS

CRITTER COUNTRY FRUIT CART: On the riverside directly across from Splash Mountain, this peddler's cart is filled with healthy selections, including fresh fruit, muffins, dill pickles, chilled bottled water, and soft drinks. It's perfect if you need some fortification before taking the big plunge. S. `$`

B breakfast **L** lunch **D** dinner **S** snacks `$` under $10 `$$` $10–$20 `$$$` $21–$45 `$$$$` $46 and up

HUNGRY BEAR: At the bottom of the bridge to Critter Country on the right, this is an immense place. Yet when you sit on the veranda, with the Rivers of America lapping so close to your feet that you could cool your toes on a hot day, the activity elsewhere in the park seems nautical miles away. Ducks dive for occasional tidbits, the *Mark Twain* towers above you as it steams downriver, and canoeists in Davy Crockett's Explorer Canoes paddle by. The menu features hamburgers, roast beef and chicken sandwiches, barbecued chicken salad, garden salad, onion rings, french fries, cookies, ice cream, and a variety of beverages. L, D, S. `$`

New Orleans Square

TABLE SERVICE

BLUE BAYOU: The lure of this popular dining spot is as much the atmosphere as it is the menu. Occupying a terrace alongside the bayou in the Pirates of the Caribbean attraction, the restaurant appears perpetually moonlit. Fireflies twinkle above bayou grasses, and stars shine through Spanish moss draped languidly over the big, old live oaks. Those who listen

carefully will be able to hear bullfrogs calling and crickets chirping. Off in the distance, an old settler rocks away on the porch of a tumbledown shack.

This enchanting restaurant, located on Royal Street, is the only eatery in Disneyland that accepts reservations (many of the tables are set aside for walk-ins, however); these arrangements must be made the day of dining, so head to the restaurant and schedule a dining time as soon as the park opens. For lunch, choose from New Orleans-style chowder, Creole gumbo, colorful Mardi Gras salad, jambalaya, and Monte Cristo sandwiches (cholesterol intense). Shrimp cocktail, calamari rings with Creole sauce, mushrooms stuffed with andouille sausage, bayou roast pork loin, Caribbean crab cakes, prime rib, and bronze chicken are served at lunch and dinner.

The dinner menu also features grilled salmon, shrimp, and steak Diane. All dinner entrées come with sautéed vegetables and a choice of salad, clam chowder, or gumbo. Be sure to save room for pecan pie or crème brûlée. Children's selections include Mickey chicken nuggets, mini-corn dogs, and Mickey pasta, served with a beverage and dessert.

The busiest periods are from noon to around 2 P.M. and again from about 5 P.M. until 9 P.M. L, D. `$$-$$$`

FAST FOOD & SNACKS

CAFE ORLEANS: Guests dine inside on small, oak-topped tables, or outside under umbrellas on a terrace overlooking a gristmill on Tom Sawyer Island, and the *Columbia* and the *Mark Twain* plying the Rivers of America. The menu features roast beef po'boys, *muffaletta* sandwiches (slices of smoked turkey, ham, salami, and provolone cheese with an olive relish), turkey and ham croissants, chowder and salad combos, Cajun chicken Caesar salad, and beef bourguignonne. There's also *poulet de la maison*, pieces of chicken sautéed in Creole sauce and served over

Happy Birthday, Disney Style

Goofy's Kitchen, at the Disneyland Hotel, hosts themed birthday parties with characters on hand to celebrate with the guest of honor. The price is $5 per person plus the cost of the meal.

If you prefer a character-filled party at Disneyland, order a cake at the Plaza Inn five days in advance; the servers will bring it out, sing "Happy Birthday," and slice it for the guest of honor and friends. (Characters are available for breakfast only.)

The Practically Perfect Tea, hosted by Mary Poppins and filled with song and tasty morsels, makes for an equally memorable birthday celebration at Disney's Paradise Pier Hotel (see "Tea Room" on page 123).

For more information, call 714-956-6755 (either hotel) or 714-781-4650 (Plaza Inn).

B breakfast **L** lunch **D** dinner **S** snacks   `$` under $10   `$$` $10–$20   `$$$` $21–$45   `$$$$` $46 and up

and frozen novelties, including Mickey's ice cream sandwiches, round out the selections. Head to one of the tables on the French Market's terrace. B, S. `$`

ROYAL STREET VERANDA: Situated opposite Café Orléans, this little snack stand has bread bowls overflowing with creamy clam chowder or vegetable or steak gumbo; fritters that come with a fruit dipping sauce; and a variety of beverages. Check out the wrought-iron balustrade above the Royal Street Veranda's small patio. The initials at the center are those of Roy and Walt Disney (this balcony belonged to an apartment that was being constructed for Walt before he died; it now houses the Disney Gallery). B, L, D, S. `$`

Frontierland

FAST FOOD & SNACKS

CLOPIN'S: Parked near Big Thunder Mountain Railroad, this food cart supplies guests on the run filling, fun fast food, like hot dogs and nachos. S. `$`

CONESTOGA FRIES: The smell emanating from this little chuck wagon is awfully familiar. Yup, McDonald's fries. S. `$`

RANCHO DEL ZOCALO: Casa Mexicana and Big Thunder BBQ fans need not shed a tear over the apparent absence of those two distinct dining spots. They've simply combined forces and reopened as a festive food court designed to resemble a grand Spanish manor. Situated by the entrance to Big Thunder Mountain Railroad, this latest addition to the Frontierland food scene features south-of-the-border specialties as well as Western barbecued favorites. Classic Mexican dishes such as tacos, quesadillas, nachos, and burritos are sure to hit the spot, while beef and pork ribs and barbecued chicken, served with substantial side dishes, are perfect for sharing. Chicken, barbecue, and Texas-style steak sandwiches are on the menu for lunch, while prime rib is featured for dinner. L, D, S. `$`

RIVER BELLE TERRACE: The terrace, between the Golden Horseshoe Stage and the entrance to Pirates of the Caribbean, offers one of the best views of the activity on the Rivers of America and of the passing throng, and the food is wholesome and hearty. Walt Disney himself used to have breakfast here most Sunday mornings. The menu features scrambled eggs, country-style potatoes, a fresh-fruit plate, and cinnamon rolls. Of the breakfast fare, the prize goes to

rice. Kids gravitate to the Mickey-shaped peanut butter and jelly sandwiches served with Mickey corn chips. L, D, S. `$ - $ $`

FRENCH MARKET: Beside the old-time train depot in New Orleans Square, this eatery is a destination in its own right (it's also the Square's largest food facility). On a pleasant day, nothing beats sitting on the open-air terrace munching on fried chicken, beef stew, fettuccine, thick clam chowder served in a bowl made from a scooped-out loaf of bread, angel hair pasta salad, Cajun chicken breast, or jambalaya, the house specialty. Roast chicken sandwiches are available at lunch only. Cakes and cheesecakes are the featured desserts. Children's portions of fried chicken and fettuccine are available. Dixieland music is played onstage periodically throughout the evening; in summer, the Royal Street Bachelors hold forth with such spirit that you could listen for hours and get far more than your money's worth. It's hosted by Stouffer's. L, D, S. `$ - $ $`

LA PETITE PATISSERIE: Located behind Café Orléans, this snack shop serves funnel cakes covered with powdered sugar, chocolate, raspberry sauce, strawberries, or nuts. Wash them down with specialty coffees, frozen nonalcoholic drinks, and cold beverages. There's limited seating. S. `$`

MINT JULEP BAR: Beside the New Orleans Square train station, this window-service bar serves fritters (doughnut-like concoctions), croissants, bagels and cream cheese, biscotti, cookies, ice cream, hot chocolate, coffee, cappuccino, and espresso. The mint juleps taste a bit like lemonade spiked with mint syrup (an acquired taste); happily, real lemonade is also on tap. A variety of sweets

the Mickey Mouse pancakes—a large flap-jack for the face, two small pancakes for the ears, a curve of pineapple for the mouth, a cherry for the nose, and berries for the eyes.

For lunch or dinner, the restaurant offers vegetable stew in a carved-out loaf of bread, steak, catfish, and salmon, ham and turkey sandwiches, a fruit plate, and kid's meals (mini-hot dogs or Mickey-shaped peanut butter and jelly sandwiches served with fresh fruit)—enough to quell hunger pangs prior to viewing Fantasmic! With its lovely interior, it's almost as pleasant to dine inside as it is to eat outside. B, L, D. $ - $ $

STAGE DOOR CAFE: This small fast-food stand adjoins the Golden Horseshoe Stage and serves hot dogs, burgers, french fries, side salads, cookies, and beverages. A children's meal is available. Grab a seat at a cafe table outside. L, D, S. $

Sweet Treats

By far the biggest treat in the park is the dessert buffet served on the Disney Gallery balcony whenever Fantasmic! is performed. Guests enjoy unlimited servings of pastries, fruit, and coffee, tea, and other beverages, plus they see Fantasmic! from the best possible vantage point. At $41 per person, this constitutes a super splurge—and an unforgettable evening. The 18 or so seats sell out quickly, so sprint to the Guest Relations window at the entrance to the park (it's to the right of the turnstiles) and make your reservation first thing.

Or make a beeline for Main Street, U.S.A., and the Blue Ribbon Bakery, the Gibson Girl Ice Cream Parlor, and the Candy Palace, which has great saltwater taffy. And by all means, sample a *churro* (fried dough rolled in cinnamon and sugar) from a food cart.

Fantasyland
FAST FOOD & SNACKS

FANTASIA GARDENS: Next to the Matterhorn, this cluster of carts can supply a quick post-ride pick-me-up in the form of a hot dog, choice of soft drinks, or bottled water. S. $

TROUBADOUR TREATS: Located within the Fantasyland Theatre, this refueling spot is open only during the theater's operating hours, dispensing cheese or pepperoni pizza, hot dogs, potato chips, pretzels, nachos, and ice cream. L, S. $

VILLAGE HAUS: Near Pinocchio's Daring Journey, this house with its gables, pointy roof, and wavy-glass windows could easily have been relocated to Fantasyland from an alpine village. Inside, wall-to-wall murals recounting the story of Pinocchio depict the wooden boy, Geppetto the wood-carver, Figaro the kitten, Monstro the whale, Foulfellow the fox, and his feline companion, Gideon. The menu features personal pizzas, burgers and fries, chef's salad, and cookies. A children's meal is available. The outdoor seating inspires lingering. It's hosted by Minute Maid. L, D, S. $

Mickey's Toontown
FAST FOOD & SNACKS

CLARABELLE'S FROZEN YOGURT: On Toon Square, adjacent to Pluto's Dog House, Clarabelle's specializes in "udderly" tasty chocolate and frozen vanilla yogurt swirled together, along with toppings, cookies, and Mickey Mouse rice crispie treats. Whet your whistle with lemonade, soft drinks, root beer, or milk. L, S. $

DAISY'S DINER: On the other side of Pluto's Dog House, Daisy's Diner serves up individual cheese and pepperoni pizzas, along with garden salads. Cookies, milk, juice, soft drinks, root beer, and lemonade round out the menu. L, D, S. $

GOOD MEALS, GREAT TIMES

B breakfast **L** lunch **D** dinner **S** snacks $ under $10 $ $ $10–$20 $ $ $ $21–$45 $ $ $ $ $46 and up

GOOFY'S FREE-Z-TIME: The vacation trailer parked by Goofy's House doubles as the dispenser of large frozen slurpy drinks. S*. $

PLUTO'S DOG HOUSE: Nestled between Clarabelle's Frozen Yogurt and Daisy's Diner, this is the place to get Pluto's Hot Dog Combo, a foot-long hot dog served with chips and a large soft drink. Extras include cookies, potato chips, Pluto's crispie treats, soft drinks, lemonade, and root beer. The kid's meal comes with a small hot dog, chips, and small soft drink. L, D, S. $

Tomorrowland

FAST FOOD & SNACKS

MOONLINER: Near the entrance to Redd Rockett's Pizza Port, this refreshment stand set in the base of the Moonliner rocket "launches" bottled beverages right into the server's hands (on request). S. $

REDD ROCKETT'S PIZZA PORT: Across from Innoventions, this upscale food court overlooks the Moonliner and Cosmic Waves. It has custom-designed tables and sparkly vinyl chairs. The colorful booths, walls, and floor; metallic paneling; floating circular chandeliers; and classic Tomorrowland posters add to the retro-futuristic ambience. Three food stations serve fresh pasta, pizza, and large salads, all prepared in an open kitchen.

Menu choices include tasty pizzas (cheese, pepperoni, and a daily special, all sold by the slice or pie), Celestial Caesar Salad, Planetary Pizza Salad, Mars-inara (spaghetti with tomato sauce), Terra Nova Tomato Basil Pasta, Count-Down Chicken Fusilli, The Mother Chip, and Midnight Oreo Cluster. A beverage counter and cooler supply drinks. The pasta dishes here are quite large and good for sharing. Indoor, outdoor, and terrace ("flight deck") seating are available. L, D, S. $ - $$

TOMORROWLAND TERRACE: Near the Premiere Shop, this is one of the largest dining facilities in Disneyland. Breakfast choices include scrambled eggs with bacon (or egg substitute with turkey sausage), potatoes, muffin, and beverage; a fruit plate with yogurt dressing, muffin, and beverage; or french toast sticks with powdered sugar, syrup, and fresh fruit.

At lunch and dinner, guests bear trays piled high with fried chicken, corn-on-the-cob, a biscuit, and wedge-cut fries; over-size deli sandwiches; smoked chicken and pepper jack cheese in a wrap with avocado, lettuce, and tomato; Caesar salad with optional grilled chicken; or charbroiled burgers. At full capacity, the eatery can—and often does—handle about 3,000 people an hour. B, L, D, S. $

A-plus for Atmosphere

Disney's talent for creating a unique and memorable setting extends to the eateries throughout the park. For atmosphere, we pick:

New Orleans Square
The Blue Bayou restaurant, for its perpetual moon glow and grown-up atmosphere, and the French Market when the Royal Street Bachelors croon.

Main Street, U.S.A.
The Plaza Inn, for its antiques, charm, and front-porch seating.

Critter Country
Hungry Bear restaurant, for a wooded setting that lets you feel in the heart of things, yet curiously removed.

Frontierland
River Belle Terrace, for its pleasant Rivers of America views.

B breakfast **L** lunch **D** dinner **S** snacks $ under $10 $ $ $10–$20 $ $ $ $21–$45 $ $ $ $ $46 and up

GOOD MEALS, GREAT TIMES

In Disney's California Adventure

With both a winery and an elegant lagoonside eatery, the tastes at Disney's California Adventure are clearly grown-up. But several fast food spots and snack stands supply theme park fare with an entertaining flair—retro Hollywood decor or a laid-back surfer setting. Guests can picnic by the Golden State's Bountiful Valley Farmer's Market, or enjoy their 15 minutes of fame (and that's just for appetizers) at a bistro set in soapland.

All three full-service restaurants here—Avalon Cove, the Vineyard Room, and ABC Soap Opera Bistro—accept reservations. Call 714-781-4560 to learn how to book a table.

Entry Plaza

BAKER'S FIELD BAKERY: Follow the enticing aroma that wafts out over California Adventure's entrance area, and you'll end up at this bustling bakery. Shelves are

filled each morning with freshly baked muffins, croissants, and pastries—each a sweet way to start the day. Brownies, large cookies, and slices of cake round out the tasty options. A variety of refreshing iced specialty coffees and steaming hot brews make the perfect pairing with your pastry of choice. S. `$`

BUR-R-R BANK ICE CREAM: Cones, shakes, and sundaes are the icy treats served up here. An extra-large, chocolate-dipped, candy-coated waffle cone piled high with ice cream is a crowd favorite. Expect the line to be long at midday, when the energy-sapping sun is at its peak. S. `$`

Hollywood Pictures Backlot

TABLE SERVICE

ABC SOAP OPERA BISTRO: Welcome to Port Charles . . . or Pine Valley . . . or Llanview, depending on the set at which you're seated. Characters from ABC's four daytime dramas, *General Hospital, All My Children, One Life to Live,* and *Port Charles,* play host to hungry soap opera fans at this entertaining bistro (well, waitstaffers *playing* character-types from ABC soaps, to be exact—did you really think Susan Lucci would be serving your lunch?). Guests enter the worlds of their favorite ABC daytime dramas as soon as they walk into the eatery, and the real drama unfolds from there. Perhaps you'll be served by the town gossip, a dashing doctor, or an amnesia victim. Menu items are themed to the shows as well (like the "One Leaf to Live" salad), and include pastas and pizzas as well as chicken, beef, and fish entrées. No need to know every storyline by heart—whether or not you tune in tomorrow, you're sure to enjoy the experience. B, L, D. `$$-$$$`

GOOD MEALS, GREAT TIMES

Fast Food & Snacks

AWARD WIENERS: Heaping cheese and chili dogs—and an autograph request or two—are the specialties here. S.　　$

FAIRFAX MARKET: A healthy selection of fresh fruit, vegetables, and beverages are provided here, for guests who want a guilt-free snack. S.　　$

HOLLYWOOD & DINE: The marquees of several classic (but now defunct) Hollywood restaurants set the stage for this nostalgic dining experience. Select from Don the Beachcomber, Villa Capri, Wilshire Bowl Grill, and Schwab's Deli. Offerings here range from soup to nuts and then some—pizzas, enormous deli sandwiches piled high with fresh ingredients, burgers and subs, and a host of kid's meals are available. Guests may dine at comfy booths inspired by those that furnished star-studded eateries in their heyday—from which many an unknown was discovered and Hollywood moments were made. B, L, D, S.　　$ - $ $

SCHMOOZIES: Yogurt-and-fruit smoothies are the specialty. For some, these chilly drinks are a meal unto themselves. Lattes, cappuccinos, and other coffees are also available. S.　　$

Golden State

Table Service

THE VINEYARD ROOM: This second-story restaurant, divided between an indoor dining area and a covered balcony at Mondavi's mission-style villa, offers some of the finest American cuisine on Disney property. A three-course, fixed-price meal is matched by some of the winery's best pressed wines (grape juice is served to guests under 21). Chefs prepare a selection of appetizers and entrées in serving skillets; the menu constantly evolves to incorporate the season's freshest ingredients. A limited à la carte menu is available on the balcony. Reservations suggested. L, D.　　$$$-$$$$

Fast Food & Snacks

BOUNTIFUL VALLEY FARMER'S MARKET: A good number of California's indigenous products are incorporated into the items available at this market's stands, from ice cream blended with dates to healthy California sandwich wraps. The local turkey and chicken leg cart provides a quick—and popular—snack, but can attract long lines at mealtimes. Picnic tables are found nearby. B, L, D, S.　　$

COCINA CUCAMONGA MEXICAN GRILL: Tasty corn and flour tortillas are the house specialties and serve as the foundation for most menu items. This *cocina* cooks steak, pork, and grilled chicken or fish tacos. A creamy, sweet rice pudding makes the perfect finale to the meal. Plan to tour the adjoining tortilla factory before dining at this fast food spot; the educational trip will make the meal all the more enjoyable. You may even snag a free sample. L, D.　　$ - $ $

PACIFIC WHARF CAFE: An extension of Boudin's display bakery, guests here have the opportunity to sample some of the country's finest sourdough bread (a secret family recipe dating back to 1850). Hearty soups and salads are served up in thick bread bowls for lunch and dinner. Croissants and muffins are offered in the morning hours. B, L, D, S.　　$ - $ $

TASTE PILOTS' GRILL: The juicy patties grilled at this Condor Flats eatery just may leave flame-broiled burger-lovers on cloud nine. (These meals are best enjoyed *after* taking an airborne trip at Soarin' Over California.) Hot stuff is the name of the game here, so expect items such as ribs, chicken wings, and onion rings to round out the menu. B, L, D, S.　　$

THE LUCKY FORTUNE COOKERY: Foods found in the Pacific Rim are featured on the menu here. Select from egg rolls, California rolls, dumplings, rice bowls, and chicken and beef noodle bowls. L, D, S.　　$ - $ $

RITA'S BAJA BLENDERS: This colorful kiosk next to Cocina Cucamonga serves up slushy fruit drinks in your choice of lemon-lime, strawberry, peach, banana, and other favorite flavors. S.　　$

WINE COUNTRY MARKET: Located on the lower level of the Mondavi's mission house, this deli provides the perfect complement to a glass of wine—cheese, soups, salads, fruit, and finger sandwiches. Dine at one of the shaded tables beside the vineyard. L, S.　　$ - $ $

Paradise Pier

TABLE SERVICE

AVALON COVE: Presented by Wolfgang Puck, this dining spot (pictured below) offers the most enchanting views of Paradise Pier's amusements and the crashing waves below (dinner here promises to be especially magical, when the boardwalk is aglow with thousands of twinkling lights). Signature dishes revolve around the catch of the day, though large salads and fresh pastas are also available. Reservations are suggested. L, D. **$ $ $**

FAST FOOD & SNACKS

BURGER INVASION: An "out-of-this-world" burger stand, it's memorable more for the cheeseburger spaceship that hovers above it than for the familiar McDonald's burgers and fries it serves up. L, D. **$**

CATCH A FLAVE: Swirl's up at this beachy ice cream stand. A selection of refreshing soft serve flavors helps guests cool off after a long day of fun in the sun. S. **$**

CORN DOG CASTLE: Hot dogs, links and cheese, fried to a golden brown and served on a stick, reign supreme. L, D, S. **$**

MALIBU-RITOS: The steaming, stuffed burritos offered here make for some of the healthier Paradise Pier meals, for vegetarians and meat-eaters alike. B, L, D, S. **$**

PIZZA OOM MOW MOW: Surf's up, dude! Venice Beach and its colorful laid-back culture (see page 149 for the real deal) are the inspiration for this pizza place's creative decor. Surfing memorabilia (circa Frankie and Annette) provide the backdrop for the cheesy entrées of choice—available plain or with a combination of toppings. L, D. **$**

California Cocktails

While Disneyland upholds a strict no-alcohol policy, Disney's California Adventure offers several spirited lounges, drink carts, and daily wine tastings (to all guests over 21; proper ID is required). Alcohol is available at all of the park's table-service restaurants and several of the fast food spots, but expect the Golden State's watering holes to be the most festive—especially in the evening hours. Cheers!

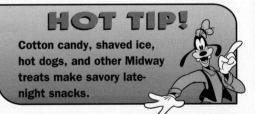

HOT TIP!

Cotton candy, shaved ice, hot dogs, and other Midway treats make savory late-night snacks.

STRIPS, DIPS, 'N' CHIPS: The deep-fried chicken and zucchini strips and fab fries (with choice of dipping sauces) are no paltry snack-on-the-go. L, D, S. **$**

| B breakfast | L lunch | D dinner | S snacks | $ | under $10 | $ $ | $10–$20 | $ $ $ | $21–$45 | $ $ $ $ | $46 and up |

GOOD MEALS, GREAT TIMES

In the Disneyland Resort Hotels

Disneyland Hotel

The diverse dining possibilities here range from grand to Goofy. For reservations or information, call 714-956-6755.

CAPTAIN'S GALLEY: Specialty coffees, muffins, bagels, cereal, fruit, kid's meals, and boxed lunches (centering on hearty salads or heaping sandwiches) are sold in this tucked-away shop. Perfect for a poolside meal. Alcohol is available. B, L, S. $

THE COFFEE HOUSE: Order biscotti, bagels, muffins, pastries, fruit, yogurt, Mickey Mouse cookies, and specialty coffees in this small coffee shop. Outside seating only. B, S. $

CROC'S BITS 'N' BITES: Part of the Never Land pool area, it's perfect for a quick burger, grilled chicken sandwich, or ice cream. There's outdoor seating nearby. S. $

PHOTO BY KEITH GROSHANS

GOOFY'S KITCHEN: This whimsical dining room features perennially popular meals and personal encounters with Goofy, Donald Duck, and other Disney friends. Service here is buffet style, so fill your plate as high and as often as you please.

Highlights at breakfast include Mickey Mouse-shaped waffles and breakfast lasagne. Lunch and dinner offer carved ham, prime rib, pasta, chicken dishes, macaroni and cheese, pizzas (including peanut butter and jelly pizza, a favorite with the young set), salads, breads, fruit, and a large selection of desserts (don't miss Goofy's Hot Chocolate Cake). Have your picture taken with one of your favorite Disney characters while you wait; it makes a terrific souvenir. Reservations suggested

HOT TIP! Expect a long line at The Coffee House in the morning, and head to Captain's Galley for breakfast on-the-go or a quick coffee.

(same-day reservations are not accepted, but you can put your name on the standby list). B, L*, D. $ $ - $ $ $

GRANVILLE'S STEAK HOUSE: This intimate dining spot is decorated with oak paneling, etched glass, and paintings that depict the American Southwest. Soft music plays as servers deliver a "3-D menu" of cuts of fresh meats, cooked to your specifications. All the entrées—juicy prime rib, fresh Maine lobster, swordfish steak, shrimp and beef brochettes, and rack of lamb, among others—come with sourdough bread and a choice of a baked potato, wild rice, or french fries. The wine list touts fine California vintages, and the desserts, including soufflés, sorbets, and the 21-layer Castle Cake with fruit filling, are delectable. Reservations suggested. D. $ $ $ $

HOOK'S POINTE & WINE CELLAR: This sophisticated, contemporary dining room overlooks the Never Land pool. Mesquite-grilled specialties include chicken breast with sweet-pea risotto and roasted garlic sauce, Chilean sea bass with a citrus-flavored glaze, and cognac-marinated rib-eye steak. Pastas, sandwiches, pizzas, salads, and turkey avocado spring rolls are also featured on the menu, along with children's selections. Reservations suggested. L, D. $ $ $

GOOD MEALS, GREAT TIMES

B breakfast **L** lunch **D** dinner **S** snacks $ under $10 $ $ $10–$20 $ $ $ $21–$45 $ $ $ $ $46 and up

Disney's Paradise Pier Hotel

It has all the bases covered—sushi, wood-fired pizza, and afternoon tea. And wait 'til you see what Minnie's cooked up for breakfast! For reservations, call 714-956-6755.

HOT TIP!

PCH Grill's fresh, hearty fare and peaceful setting make it the perfect place to take a lunch break when the parks are packed and the midday sun seems inescapable.

DISNEY'S PCH GRILL: Besides hosting a character breakfast with Minnie & Friends that offers both table service and a buffet, Disney's PCH Grill—the initials stand for Pacific Coast Highway—reflects California tastes with Asian influences. The focal point is the open kitchen, which features a large pizza oven. The whimsical decor incorporates primary colors and Mickey silhouettes, while the menu, designed like a road map, features tasty American and

Asian dishes. For lunch or dinner, consider sampling the sake-marinated sea bass, hoisin-grilled baby-back ribs, wonton chicken salad, juicy burgers, healthy sandwiches, or wood-fired specialty pizzas such as Mongolian chicken. Kids can "design" their own pizzas. Reservations suggested. B, L, D. $$

TEA ROOM: There's no more delightful way to spend an afternoon than at the Practically Perfect Tea, which is hosted by Mary Poppins herself. The ever-so-elegant nanny sings and drops by each table to chat with guests as they sip tea and nibble dainty sandwiches and scones in Victorian surroundings. For some, the fare is filling enough to take the place of a meal; for most, it's a substantial snack. Everybody gets to play dress-up for a photo op, so be sure to have your camera with you.

Tea time is at 12:30 P.M. on Wednesday, Saturday, and Sunday (daily during summer and holidays), with additional 10 A.M. and 3 P.M. seatings on Saturday and a 3 P.M seating on Sunday. The tea tends to be rather weak, so let your server know if you prefer to drink it strong. Reservations are necessary. S. $$$

HOT TIP!

For Japanese dining in the most traditional setting, ask to sit in the Tatami room at Yamabuki.

YAMABUKI: This restaurant is named after a flower known as the Japanese rose. Authentic traditional and contemporary Japanese dishes, described clearly and concisely on the menu, are served à la carte or as part of a set menu, almost always with miso soup, salad, and steamed rice or a California roll. Japanese beers and sake are served, along with wine and other beverages. The à la carte items include tiger prawns, shrimp and vegetable tempura, sushi, and sashimi, as well as New York steak cooked to order, a daily grilled fish special, and children's portions of chicken or beef teriyaki. Some dishes are cooked at your table. The sushi bar offers a fine selection of fresh fish and rarely has a wait. Reservations suggested for the dining room. L (weekdays), D. $$$

GOOD MEALS, GREAT TIMES

B breakfast **L** lunch **D** dinner **S** snacks **$** under $10 **$$** $10–$20 **$$$** $21–$45 **$$$$** $46 and up

Disney's Grand Californian Hotel

The restaurants at Disney's newest hotel offer a taste of (and a twist on) California cuisine. For reservations call 714-956-6755.

HOT TIP! Napa Rose's adjoining lounge offers several of the restaurant's appetizers as well as an impressive wine list.

NAPA ROSE: This elegant restaurant features a menu of market-fresh, wine country-inspired dishes flavored by fruits of the sea and vine (the eatery is named after California's most famous valley of vineyards). A striking 20-foot stained glass window offers sweeping views of Disney's California Adventure, while the open kitchen gives insight into California cooking. The offerings evolve as new items are introduced each season. Consider grapevine smoked salmon with lemon, capers, and goat cheese panini, or grilled free-range veal with truffled white beans and a black-trumpet cabernet vinaigrette. The dessert tray offers a trio of citrus temptations: Key lime custard, orange napoleon, and a lemon cream nut tart. The California wine list is one of the most extensive on property. Reservations suggested. L, D. $$$-$$$$

HEARTHSTONE LOUNGE: Though primarily a drinking spot, this lounge is open in the morning for early risers in search of hot coffee and the day's paper. Continental breakfast items are also available. B, S. $

STORYTELLERS CAFE: It's hard to imagine a time before computers and television (especially for the youngest members of the group), when children were exposed to new cultures and histories only through the stories of others. This restaurant salutes tales set in California, like "The Jumping Frogs of Calaveras County" and "Island of the Blue Dolphin," through seven-foot murals that act as backdrops to the chefs at work in the exhibition kitchen. In the morning, the stage is set for a festive character-hosted buffet. Chip, Dale, and other Disney characters entertain guests while the buffet offers a bounty of breakfast options, from pancakes and waffles to eggs, sausage, and a selection of fresh fruit. Lunch and dinner offer such pleasers as wood-fired pizzas, homemade pastas, and burgers, plus salads, grilled fish, and spit-roasted chicken, all prepared and served by chefs from their cooking islands. Reservations suggested for breakfast. B, L, D. $$-$$$

WHITE WATER SNACKS: The splish-splash of the waterfall and kids soaring down the slide at the Redwood pool set the mood for this dining spot. Open for breakfast, lunch, and dinner, the fast food restaurant serves up more than snacks and drinks (though it supplies these as well). Specialty coffees, muffins, bagels, sweet rolls, and breakfast burritos are available in the morning. Large salads, deli sandwiches, pizzas, burgers, hot dogs, and grilled chicken are lunch and dinner options. B, L, D, S. $

HOT TIP! Any full-service dining spot at a Disneyland Resort hotel will validate your parking at that hotel; remember to get your parking pass stamped before you leave.

B breakfast **L** lunch **D** dinner **S** snacks   **$** under $10   **$ $** $10–$20   **$ $ $** $21–$45   **$ $ $ $** $46 and up

124

GOOD MEALS, GREAT TIMES

In Downtown Disney

The settings and menus of the restaurants at Downtown Disney each focus on a different theme, but they certainly have something in common—their meals are all served with a side of entertainment. To learn more about the amusing options at Downtown Disney, refer to page 128.

CATAL RESTAURANT AND UVA BAR: A sun-kissed balcony, outdoor tapas bar, and villa-style dining room set the Mediterranean mood at this casual but elegant restaurant. The menu focuses on grilled seafood, chicken, and vegetables, infused with olive oil and citrus accents. With several pastas and salads available, vegetarians have much to choose from here. The large courtyard bar, which also serves appetizers into the evening, offers coffee and a continental breakfast in the morning. Reservations suggested for lunch and dinner; 714-774-4442. B, L, D.   `$ $ $`

HOUSE OF BLUES: Diners with a craving for Cajun cookin' will find bliss at this Delta dive (all part of the theme). With a menu set deep in the south, but not so spicy that it won't please all palates, the eatery offers items such as Memphis-style ribs, voodoo shrimp, jambalaya, and tasty thin-crust pizzas. On Sundays guests sing hallelujah for the all-you-can-eat southern-style Gospel Brunch (local and national gospel touring groups provide the stirring entertainment). Reservations suggested; 714-778-2583. L, D, S.   `$ $ $`

LA BREA BAKERY: Since it opened in 1990, Southern Californians have flocked to the original La Brea Bakery for its selection of fresh breads and sweet pastries. The offerings at this casual Downtown Disney spot— breakfast treats, grilled panini sandwiches, and crostini (small, open-face sandwiches)— are built on the legendary bread. A juice and coffee bar blends up healthy concoctions and icy smoothies, plus espresso, cappuccino, iced coffees, and specialty roasts. Wine by the glass and microbrewed beers are also available. B, L, D, S.   `$-$ $`

NAPLES RISTORANTE E PIZZERIA: Dine indoors or alfresco at this contemporary Italian trattoria. A large outdoor terrace provides perfect views of the Disney landscape, plus a peaceful and romantic setting for lunch or dinner. Two *bocce* courts (the Italian equivalent of bowling and inspiration for the country's classic ice cream dessert with the same name) keep guests entertained. Pizzas are served in individual portions or *al metro* (one meter long and perfect for a hungry family to share). The menu also includes *piccoli piatti* (small salads served tapas-style), fresh pasta dishes, and seafood entrées. Reservations suggested; 714-776-6200. L, D.   `$ $ $`

RAINFOREST CAFE: It's a jungle inside this tropical paradise of a restaurant. Lush greenery, misty waterfalls, tropical storms, life-size Audio-Animatronic animals, and several real-life creatures create a sometimes-hectic, always-colorful atmosphere. An elaborate menu features sizable, environmentally conscious appetizers and entrées, including pastas, thick burgers, and hearty sandwiches. Reservations suggested; 714-772-0413. L, D, S.   `$ $-$ $ $`

HOT TIP! Many Downtown Disney dining spots serve simple breakfasts. Grab a bite to eat before heading to Disney's California Adventure or Disneyland.

RALPH BRENNAN'S JAZZ KITCHEN: Sample some homestyle New Orleans specialties at this comfy cafe while listening to the soothing sounds of jazz. Gumbo, jambalaya, Cajun chicken, and fresh pasta dishes are house favorites. Reservations suggested; 714-776-5200. L, D, S.   `$ $-$ $ $`

STUDIO GRILL: Set inside California's first ESPN Zone, this sporty spot serves up baskets full of ballpark fare, plus more sophisticated items like cajun fettuccine, grilled chops, and New York strip steaks. Sports fans will want to catch a taping of *Up Close*, ESPN's daily interview program hosted by Gary Miller, recorded here most weekday afternoons. Reservations accepted; 714-300-3776. B (weekends only), L, D, S.   `$ $`

Y ARRIBA Y ARRIBA: This hot spot cooks up spicy Spanish and South American staples. Appetizers are served tapas-style, followed by chicken, beef (carved at the table), or vegetable dishes, plus sides of rice and beans, fried bananas, or salad. A tapas-toting trolley makes rounds, and specialty acts perform throughout the day. Reservations suggested; 714-533-8272. L, D, S.   `$ $-$ $ $`

GOOD MEALS, GREAT TIMES

B breakfast **L** lunch **D** dinner **S** snacks   `$` under $10   `$ $` $10–$20   `$ $ $` $21–$45   `$ $ $ $` $46 and up

RESTAURANT ROUNDUP

There are more dining choices than ever before at the Disneyland Resort. We've picked our favorites based on food quality, restaurant atmosphere, and overall value. Use these Birnbaum's Bests to help you decide where to grab a quick bite or have a hearty meal.

BEST RESTAURANTS FOR FAMILIES

TABLE SERVICE

Blue Bayou . . . . .Disneyland Park (p. 115)
ABC Soap Opera Bistro . .California Adventure (p. 119)
Disney's PCH Grill . . . . . . .Paradise Pier Hotel (p. 123)
Rainforest Cafe . . . . .Downtown Disney (p. 125)

FAST FOOD

Royal Street Veranda . . . . . .Disneyland Park (p. 116)
Rancho del Zocalo . . . . .Disneyland Park (p. 116)
Hollywood & Dine . . . . .California Adventure (p. 120)
Pacific Wharf Cafe . . . . .California Adventure (p. 120)
Award Wieners . . . . .California Adventure (p. 120)

BEST PIZZA

Naples Ristorante e Pizzeria
Downtown Disney (p. 125)

BEST SUSHI

Yamabuki
Paradise Pier Hotel (p. 123)

BEST STEAK

Granville's Steak House
Disneyland Hotel (p. 122)

BEST CHARACTER MEAL

Goofy's Kitchen . . . . .Disneyland Hotel (p. 122)

RUNNERS-UP

Plaza Inn . . . . .Disneyland Park (p. 114)
Storytellers Cafe . . .Grand Californian Hotel (p. 124)

BEST RESTAURANTS FOR ADULTS

Napa Rose .Grand Californian Hotel (p. 124)
Ralph Brennan's Jazz Kitchen . . . . .Downtown Disney (p. 125)

RUNNERS-UP

The Vineyard Room . . . . .California Adventure (p. 120)
Granville's Steak House . . . . .Disneyland Hotel (p. 122)
Catal Restaurant and Uva Bar . . . . .Downtown Disney (p. 125)

BEST SNACKS

Blue Ribbon Bakery . . . . .Disneyland Park (p. 113)
Bur-r-r Bank Ice Cream . . . .California Adventure (p. 119)

GOOD MEALS, GREAT TIMES

ENTERTAINMENT

There's more to Disney than thrill rides and character greetings. Whether you're looking for a midday break from the parks or a place to party the night away, the following options are sure to please. There's plenty to do at Disney's three hotels and in Downtown Disney—an entertainment district with adult appeal. We've also included some Anaheim-area options for those interested in venturing beyond Disney borders.

Note: For information on nighttime theme park happenings, refer to the "Entertainment" section at the end of the *Disneyland Park* and *Disney's California Adventure* chapters of this book.

Disney Hotels

Lounges

DISNEYLAND HOTEL: The cozy **Wine Cellar** (pictured below) is located on the lower level of Hook's Pointe & Wine Cellar and serves California wines by the bottle, glass, or taste.

Sophisticated, semicircular **Top Brass** bar, with its leaded-glass door, brass rails, and striking watercolor of the Anaheim orange groves circa 1962, provides an intimate meeting place.

An open-air lounge, offering a menu long enough that the place should almost be called a restaurant (burgers, sandwiches, and such are served throughout the day and night), the **Lost Bar** is this hotel's most happening hot spot, especially when the resident musicians are performing. Several outdoor tables are kept toasty-warm by the heat lamps that are lit each evening.

DISNEY'S PARADISE PIER HOTEL: The lobby **Coffee Bar & Lounge** has perhaps the only cappuccino maker and "Henri Rousseau" print in existence with Mickey ears.

The small lounge inside the **Yamabuki** restaurant is a quiet retreat and the perfect place to join friends for a nightcap.

DISNEY'S GRAND CALIFORNIAN HOTEL: The lounge adjoining the elegant **Napa Rose** restaurant offers an extensive selection of wines by the glass and a soothing atmosphere.

At the handsome **Hearthstone Lounge**, you can sip a cocktail or after-dinner cordial opposite a roaring fireplace.

Live Entertainment

DISNEYLAND HOTEL: At the free **Fantasy Waters**, fountains and lights dance in rhythm to Disney tunes; it occurs twice nightly. Hear music most nights in summer and on weekends the rest of the year at **The Lost Bar**; other performers croon at various locations.

DISNEY'S GRAND CALIFORNIAN HOTEL: As a tribute to the early 1900s storytelling tradition, entertainers tell tall tales in the hotel's main lobby throughout the day.

Fun & Games

DISNEYLAND HOTEL: Kids can steer small, remote-control **Jungle Cruise Boats** by the hotel's lagoon. The beach's volleyball court is a hit, especially in the afternoon; the **Game Arcade** in the shopping enclave scores high points on evenings when the parks close early.

DISNEY'S PARADISE PIER HOTEL: Youngsters have a blast at this hotel's arcade, located off the main lobby.

DISNEY'S GRAND CALIFORNIAN HOTEL: The **Grizzly Game Arcade**, a brand-new game room, features all the latest whistles and bells.

GOOD MEALS, GREAT TIMES

Downtown Disney

Easily accessed by foot (from the Disney-land Resort hotels or theme parks) or monorail (from Disneyland Park's Tomorrowland), this entertainment district offers escape from the hustle and bustle during the day, and a place to mix and mingle in the evening hours. Many Downtown Disney venues serve double (or triple) duty—as dining and dancing (and sometimes shopping) spots. For more information on the restaurants' offerings, see page 125.

Shops open early and don't close until late in the evening. Club performers generally hit the stage post dinner and wrap past midnight.

Clubs & Concerts

HOUSE OF BLUES: Don't let the name of this jumping joint fool you—the lineup features a rousing mix of rock, R&B, hip-hop, reggae, and latin music, along with a touch of the blues. Big-name bands and local acts are slotted to perform throughout the week.

Call 714-778-2583 to learn the House's schedule during your visit. Ticket prices range from about $5 to $30, depending on the performer. Call TicketMaster or visit *www.ticketmaster.com* to purchase tickets in advance, or stop by the club's box office the day of the performance.

RALPH BRENNAN'S JAZZ KITCHEN: The soothing sounds of jazz set the tone for the relaxed atmosphere at this restaurant's performance lounge. Big band acts and classic songsters entertain on select days of the week. A smooth soundtrack provides background music when the stage is dark. Special tickets may be required for certain performances. Call 714-776-5200 to inquire about ticket reservations.

Y ARRIBA Y ARRIBA: The entertainment here comes in all forms, each with its own Latin flair. A troupe of in-house performers demonstrates traditional Spanish and South American dance styles—that is, when the main stage isn't occupied by famous Latin performers or the Y Arriba orchestra (guests can discover their own Latin flair out on the dance floor). Fashion shows, vignettes, and poetry and literature readings are staged here during the day. Special tickets may be required for certain performances; call 866-611-7469 to inquire about ticket reservations.

Lounges

CATAL RESTAURANT AND UVA BAR: Designed to resemble the Art Nouveau-style of a Paris metro station, this large wine and tapas bar tempts guests with the fruits of the vine and sea. Guests can drink under the stars at the outdoor bar or mingle indoors, and can select from the extensive wine list (each wine can be sampled by the glass).

MAGIC MUSHROOM BAR: Part of the lush Rainforest Cafe, this circular drinking hole is capped by a giant mushroom, and serves up aptly named blended beverages, such as the Margarilla and the Tropical Toucan (nonalcoholic versions are also available). Known as a family-friendly spot, don't be surprised if a tiny tot is sitting at the zebra-legged bar stool beside you, especially at lunch or dinnertime.

ESPN ZONE: Stop by the bar area of the Zone's Studio Grill for a tall one before heading upstairs to play arcade games at the Sports Arena. With large-screen TVs blaring from each section of the room, expect the joint to be jumping on big-game nights.

Shopping

BASIN: Indulge in the lavish bath and body products available at this inviting boutique.

COMPASS BOOKS AND CAFE: This branch of the West's oldest (since 1851) independent bookstore is heavy on the travel tomes, and also features a coffee bar and outdoor newsstand.

DEPARTMENT 56: 'Tis always the season to be jolly at this shop featuring hand-crafted miniature houses, villages, and other holiday collectibles.

HOUSE OF BLUES COMPANY STORE: A slew of spicy sauces lets you take a bit of this House back to your house. Home accessories and House of Blues logo merchandise round out the options here.

HOYPOLOI: This gallery, which displays ceramics, sculptures, and other decorative items, provides the perfect retreat on a crowded day.

ILLUMINATIONS: Light up your life with an assortment of hand-crafted candles, aromatherapy products, and accessories.

ISLAND CHARTERS: Ahoy! This shop offers one-of-a-kind nautical and aviation gifts for seafarers and landlubbers alike.

LEGO IMAGINATION CENTER: Four hundred of the world's most famous building brick sets and products are for sale, along with LEGO shirts, hats, and other apparel (and no, they're not made of LEGO bricks).

LIQUID PLANET: Simple surfer-wear and accessories help guests dress the part of the laid-back beachcomber.

MAINSPRING: Time never stands still at this watch shop, where more than 5,000 brands and styles are on display.

MARCELINE'S CONFECTIONERY: Named for Walt Disney's hometown, this sweet shop offers classic and contemporary candies.

PETALS: Leather is the look of choice at this cozy boutique. Jackets, handbags, and other accessories are for sale.

RAINFOREST SHOP: Large butterflies and vibrant Amazon parrots perched atop looping jungle vines define this tropical shopping paradise, adjacent to the Rainforest Cafe. Plush animals and environmentally themed toys, plus Rainforest Cafe logo merchandise and packages of tasty candy, cookies, and coffee are for sale.

SEPHORA: A black-and-white motif provides a perfect backdrop for the colorful palette of products available at this cosmetics mecca. Sephora's own line of makeup and bath products is complemented by a wide selection of popular and hard-to-find beauty products and perfumes.

SOLITON: Southern California style would not be complete without a cool pair of shades—head here for the ideal eyewear.

SOMETHING SILVER: Perfect for celebrating a 25th anniversary, or just creating a look, the jewelry here is simple and stylish.

SPORTS CENTER STUDIO STORE: Sports fans and couch potatoes alike will cheer over the ESPN, *SportsCenter*, and *Monday Night Football* branded apparel and other merchandise at this gift shop located inside the ESPN Zone.

STARABILIAS: Shoppers can take a walk down memory lane at this shop, which showcases television, movie, music, and political memorabilia.

TIN PAN ALLEY: Nostalgia buffs will enjoy this collection of metal gifts and novelty items. Featured is a large selection of magnets in every size and shape.

WORLD OF DISNEY: Shelves are stacked sky-high (airplanes piloted by familiar Disney characters dangle from the cloud-covered ceiling) at this souvenir shopper's dream-come-true. Each overflowing room features a different theme and type of merchandise: The Lion King room is well suited to adult apparel, while Disney Villains add dastardly decor to the watch and accessory department. With an entire room dedicated to plush toys (the 20-foot wall of plush features more than 15,000 characters), and rooms for dolls, figurines, toys, videos, clothing, accessories, and collectibles, everyone is bound to find what they are looking for here. Classic Disney films play continuously on the big screen to occupy restless young (and old) shoppers. Expect the place to be packed most evenings and all day on the weekends.

Fun & Games

AMC MOVIE THEATRES: Moviegoers enjoy wall-to-wall movie screens and comfy stadium seating at each of the 12 cinemas located inside this 60,000-square-foot megaplex. Current releases are shown throughout the day, with special matinee and late-night screenings.

ESPN ZONE: This sports shrine offers dining options (see page 123) and a lounge area, plus two distinct fun zones. In the **Screening Room**, sports fans can cheer their team to victory, as games from around the world are televised on one central 16-foot screen and a dozen additional 36-inch video monitors. With multi-game viewing capabilities and direct audio control, picture-in-picture is taken to a whole new level. Even bathroom breaks won't mean a minute missed—the restrooms are all equipped with TVs tuned to the main event.

The **Sports Arena** challenges armchair athletes and jocks alike with interactive sports-themed games that put your skills, strength, and smarts to the test. Game cards (necessary to play the arena's games) can be purchased in $5 increments.

Beyond the Disneyland Resort

Clubs & Concerts

ARROWHEAD POND OF ANAHEIM: Besides being the home of the Mighty Ducks hockey team, "the Pond" accommodates 19,400 fans for major concerts, from rock to rap to country. Barbra Streisand, Neil Diamond, Reba McEntire, Phil Collins, Billy Joel, Kenny G, Smashing Pumpkins, and Alanis Morissette have headlined here. 2695 E. Katella Ave.; Anaheim; 714-704-2500.

BILL MEDLEY'S MUSIC CITY: Music and special events provide a nostalgic trip through the 1950s, '60s, and '70s. 18774 Brookhurst St.; Fountain Valley; 714-963-2366.

CERRITOS CENTER FOR THE PERFORMING ARTS: This state-of-the-art theater presents popular artists, musicians, dance companies, and Broadway shows. Performers have included Isaac Stern, the Alvin Ailey American Dance Theater, Whitney Houston, Peabo Bryson, Trisha Yearwood, and Bernadette Peters. 12700 Cerritos Court Dr.; Cerritos; 562-916-8500 or 800-300-4345.

CRAZY HORSE STEAKHOUSE/SALOON: Known for western music, Crazy Horse often features famous country entertainers. 1580 Brookhollow Dr.; Santa Ana; 714-549-1512.

FULLERTON CIVIC LIGHT OPERA: When it comes to musical comedy and operetta, anything goes at the Fullerton Civic Light Opera. Plummer Auditorium; Lemon Street and Chapman Ave.; Fullerton; 714-526-3832.

HYATT NEWPORTER SUMMER JAZZ SERIES: On Friday nights from June through September, jazz artists perform in the hotel's amphitheater. Tickets cost $25 to $35. 1107 Jamboree Rd.; Newport Beach; 949-729-1234.

IMPROVISATION COMEDY CLUBS: Two sister clubs present shows five or six nights a week; call for schedules and headliners. 945 E. Birch St.; Brea; 714-529-7878; and 4255 Campus Dr., Irvine; 949-854-5455.

ORANGE COUNTY PERFORMING ARTS CENTER: This acoustically impressive 3,000-seat theater hosts symphony orchestras, opera and dance companies, and entertainers, and mounts musical-theater productions. Jazz, cabaret, and Broadway reviews are staged in the intimate 300-seat Founder's Hall, where drinks are served. 600 Town Center Dr.; Costa Mesa; 714-556-2787.

Dinner Theater

MEDIEVAL TIMES: Guests feast on four courses served by wenches and knaves while knights on horseback twist and joust. 7662 Beach Blvd.; Buena Park; 714-521-4740.

PLAZA GARIBALDI: It's a Mexican fiesta with mariachis, singers, folkloric dancers in authentic costumes, traditional food, margaritas, and more. 1490 S. Anaheim Blvd.; Anaheim; 714-758-9014.

WILD BILL'S WILD WEST DINNER EXTRAVAGANZA: Feast on an all-you-can-eat four-course meal of ribs, chicken, and the fixings, while Miss Annie and Wild Bill host a western hoedown with Native American dancers, a comely rope artist, and a magician. 7600 Beach Blvd.; Buena Park; 714-522-6414.

Lounges

In Anaheim, **J.T. Schmid's Brewhouse & Eatery**, across the road from the Pond, has handcrafted ales, with gleaming vats on view; 2610 Katella Ave.; 714-634-9200. In nearby Orange, the **Alcatraz Brewing Company** is ensconced in the lively Block at Orange (see "Fun & Games," below); 20 City Blvd. West; Orange; 714-939-8686. On the coast, the **Huntington Beach Beer Company** mixes brews with free live blues on Thursday nights, and its indoor and outdoor seating offer ocean views all the time; 201 Main St.; Huntington Beach; 714-960-5343.

Across the road from Edison Field, the authentically old-fashioned sports bar at **The Catch** restaurant has 11 TV monitors and autographed photos of baseball greats on the walls. It provides round-trip shuttle service to Arrowhead Pond; 929 S. State College Blvd.; Anaheim; 714-634-1829. The **National Sports Grill** hosts a radio call-in show, "Mighty Ducks Live," after every local game. It also has sports memorabilia, 4 big-screen TVs, 63 TV monitors, and 11 pool tables; 450 N. State College Blvd.; Anaheim; 714-935-0300.

Fun & Games

THE BLOCK AT ORANGE: This outdoor entertainment complex, only five miles from Disneyland, has a 30-screen **AMC Cinema**, **Dave & Buster's** billiards parlor, and movie-set-themed **GameWorks**, a state-of-the-art arcade. Valet parking available. 20 City Blvd. West; Orange; 714-769-4001.

GOOD MEALS, GREAT TIMES

Sports

SPORTS

Southern California's appealing combination of warm, sunny weather and invigorating ocean breezes has created a population of outdoors and exercise enthusiasts. Well-toned athletes flex their muscles on golf courses and tennis courts; atop surfboards, bicycles, and in-line skates; on hiking and jogging trails; or 15-feet underwater, mingling with schools of fish.

In Orange County alone, there are more than 10,000 acres of parkland and several hundred miles of bike trails. Hiking paths and fishing streams crisscross 70,000 acres of mountain terrain in Cleveland National Forest. Just 15 miles south of Anaheim, prime Pacific Ocean beaches, perfect for basking in the sun or catching the ultimate wave, await the wayfarer. In fact, 42 miles of glistening sand and sleepy seaside communities lie within an hour's drive of Anaheim.

Those who delight in spying on Mother Nature can catch glimpses of California's gray whales as they migrate to Mexico in winter, or ospreys, blue herons, and swallows returning to the area in the spring. A team of Orange County's most entertaining creatures, the Mighty Ducks, can be spotted on the ice at the Arrowhead Pond of Anaheim, September through April. Even Angels have been sighted, gracing the bases at Edison International Field, April through September.

To be sure, the sporting life in Orange County is heavenly.

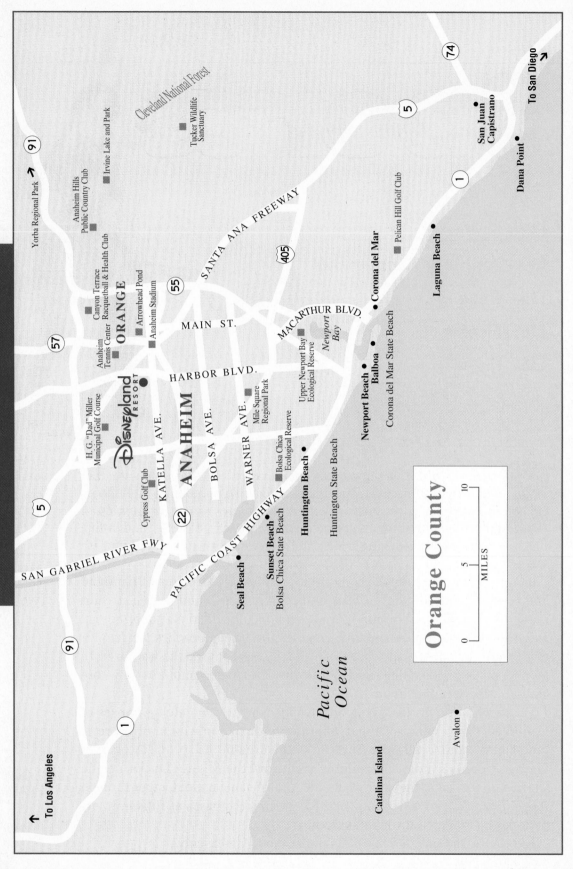

Orange County

Cleveland National Forest

Tucker Wildlife Sanctuary

Irvine Lake and Park

Yorba Regional Park

91

Anaheim Hills Public Country Club

57

Canyon Terrace Racquetball & Health Club

Anaheim Tennis Center

Arrowhead Pond

Anaheim Stadium

ORANGE

55

MAIN ST.

SANTA ANA FREEWAY

405

MACARTHUR BLVD.

Newport Bay

Corona del Mar

HARBOR BLVD.

H. G. "Dad" Miller Municipal Golf Course

Disneyland RESORT

Mile Square Regional Park

Upper Newport Bay Ecological Reserve

Newport Bay

Newport Beach

Balboa

Corona del Mar State Beach

Pelican Hill Golf Club

Laguna Beach

1

5

San Juan Capistrano

Dana Point

To San Diego

74

Cypress Golf Club

WARNER AVE.

BOLSA AVE.

KATELLA AVE.

ANAHEIM

22

Bolsa Chica Ecological Reserve

Huntington Beach

Huntington State Beach

5

SAN GABRIEL RIVER FWY

PACIFIC COAST HIGHWAY

Sunset Beach

Bolsa Chica State Beach

Seal Beach

91

1

To Los Angeles

Pacific Ocean

Catalina Island

Avalon

MILES

0   5   10

132

EYE ON THE BALL

Golf

ANAHEIM HILLS PUBLIC GOLF CLUB: This challenging championship course is a hilly, par-71, 6,245-yard layout nestled in the valleys and slopes of Santa Ana Canyon. Greens fees are $40 Monday through Thursday and $50 Friday through Sunday and holidays, cart included. Guests 62 and older can play standby for $32. Clubs (matched sets) can be rented for $15. The golf course is busiest on weekends; the least crowded days are Monday, Tuesday, and Wednesday, but even then reservations are recommended (call seven days ahead for both weekday and weekend play). 6501 Nohl Ranch Rd.; Anaheim; 714-998-3041 (pro shop); 714-765-4653 (reservations).

CYPRESS GOLF CLUB: Lakes, streams, bunkers, trees, and scenic vistas decorate this serene par-71, 6,500-yard course, which is designed to harmonize with the environment by Perry O. Dye, son of the legendary Pete Dye. Fees are $55 ($45 before 7:30 A.M.) to play Monday through Thursday, $65 Friday, and $80 weekends, cart included. Twilight rates ($45 to $65), early-bird discounts ($45 Monday through Thursday), and birthday specials ($35 to $45 with ID) are also available. Reservations are recommended and can be made up to two weeks in advance. Collared shirts and soft spikes are required; no jeans or sneakers. It's a 15-minute drive from the Disneyland Resort. 4921 E. Katella Ave.; Los Alamitos; 714-527-1800 (pro shop and reservations).

H. G. "DAD" MILLER MUNICIPAL GOLF COURSE: "Dad" Miller made a hole in one on this course (on the 112-yard 11th hole) when he was 101 years old, and it's still a favorite with older guests, who appreciate the flat, walkable terrain. But if you're a tad younger, don't let that keep you from playing here. This par-71, 5,756-yard golf course is one of the busiest in California—partly because of its convenient location in the middle of the city, but also because it's just right for the strictly recreational golfer. The cost to play here is $23 Monday through Thursday, $32 Friday through Sunday and holidays. Guests 62 and older can play standby for only $12 Monday through Thursday. Carts cost $24 for 18 holes, $15 for nine holes. Reservations are suggested, and may be made a week in advance. 430 N. Gilbert St.; Anaheim; 714-765-3481 (pro shop); 714-765-4653 (reservations).

PELICAN HILL GOLF CLUB: Test your skills here on two gorgeous Tom Fazio-designed courses. The 6,634-yard, par-70 Ocean South course features two holes that play right along the water, while the 6,856-yard, par-71 Ocean North course, which is set above the ocean, provides panoramic views from every hole, especially the 12th. For reservations made 8 to 60 days in advance, the cost to play at either course is $175 Monday through Thursday, and $250 Friday through Sunday, cart included (these reservations cannot be canceled). Arrangements

Practice Makes Perfect

Check out **The Greens at Park Place**, a PGA-approved, 18-hole championship putting course (a small golf course, really), for $10 a round Monday through Thursday, and $13 Friday through Sunday and holidays (near Newport Beach, at 3301 Michelson Dr.; Irvine; 949-250-7888).

Harbor Greens Golf Practice Center is a 60-tee driving range open long hours, with free shuttle and use of clubs for area hotel guests, grass and mat tees, a large pro shop that lets you test out any of its clubs, night lighting, and buckets of balls for $8 (behind the Hyatt Regency Alicante, at 12261 Chapman Ave.; Garden Grove; 714-703-1200 [pro shop] or 714-663-8112).

made one to six days in advance cost $20 less and can be canceled with 48-hour notice. Twilight rates (between noon and 4 P.M., depending on the time of year) are $95 Monday through Thursday, and $135 Friday through Sunday and holidays. The club has a great pro shop, with golf attire for men, women, and children. 22651 Pelican Hill Rd. South; Newport Coast; 949-760-0707 (pro shop and reservations).

Tennis & Racquetball

ANAHEIM TENNIS CENTER: This public facility has all the perks of a private club—an inviting clubhouse, a well-stocked pro shop, computerized practice machines, lockers, and showers. The accommodating staff will even try to pair you with a suitable partner if you make a request in advance. There are 12 fast, hard-surface courts, all lighted for night play. Singles and doubles rates range from $5 to $7 per person per hour, depending on time of day. Use of ball machines is $5; they are separated from the courts, but this area is still a good place to practice forehand and backhand strokes.

Playing hours begin at 8 A.M. and end at 10 P.M. Monday through Thursday, 9 P.M. Friday, and 6 P.M. weekends and holidays. Racquets rent for $3. Locker and shower facilities are free (you must supply towels). A half-hour private lesson with the resident pro costs $22; call for rates for semiprivate and group lessons. Reservations (bookable up to five days in advance) are suggested, especially for court times after 5 P.M. It's about three miles from the Disneyland Resort. 975 S. State College Blvd.; Anaheim; 714-991-9090.

CANYON TERRACE RACQUETBALL AND HEALTH CLUB: In existence since 1977 and a real find for visitors, this facility has six air-conditioned racquetball courts and low court fees—$6 to $8 per person per hour for nonmembers ($5 per person for three players, and $4.50 per person for four players). The rates are lower on weekends and before 4 P.M. weekdays. The club rents racquets and offers its full-size weight room to nonmembers for $5. The hours are 6 A.M. to 10 P.M. Monday through Thursday, 6 A.M. to 9 P.M. Friday, 7 A.M. to 7 P.M. weekends. 100 N. Tustin Ave.; Anaheim; 714-974-0280.

Spectator Sports

BASEBALL
Anaheim Angels (April–September): Edison International Field of Anaheim; 2000 Gene Autry Way; Anaheim; 714-634-2000; *www.angelsbaseball.com*
Los Angeles Dodgers (April–September): Dodger Stadium; 1000 Elysian Park Ave.; Los Angeles; 323-224-1448; *www.dodgers.com*

BASKETBALL
Los Angeles Clippers (October–April): Staples Center; 1111 S. Figueroa St.; Los Angeles; 213-742-7500
Los Angeles Lakers (October–April): Staples Center; 1111 S. Figueroa St.; Los Angeles; 310-419-3865

Los Angeles Sparks (May–August): Staples Center; 1111 S. Figueroa St.; Los Angeles; 310-330-2434 (tickets)

HOCKEY
Los Angeles Kings (September–April): Staples Center; 1111 S. Figueroa St.; Los Angeles; 213-480-3232
Mighty Ducks of Anaheim (September–April): Arrowhead Pond of Anaheim ("the Pond"); 2695 E. Katella Ave.; Anaheim; 714-704-2701; 714-740-2000 (tickets)

Surf & Sun

Beaches

Orange County's public beaches cover 40 miles of coastline—some dramatic, with high cliffs and crashing waves; others tranquil, with sheltered coves and tide pools. In summer, the water temperature averages 65 degrees but can get as high as 75 or 80; in winter, it's a nippy 57 to 60 degrees. Beaches are open from around 6 A.M. to 10 P.M., with lifeguards on duty in summer, and bicycles, in-line skates, and roller skates available for rent. Public access is free, but expect to pay around $6 for parking in beach lots.

BALBOA/NEWPORT BEACH: The Balboa Peninsula juts into the Pacific, creating beaches—Newport on the mainland, Balboa on the peninsula—that are long and horseshoe shaped, pleasant and sandy, and popular with families, surfers, and sightseers alike.

HOT TIP!

For a scenic 45-minute walk, follow the harbor-hugging pathway around Balboa Island. For a mini-expedition, head to Little Balboa Island—it can be easily circumnavigated in about 20 minutes.

The largest small-craft harbor in the world, Newport Harbor shelters almost 10,000 boats. For the best view, drive south along the peninsula on Newport Boulevard to Balboa Boulevard; turn right on Palm Street, and you'll find parking for the Balboa Pier.

Throughout the fall and winter months, the 750-acre Upper Newport Bay Regional Park and Ecological Reserve teems with great blue herons, ospreys, and other glorious winged creatures. The park's partially subterranean Interpretive Center, at Irvine Avenue and University Drive, features several exhibits on bird life, the watershed, and the history of Newport Bay.

During the migratory season (October through March), Friends of Newport Bay leads free walking tours through the reserve on the second Saturday of the month, pointing out interesting birds, as well as fossils, marsh plants, and fish.

The reserve is open daily from 10 A.M. to 4 P.M. To get there from Anaheim, follow I-5 south to Highway 55 to the Pacific Coast Highway; turn left onto Jamboree Road, take the first left onto Back Bay Drive, and follow it to the Ranger Station. Friends of Newport Bay can confirm bird-watching dates and monthly tour times; 949-646-8009. To obtain updated information about guided tours and special events year-round, contact Upper Newport Bay headquarters weekdays; 949-640-6746; *www.newportbay.org.*

CORONA DEL MAR STATE BEACH: Pretty, secluded, and pristine, Corona del Mar State Beach is a favorite for swimming, snorkeling, and family gatherings; and the lookout point above the beach is a great place to watch the sun set. There are picnic tables, grills, fire rings, a snack bar, and showers. For more information, call 949-644-3295.

HUNTINGTON BEACH: The self-proclaimed "Surfing City" hosts annual competitions, and on any summer day, enthusiasts make a beeline for the water; only diehards in wet suits venture out in winter. Concessions on the beach rent and sell surfboards and wet suits. The long stretch of sand fronting the town is a popular place for jogging and beach volleyball. The pier provides an ideal spot for fishing and a good vantage point for observing the passing scene. Check out the small surfing museum at 411 Olive Avenue; 714-960-3483. For surf information, call 714-536-9303.

Bolsa Chica Ecological Reserve, 1,200 acres of Pacific Ocean marshland a mile north of Huntington Beach pier on Pacific Coast Highway, harbors fish, sea hares, and wetland birds. To get there, walk across the bridge from the beach's parking lot and follow a trail that loops through the marsh; 714-846-1114.

LAGUNA BEACH: Thirty different beaches and coves line this six-mile coastline, popular with surfers, kayakers, body boarders, and snorkelers. Laguna is the best spot in Orange County to scuba dive, though you'll

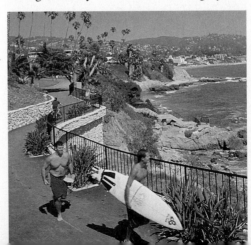

need a wet suit no matter what time of year you visit. Laguna Sea Sports (925 N. Coast Hwy.; 949-494-6965) offers full rentals, guided beach dives, classes, general information, and much more; there's a pool on the premises, and it's only about one block from the beach. Main Beach (the central strip of sand) offers basketball and volleyball courts as well as a playground.

A short walk from here, Heisler Park has picnic areas, beaches for swimming and sunning, cliff-top lookout points, lawn bowling, and shuffleboard; stairs lead to tide pools. Serious hikers like to head for Crystal Cove State Park, Aliso and Wood Canyons Wilderness Park, or Laguna Coast Wilderness Park. Watch the sun set from the gazebo near the art museum or from Laguna Village.

Fishing

In Orange County, you can cast for bass, catfish, and trout in tranquil lakes; troll the Pacific for bonitos, barracuda, calico bass, sand bass, halibut, mackerel, whitefish, and yellowtail; and scoop grunions off the beach.

SPORTFISHING: Boats set out from Davey's Locker, at the Balboa Pavilion in Balboa (call 949-673-1434), and from Dana Wharf Sportfishing, at Dana Point Harbor (named for Richard Henry Dana, who wrote *Two Years Before the Mast);* call 949-496-5794, ext. 18. Reservations are suggested. Licenses, necessary for deep-sea sportfishing, are available at either location and cost about $8 per day.

FRESHWATER ANGLING: At Irvine Lake, no fishing license is required and there is no charge for fish caught, unless you visit the "pay-per-pound" pond. Monday through Thursday the gate fee is $13 for adults ($12 for guests 62 and older) and $7 for children 4 through 12; under 4 free. Friday through Sunday, and holidays, it's $15 for all adults and $8 for children 4 through 12. Fishing poles, motorboats, rowboats, and pontoons may be rented, or you can launch your own craft for an $8 fee. A tackle shop and cafe are on-site. No pets allowed. 4621 Santiago Canyon Rd.; Silverado; 714-649-2168 (for detailed recorded information) or 714-649-9111.

GRUNION ALERT: You can try your hand—literally—at catching grunions at Bolsa Chica State Beach from March through September, when the tiny fish come ashore to lay eggs in the sand and then head back to sea on outgoing waves. They're slippery, and you have to catch them with your bare hands; fortunately, they also shimmer in the moonlight so they're fairly easy to spot. The best time: about an hour after high tide on the second, third, fourth, and fifth nights after a full moon.

Note: Catching grunions is illegal in April and May; any other time of year, feel free to help yourself. A fishing license is required for anyone older than 16. No parking after 10 P.M. at Bolsa Chica State Beach.

Parks

IRVINE PARK: Located in Santiago Canyon, near Irvine Lake, this peaceful place has hiking and equestrian trails that wind through 477 hilly acres and 800-year-old sycamores and oaks. The oldest county park in California, it offers several miles of bike trails, plus a petting zoo, playground, waterfall, lake, and plenty of picnic facilities. Tandem bicycles may be rented for $12 an hour on weekends only. There is a $2 to $5 parking fee per vehicle year-round. 1 Irvine Park Rd.; Orange; 714-633-8074.

MILE SQUARE REGIONAL PARK: It's one square mile in area—thus the name. Besides 15 miles of winding bike trails, the park features a fitness course with 20 stations, a nature area with bulletin boards detailing the park's plant and animal life, and an assortment of picnic areas and shelters. Bikes may be rented here on weekends and holidays. 16801 Euclid Ave.; Fountain Valley; 714-962-5549.

TUCKER WILDLIFE SANCTUARY: This 12-acre sanctuary in the Santa Ana Mountains' Modjeska Canyon is an oasis of trees, flowers, plants, and wildlife. Naturalists are on duty to answer questions, and there are two short nature trails. A small donation is suggested. 29322 Modjeska Canyon Rd.; Silverado; 714-649-2760.

YORBA REGIONAL PARK: These 175 acres in the Anaheim Hills cradle four lakes, picnic areas, playgrounds, and trails for hiking and biking (bike rentals are available during the summer). The five miles of trails provide a pleasant, not-too-tough workout, and they link up with the Santa Ana River Trail, a safe bike route through Orange County to Huntington Beach. Visitors can walk or bike into the park without charge; however, there is a $2 to $5 parking fee for vehicles. 7600 E. La Palma Ave.; Anaheim; 714-970-1460.

Orange County & Beyond

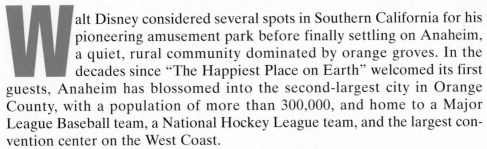

Walt Disney considered several spots in Southern California for his pioneering amusement park before finally settling on Anaheim, a quiet, rural community dominated by orange groves. In the decades since "The Happiest Place on Earth" welcomed its first guests, Anaheim has blossomed into the second-largest city in Orange County, with a population of more than 300,000, and home to a Major League Baseball team, a National Hockey League team, and the largest convention center on the West Coast.

Like Anaheim, Buena Park is filled with family-oriented attractions; Santa Ana, the county's largest city, is developing an impressive museum mile; and Orange emanates small-town charm, with cafes, one-of-a-kind shops, and even an old-fashioned soda fountain. The beach communities of Newport and Laguna mix seaside culture with a vibrant arts scene, while nearby San Juan Capistrano bears witness to the area's mission heritage.

An hour's drive north from Anaheim, and a fun excursion, Los Angeles is a dynamic mix of culture, glamour, museums, shops, restaurants, and entertainment venues, interspersed with parks, palm trees, and traffic. Due west of L.A., legendary beaches attract beauty and brawn like a magnet. A 90-minute drive south from Anaheim, along coast-hugging I-5, leads to Legoland California, in Carlsbad, and to San Diego, with its world-famous zoo. No doubt about it: Southern California has something for everyone.

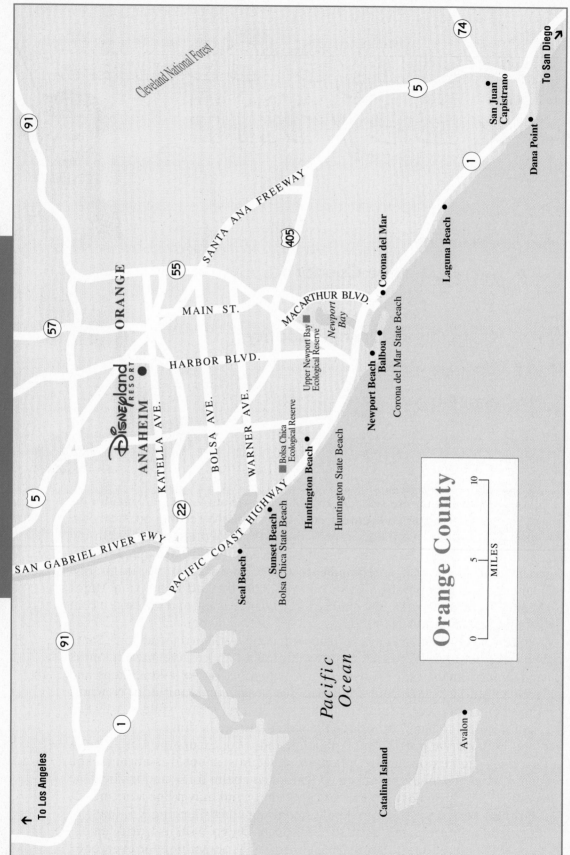

Cleveland National Forest

91

57

5

91

1

To Los Angeles

San Gabriel River Fwy

PACIFIC COAST HIGHWAY

KATELLA AVE.

BOLSA AVE.

WARNER AVE.

Disneyland RESORT

ANAHEIM

ORANGE

55

MAIN ST.

HARBOR BLVD.

22

Santa Ana Freeway

405

MACARTHUR BLVD.

Seal Beach

Sunset Beach
Bolsa Chica State Beach

Bolsa Chica
Ecological Reserve

Huntington Beach

Huntington State Beach

Upper Newport Bay
Ecological Reserve

Newport Bay

Newport Beach

Balboa

Corona del Mar

Corona del Mar State Beach

Laguna Beach

5

1

74

San Juan
Capistrano

Dana Point

To San Diego

Pacific
Ocean

Catalina Island

Avalon

Orange County

MILES

0   5   10

ORANGE COUNTY

Anaheim

ADVENTURE CITY: This sweet little theme park was created for children ages 2 through 12, but parents are welcome to go on every ride except one, the kid-powered Crank 'n' Roll. There are 17 attractions and activities in all, including puppet shows, children's theater, a petting farm, and a 25-foot rock-climbing wall for kids ages five and older. Adventure City is within walking distance of Hobby City (see the Doll and Toy Museum, on this page). Open daily; hours vary; admission charge. It's located four miles from the Disneyland Resort and two miles from Knott's Berry Farm (see page 141). 1238 S. Beach Blvd.; 714-236-9300.

ANAHEIM MUSEUM: Housed in the only remaining Carnegie library building in Orange County (there used to be five), the museum depicts Anaheim's history from its beginnings as a rural society to the opening of Disneyland in 1955. It also pays tribute to the area's original German settlers. Changing exhibits focus on different aspects of Southern California's history. Open Wednesday through Saturday, limited hours; admission is free, but a small donation is suggested. About a mile from the Disneyland Resort. 241 S. Anaheim Blvd.; 714-778-3301.

DISNEY ICE: Forget mild-weather outdoor pursuits for a moment to consider gliding over the ice in a building that resembles an escapee from Mickey's Toontown. Designed by noted architect and hockey fan Frank Gehry, Disney ICE houses an Olympic-size rink for public skating for all ages and skill levels, plus an adjacent NHL regulation rink

where the Mighty Ducks train. There's also drop-in hockey for men and women 18 and older, a pro shop, snack bar, and lockers. Day and evening skating sessions are available; birthday parties can be held here. Admission charge for skating. It's two miles north of the Disneyland Resort. 300 West Lincoln Avenue; 714-535-7465; *www.disneyice.com.*

DOLL AND TOY MUSEUM: Collector Bea DeArmond has been gathering dolls and toys for more than 70 years, and the results are displayed in a building that is a half-scale replica of the White House. Inside are more than 5,000 dolls and other toys, including teddy bears dating from 1907 and 500 Barbies that fill an entire wall. Old and new dolls are for sale in the gift shop. The museum is part of Hobby City, a group of 20 hobby, crafts, and collector shops. Open daily; admission charge. Four miles from the Disneyland Resort and two miles from Knott's Berry Farm. 1238 S. Beach Blvd.; 714-527-2323.

BOWERS MUSEUM OF CULTURAL ART: The original Mission-style Bowers building dates back to 1936, and with two major expansions since that time, the museum has become the largest in Orange County. It celebrates the fine arts of indigenous peoples—notably pre-Columbian, Native American, Oceanic, and African—and reflects the multicultural population of the Golden

State. The Bowers is also a repository for early California artifacts. Tangata, far more sophisticated than most museum eateries, features creative ethnic dishes, while the outstanding museum shop sells artwork, jewelry, clothing, and other gift items from around the world.

Kidseum, part of the Bowers Museum but a short walk away (at 1802 N. Main St.), is a large, airy space where children get to learn in a hands-on way about the cultures of other places and people. Supervised activities here focus on art and music, and costumes are plentiful, colorful, and fun.

The Bowers Museum is open Tuesday through Sunday; Kidseum, Tuesday through Sunday in summer and weekends in winter (limited hours). Admission charge for both. They are five miles from the Disneyland Resort. 2002 N. Main St.; Santa Ana; 714-567-3600; 714-480-1520 (Kidseum info line); *www.bowers.org.*

CRYSTAL CATHEDRAL: More than 10,000 panes of glass cover a web-like steel skeleton and 236-foot tower in this startling structure created by the architect Philip Johnson.

Established in 1980 by the Reverend Robert H. Schuller and affiliated with the Reform Church of America, the Crystal Cathedral houses a 16,000-pipe organ, 52-bell carillon, Steuben-glass cross, 33 marble columns, and 3,000 seats. Schuller began his ministry in a drive-in theater, and those attending services today still have the option to sit in their cars and watch on a giant television screen. Worship here has definite theatrical elements, and the Easter and Christmas pageants border on Broadway productions. A large gift shop sells inspirational music, books, cards, and gifts.

The visitors center is open from 9 A.M. to 3:30 P.M. Monday through Saturday, and free tours are available. Sunday services are at 8:30 A.M. in the small Chapel-in-the-Sky, and in the main cathedral at 9:30 A.M., 11 A.M., 1 P.M. (in Spanish), and 6 P.M., with free coffee and juice afterward. It's two miles southeast of the Disneyland Resort. 12141 Lewis St. (entrance on Chapman); Garden Grove; 714-971-4000; 714-971-4013 (tour information).

DISCOVERY SCIENCE CENTER: Part science center, part amusement park, this place gives new meaning to the term "hands-on." In eight themed areas with 100 exhibits, guests get to experience an earthquake, lie on a bed of nails, climb a

PHOTO BY ALICE GARRARD

rock wall, create clouds, walk through a tornado, tread on a musical floor, deconstruct a computer, fingerpaint electronically, pilot a plane, and make an impression in a pin wall. A shop offering a selection of science-related merchandise is on the premises. Open daily, except major holidays. Admission charge; 3-D laser theater extra. It's only five miles from the Disneyland Resort; look for the giant cube outside. 2500 N. Main St.; Santa Ana; 714-542-2823; *www.discoverycube.org.*

KNOTT'S BERRY FARM: This is not a farm at all, but a themed amusement park depicting much of the history and culture of California. It began in 1920 as the Knott family's boysenberry patch (hence the name). During the Great Depression, Walter Knott's wife, Cordelia, started a tearoom to help make ends meet, and her chicken dinners were such a success that Walter built a wander-through ghost town to keep hungry patrons from getting impatient. Things progressed from there.

Owned by the Knott family until 1998, the 160-acre park now offers 165 rides (including six roller coasters), shows, attractions, restaurants, and shops in six themed areas: Ghost Town (the original park), home to GhostRider, a massive wooden roller coaster created from 2.5 million feet of yellow pine and 310 tons of steel; Fiesta Village, a re-creation of colonial Spanish America; The Boardwalk, a combination California beach enclave and seaside amusement park, featuring the Supreme Scream tower, the world's tallest descending thrill ride (with a 30-story, three-second drop), and Perilous Plunge, the world's tallest, deepest water drop ride (with a 115-foot drop at a 75-degree angle); Wild Water Wilderness, a turn-of-the-century river wilderness park with California flora; and the Indian Trails area, which celebrates the arts, crafts, and traditions of Native Americans. Camp Snoopy, a six-acre play area themed around the world's most beloved beagle, features Woodstock's Airmail (a mini-Supreme Scream), the Red Baron biplane ride, a petting zoo, pontoon bridges, a treehouse, and Thomas Edison Inventor's Workshop, with hands-on science exhibits. Best of all, children get to meet Snoopy and his *Peanuts* pals here.

Across Beach Boulevard from the park's main gate stands Independence Hall West, Knott's replica of Independence Hall in Philadelphia, completely renovated in late 1998 (enter through a tunnel in the main parking area near the shops; there's never a charge to visit it). Chandeliers, furniture, and the shape and size of the rooms are precisely

reproduced, and there is a replica of the Liberty Bell, crack and all.

Also adjacent to the park, you'll find Knott's newest "splash": Knott's Soak City USA. This 13-acre water park boasts 21 rides, including tube and body slides, vertical chutes, wave pool, and children's pool, all designed in the style of the longboards and surf woodies of the 1950s California coast.

Knott's California MarketPlace is filled with shops and eateries. Chicken dinners and boysenberry pies are still on the menu here, but try to dine early to avoid the crowds.

Knott's Berry Farm is open daily except Christmas; Soak City USA is open daily from mid-June to early September and weekends through late September. A show with fireworks and lasers takes place on nights the park is open late. Admission charge; the price drops after 4 P.M. in summer, and on weekends year-round. Parking is extra, but if you come only to shop, dine, or visit Independence Hall, you get three hours free (four during holidays). 8039 Beach Blvd.; Buena Park; 714-220-5200.

OLD TOWNE ORANGE: For an idea of what Southern California was like before the advent of the freeway (or of Disneyland, for that matter), visit the historic area of Orange. Highlights include a pharmacy (and old-fashioned soda fountain) that's been in business since 1900, art galleries, lots of antiques shops, Victorian manors that serve afternoon tea, a church that's now a restaurant and dinner theater, a bridal museum where you can order a vintage-style gown, and Victorian and Craftsman houses galore. Old Towne Orange is 15 minutes due east of Anaheim via Chapman Avenue. The Visitor Bureau is located at 439 E. Chapman Avenue; 714-538-3581 or 800-938-0073; *www.orangechamber.com.*

ROBERT MONDAVI WINE AND FOOD CENTER: Named after the California vintner, the center is not a winery, nor does it offer tours and tastings (head to Disney's California Adventure, in the Disneyland Resort, for that). But it provides nine special events each month, including wine seminars, cooking demonstrations, art exhibits, and black-tie dinners. Thanks to the elegant setting (including a rose garden), events book up quickly, so reserve in advance. The gift shop sells wines and books. Open weekdays. 1570 Scenic Ave.; Costa Mesa; 714-979-4510; *www.robertmondavi.com.*

MOVIELAND WAX MUSEUM: Silver-screen star Mary Pickford dedicated Movieland when it opened here in 1962. Today more

than 275 film and TV performers are portrayed in scenes from their best-known roles: Judy Garland in *The Wizard of Oz*, Robert Redford and Paul Newman in *Butch Cassidy and the Sundance Kid*, and Marilyn Monroe in *Some Like It Hot*. More recent additions to the star-studded lineup include Clint Eastwood, Whoopi Goldberg, Sharon Stone, Brad Pitt, John Travolta, and Hulk Hogan.

Many of the costumes and props on display were donated by the stars themselves. During a visit, you'll walk under marquees and lights, along a yellow brick road, and through watery wreckage from *The Poseidon Adventure*. Open daily. Admission charge; combination tickets with Ripley's Believe It or Not (across the street) are available. The museum is seven miles from the Disneyland Resort. 7711 Beach Blvd.; Buena Park; 714-522-1154; *www.movielandwaxmuseum.com.*

RICHARD NIXON PRESIDENTIAL LIBRARY AND BIRTHPLACE: In the restored house built by his father, this 22-room library chronicles the life of the 37th

president of the United States, from boyhood on. There are changing exhibits, and a 22-foot-long, 7-foot-wide Lincoln Continental used by four American presidents is on permanent display. Both Richard Nixon and former first lady Pat Nixon are buried here. Open daily; admission charge. It's a 15-minute drive from the Disneyland Resort. 18001 Yorba Linda Blvd.; Yorba Linda; 714-993-3393; *www.nixonlibrary.org.*

RAGING WATERS: The largest water park west of the Mississippi, Raging Waters has acres of rides, slides, chutes, and lagoons. Highlights include El Niño, the 109-foot High Extreme II, and Volcano FantaSea. Open weekends only from late April through May and in September; daily from June through August. Admission charge for anyone over 42 inches tall; discounts available after 4 P.M.; parking is extra. It's about a half hour drive from the Disneyland Resort (it's not actually in, but next door to, Orange County). 111 Raging Waters Dr.; San Dimas; 909-802-2200.

RIPLEY'S BELIEVE IT OR NOT: Here you'll discover 10,000 square feet of curiosities amassed by cartoonist, world traveler, and collector of oddities Robert Ripley. The Riddler Room is an interactive area for kids. Open daily. Admission charge; combination tickets with the Movieland Wax Museum (across the street) are available. Seven miles from the Disneyland Resort. 7850 Beach Blvd.; Buena Park; 714-522-1152.

WILD RIVERS WATERPARK: More than 40 attractions include two wave pools, a seven-story "mountain" with sheer-drop and high-speed slides, an inner-tube trip, and small-scale rides and pools for young visitors. Open weekends only from mid-May through early June and in late September; daily from early June through early September. Admission charge. It's about 20 minutes from the Disneyland Resort. 8770 Irvine Center Dr.; Irvine; 949-768-9453.

On the Coast

Corona del Mar

ROGER'S GARDENS: This public nursery fills 7½ acres of landscaped grounds with splendid flowers, plants, shrubs, and trees; and from mid-October through December 30, themed holiday trees draw enthusiastic crowds. Free lectures and demonstrations are given in the amphitheater on Saturday and Sunday year-round (lecture subjects and times vary, call for specifics). The gift shop sells a selection of items for the home, as well as holiday decorations year-round, including hand-painted glass ornaments designed by the world-famous Christopher Radko. Open daily 9 A.M. to 9 P.M. in spring, 9 A.M. to 7 P.M. in summer; 9 A.M. to 5 P.M. in fall and winter. It's a 35-minute drive south of the Disneyland Resort. 2301 San Joaquin Hills Rd.; Corona del Mar; 949-640-5800; *www.rogersgardens.com.*

SHERMAN LIBRARY AND GARDENS: The gardens are a veritable museum of plants and flowers ranging from desert flora to exotic tropical vegetation, displayed amid fountains and sculptures, brick walkways, and manicured lawns. They surround the library, which is a major research center devoted to the history of the Pacific Southwest, particularly the past 100 years. A gift shop and cafe are on the premises. The gardens are open daily from 10:30 A.M. to 4 P.M.; the library, from 9 A.M. to 4:30 P.M. Tuesday, Wednesday, and Thursday. Admission is $3 for adults, $1 for children 12 through 16; free for children under 12; free to all on Monday. It's a 35-minute drive southeast of the Disneyland Resort. 2647 E. Pacific Coast Hwy.; Corona del Mar; 949-673-2261.

Dana Point Area

OCEAN INSTITUTE: There's a lab to visit at this institute (previously known as the Orange County Marine Institute), and a whale skeleton to admire; plus the tall ship *Pilgrim* may be toured, but only on Sunday, from 10 A.M. to 2:30 P.M. Educational cruises take place on weekends aboard the RV *Sea Explorer*. It's equipped with video microscopes and state-of-the-art electronics; prices, times, and themes vary. The lab is open to the public 10 A.M. to 4:30 P.M. on weekends; the gift shop is open daily. Free admission, but donations are always accepted. It's 45 minutes from the Disneyland Resort. 24200 Dana Point Harbor Dr.; Dana Point; 949-496-2274; *www.ocean-institute.org.*

LOS RIOS HISTORIC DISTRICT: Situated beside the Capistrano train depot (1894), just three miles from the coast, this small enclave captures the flavor of Southern California at the turn of the century. The district encompasses 31 adobe homes built between 1794 and the 1880s. Among them is the O'Neill Museum, a Victorian house built in the 1870s, filled with period furniture, and open to the public.

The district is within walking distance of Mission San Juan Capistrano. Take I-5 south (or the train) to the mission; about 50 minutes from Anaheim. For more information, contact the San Juan Capistrano Chamber of Commerce; 949-493-4700.

MISSION SAN JUAN CAPISTRANO: The famous mission at the southern tip of Orange County retains a wistful air of grandeur, even though these five buildings on 10 acres are all that remain of the original 225,000-acre tract. Highlights of the self-guided walking tour include a 350-year-old gilt altar, a Moorish fountain, ancient pepper trees, a mission cemetery, the quarters of the early padres, and the Spanish soldiers' barracks. Once the most remarkable in the entire mission chain, the church was shattered by a powerful earthquake in 1812. The four bells of the tower and a small sanctuary called the Serra Chapel were miraculously spared; the chapel still holds services daily in English and Spanish (call for schedules).

The other miracle is the return of the swallows to Capistrano every year on March 19 (Saint Joseph's Day). Christians take this as a sign of the holiness of this place, while ornithologists explain it as no more than a predictable natural phenomenon. Open from 8:30 A.M. to 5 P.M. daily. Admission is $6 for adults, $5 for seniors 60 and older, and $4 for children 4 through 11. Take I-5 (or the train) south to the mission, which is about 50 minutes from Anaheim. Corner of Ortega Hwy. and Camino Capistrano; San Juan Capistrano; 949-234-1300; *www.missionsjc.com.*

Note: During your visit, don't miss the *other* gem of San Juan Capistrano, its award-winning regional library, designed by architect Michael Graves in 1983; 31495 El Camino Real; 949-493-1752.

Huntington Beach

Life at Huntington Beach revolves around the surf—it's the perfect spot for catching a wave, or watching others do so. For more information on the beach itself, see page 135.

HUNTINGTON BEACH ART CENTER: Founded in 1995, this is one of the few venues in Orange County where you can find performance art. It's also the place to see avant-garde and cutting-edge work: art installations, videos, sculpture, and group and solo exhibitions of emerging American artists. The center has three galleries and a theater that seats 100 people. Open Wednesday through Sunday, in the afternoon. Small admission charge; free for children 12 and younger. It's a 40-minute drive south of the Disneyland Resort. 538 Main St.; Huntington Beach; 714-374-1650.

INTERNATIONAL SURFING MUSEUM: You'll find all that's surfing-related here—artwork, jewelry, vintage surfboards and paddleboards, even skateboards. Expect some surfer music, too. Open afternoons daily in summer; Thursday through Monday the rest of the year. Small admission charge. 411 Olive St.; Huntington Beach; 714-960-3483l; *www.surfingmuseum.org.*

PIER PLAZA: In the heart of town, this sweeping oceanfront plaza has a palm tree grove with benches, widened bike and pedestrian paths, and an amphitheater for weekend entertainment (call 714-374-1657 to get the performance schedule). It's about a half hour from the Disneyland Resort. The Huntington Beach Visitor and Information Center is at 417 Main Street; 714-969-3492 or 800-729-6232; *www.hbvisit.com.*

Laguna Beach

A professional artist's colony since 1917, Laguna Beach continues to thrive as Orange County's leading artistic hot spot, with over 90 galleries, antique shops, and boutiques displaying local artists' masterpieces. Painters find inspiration in the dramatic cliffs, carved-out coves, and pearl-white sand that define the beach's setting (see page 135 for details on the maritime activities offered year-round off the shores of Laguna).

LAGUNA ART MUSEUM: Founded in 1918 (a year after the town itself), California's oldest museum focuses its energies on and devotes its gallery space to work produced by the state's artists, past and present. Permanent exhibitions highlight California Impressionism, while several changing exhibits feature contemporary artists. A visit here can easily be combined with browsing in some of the local art galleries, most within walking distance of the museum. Closed Wednesday. Admission charge. It's about a 40-minute drive south of the Disneyland Resort. 307 Cliff Dr.; Laguna Beach; 949-494-6531.

LAGUNA PLAYHOUSE: Now in its 81st season, this is the oldest continuously operating theater company on the West Coast. Since 1969, the Laguna Playhouse has called the 420-seat Moulton Theater home. Screen legend Harrison Ford was discovered in a Laguna Playhouse production in 1965; Julie Harris has also appeared here, as did Bette Davis. The theater stages dramas, musicals, and comedies, often to glowing reviews in the *Los Angeles Times.* The season runs from August through mid-June. It's about a 40-minute drive south of the Disneyland Resort. 606 Laguna Canyon Rd.; Laguna Beach; 949-497-2787; *www.lagunaplayhouse.org.*

Newport/Balboa

Sun-kissed beaches and an ample small-craft harbor make this area of the coast a haven for sailors and vacationers alike (see page 135 to learn about the many seaside activities), but the pastimes here extend beyond the beach to celebrate the worlds of sports, history, and the arts.

BALBOA FUN ZONE: Established in 1936, this area looks like an old-fashioned boardwalk, complete with amusements, shops, cotton candy, and candied apples. But most people come here to admire the historic pavilion, take a harbor cruise, or board the car ferry to tiny Balboa Island to shop or dine. Ferry service is continuous. It's a half hour drive south of the Disneyland Resort. 600 E. Bay St.; Balboa Peninsula; for harbor tour information, call 949-673-0408; *www.thebalboafunzone.com.*

BALBOA PAVILION: This landmark building is the departure point in Orange County for Catalina Island, via Catalina Passenger Service; 400 Main Street; 949-673-5245. The company also offers regularly scheduled harbor cruises, supplying wonderful views of the multimillion-dollar shorefront houses in the harbor, including the former summer residence of George Burns and Gracie Allen. It's about a half hour drive south of the Disneyland Resort.

NEWPORT HARBOR NAUTICAL MUSEUM: The *Pride of Newport* stern-wheeler has housed this museum since 1995 as a tribute to Newport Harbor, Southern California, and the Pacific. The Newport Gallery details the history of the harbor, the extensive Model Gallery incorporates interactive screens, and special exhibitions highlight the work of contemporary marine artists. The Riverboat restaurant serves lunch and dinner onboard, as well as brunch with music on weekends. The museum is closed Monday. Admission charge. It's 30 minutes south of the Disneyland Resort. 151 East Coast Hwy., at Bayside, Newport Beach; 949-673-7863 (museum); 949-673-3425 (restaurant).

NEWPORT SPORTS COLLECTION FOUNDATION: View Muhammed Ali's gloves; jerseys worn by Mark McGwire, Michael Jordan, Shaquille O'Neal, 19 Norris Trophy recipients, and all Cy Young Award winners; footballs signed by all Heisman Trophy winners; Dwight Eisenhower's golf clubs; seats from Ebbets Field, Fenway Park, and Yankee Stadium; and more. Closed Sunday. Free admission. About a half hour drive south from the Disneyland Resort. Located in Fashion Island; 100 Newport Center Drive; Newport Beach; 949-721-9333.

ORANGE COUNTY MUSEUM OF ART: Founded in 1961, the former Newport Harbor Art Museum, now triple its original size, is the county's premier contemporary and modern-art museum. It focuses primarily on post-World War II California art and sculpture. California artists were isolated from the East Coast and European centers of art for the first half of the 20th century, and the influences of the Mexican and Pacific Rim cultures are notable.

The museum has an installation gallery and bookstore, as well as an admission-free satellite gallery with a large shop at South Coast Plaza in Costa Mesa. It's closed Monday. The museum is about a 20-minute drive south from the Disneyland Resort. 850 San Clemente Dr.; Newport Beach; 949-759-1122; *www.ocma.net.*

Catalina Island

A delightful day trip from Anaheim, this large island off the coast of Southern California resembles an unspoiled Mediterranean isle. Snorkeling, scuba diving, kayaking, whale watching, sportfishing, golf, hiking, and horseback riding keep the more athletically inclined guests on their toes. Less active folks will enjoy a tour of the local "casino," an entertainment complex built in Avalon, the island's center, by William Wrigley, Jr., in 1919 (dancing, not gambling, was the preferred form of entertainment here). Other island exploring possibilities include a marine tour in a glass-bottom boat, a voyage on a semi-submersible vessel for a fish's perspective of underwater life, and an island "safari" in a jeep for glimpses of buffalo (300 roam the island), bald eagles, wild goats, deer, and boars.

From the Balboa Peninsula, Catalina Passenger Service makes the 26-mile trip on the *Catalina Flyer* in about 75 minutes; 949-673-5245. The *Catalina Express* offers round-trip service to the island from Dana Point, Long Beach, and San Pedro; 800-618-5533. The ride over can sometimes be choppy, so those prone to seasickness should take precautions.

For more information, contact the Catalina Island Visitors Bureau; 310-510-1520.

Shopping in Orange County

Malls may not have been invented in Southern California, but they were perfected here to appeal to a discerning, largely suburban population. Most are open from 10 A.M. to 9 P.M. weekdays, from 10 A.M. to 7 P.M. Saturdays, and from 11 A.M. to 6 P.M. Sundays. Call for exact hours. Sales tax is 7.75 percent in Orange County.

FASHION ISLAND: This sophisticated outdoor mall has more than 200 stores and restaurants in a Mediterranean-themed setting of potted flowers, towering palms, and plazas with fountains, fish pools, and umbrella-topped tables. The four major department stores are Bloomingdale's, Neiman Marcus, Robinsons-May, and Macy's; the enclosed Atrium Court houses many small shops and the Farmer's Market. The mall also features a full-service spa, six cinemas, Hard Rock Cafe, Wolfgang Puck Cafe, California Pizza Kitchen, and Cheesecake Factory. On Newport Center Drive in Newport Beach, about a half hour drive south of the Disneyland Resort; 949-721-2000.

MAINPLACE MALL: It's home to the Disney Store, with its character-conscious toys, videos, books, gift items, collectibles, and clothing for adults and children. The MainPlace Mall also houses the first Walt Disney Gallery. Adjacent to the Disney Store, it features animation art, vintage Disney posters and other memorabilia, upscale character-inspired jewelry, and contemporary home and gift items—as well as the Fantasy Video

Timeline, the Interactive Disney Storybook, and the Animation Kaleidoscope. Also at the MainPlace Mall, you'll find Macy's, Nordstrom, Robinsons-May, Barnes & Noble Bookstore, and Crate & Barrel, along with many other shops and restaurants, one-hour photo development, shoe repair, cinema complex, concierge desk, and American Express Travel Service. A shuttle runs often between the Anaheim hotels and the mall. 2800 N. Main St. (at the intersection of I-5 and Hwy. 22); Santa Ana, approximately four miles from the Disneyland Resort; 714-547-7000.

SOUTH COAST PLAZA: Festive, airy, upscale, and enormous, it's home to more than 260 restaurants and shops, including the Disney Store, Macy's, Nordstrom, Saks Fifth Avenue, Coach, Hermès, Chanel, Christian Dior, Escada, Jil Sander, Gianni Versace, Alfred Dunhill, the Rainforest Cafe, and Wolfgang Puck Cafe. A bridge connects the two sides of South Coast Plaza. Shuttles operate to and from Anaheim hotels. At the intersection of the San Diego Freeway and Bristol Street in Costa Mesa, about ten miles from the Disneyland Resort; 714-435-2000 or 800-782-8888.

TRIANGLE SQUARE: This boldly modern shopping complex is home to the only Nike Town in California. It also has an enormous Barnes & Noble Bookstore, Virgin Megastore, eight cinemas, and a supermarket. Adults dine on sushi and California cuisine at Zen Bistro, while kids head for Johnny Rockets. The Costa Mesa Freeway (55) dead-ends into Triangle Square, at Newport and Harbor boulevards in Costa Mesa, a 45-minute drive from the Disneyland Resort; 949-722-1600.

"MALL-TERNATIVES": If malls appall you, check out The Lab, a self-proclaimed "anti-mall" with indoor/outdoor shops, cafes, and free entertainment for teens and families; 2930 Bristol St.; Costa Mesa (714-966-6660). Or try the fine Gallery Shop at the Bowers Museum of Cultural Art; 2002 N. Main St.; Santa Ana (714-567-3643); Doll City U.S.A., 6,000-square-feet of dolls, at 2080 S. Harbor Blvd.; Anaheim (714-750-3585); and all the fun shops at the Disneyland Resort.

146

LOS ANGELES

From the rugged ridges of the Santa Monica Mountains to the vast San Fernando Valley to downtown L.A. itself, Los Angeles County spreads close to 5,000 square miles (including 72 miles of shoreline), knit together by 500 miles of freeways. To get to L.A. from Anaheim, take I-5 north and Route 101 or 10 west. All of the places described below can be reached in about 45 minutes to 2 hours. For more information or maps, contact the Visitor Information Center; 685 S. Figueroa St., Los Angeles, CA 90017; 213-689-8822; *www.lacvb.com*.

Attractions

DOWNTOWN

EXPOSITION PARK MUSEUMS: Here you get three museums for the price of one. At the California Science Center, hands-on exhibits probe the inner workings of everything from a single-cell bacterium to a 100-trillion-celled human being. Don't miss the high-wire bicycle; Gertie's Gut; or Tess, the 50-foot marvel. There's also an IMAX theater; 213-744-7400 (it's free, except for IMAX movies; open daily). The California African-American Museum highlights the art and achievements of African Americans; 213-744-2060 (free; closed Monday). The Natural History Museum features dueling dinosaurs and an insect zoo; 213-763-3466 (admission charge; open daily). The museums are within walking distance of one another. Closed on major holidays. Parking (about $5) is at Figueroa and 39th Street.

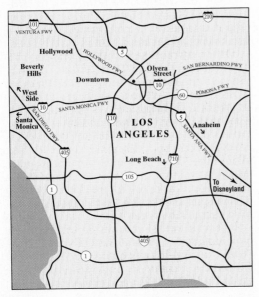

FARMERS MARKET: An L.A. fixture since 1934 and popular with locals for Sunday brunch, it's filled with stands piled high with fresh produce, plus all manner of prepared foods. The French Crepe Company's sweet and savory crepes are not to be missed. Tables allow for casual outdoor dining. In a separate area, there's indoor shopping for clothing and souvenirs. Open daily. Free parking. 6333 W. Third St. and Fairfax Ave.; 323-933-9211.

LA BREA TAR PITS: If you have ever wondered what L.A. looked like before the studios and skyscrapers, visit the 40,000-year-old pools of *brea* (Spanish for "tar"), in Hancock Park, where a replica depicts one unlucky mastodon perpetually trapped in the mire. Free. Open daily. Inside the tar pits sits the George C. Page Museum (open daily; admission charge) displaying bones excavated from the area and (living) paleontologists doing research in a "fishbowl" lab. 5801 Wilshire Blvd.; Park La Brea; 323-934-7243; *www.tarpits.org*.

LOS ANGELES COUNTY MUSEUM OF ART: Expect to be dazzled by the permanent collection of pre-Columbian, Islamic, and African art; costumes and textiles; and a distinguished collection of 19th- and 20th-century art and photography. Admission charge. Closed Wednesday. 5905 Wilshire Blvd.; 323-857-6000; *www.lacma.org*.

OLVERA STREET: The name of this small pedestrian street commonly refers to the area where the city began in 1781. Today it's home to strolling mariachis, colorful Mexican shops, and food stalls selling spicy tacos, burritos, and enchiladas. Free walking tours are offered some mornings. Union Station (built in 1939) is across the street. 125 Paseo de la Plaza; 213-628-1274.

HOLLYWOOD

GRIFFITH PARK ATTRACTIONS: The largest park in the United States that is surrounded by a city, 4,063-acre Griffith Park is home to the Los Angeles Zoo and its more than 1,200 inhabitants; the Autry Museum of Western Heritage, which salutes the American West; the Griffith Observatory; an equestrian center; and many walking trails. In 2000, the restored Carolwood Barn, part of Walt Disney's beloved backyard miniature railroad, was moved to the L.A. Live Steam facility. Ranger Station; 4730 Crystal Springs Dr.; 323-913-4688.

HOLLYWOOD ENTERTAINMENT MUSEUM: The sets from *Star Trek* and *Cheers* are highlights at this unabashedly starstruck museum. In the Main Hall, you can hear a recording of Walt Disney talking about animation. Admission charge; closed Wednesdays. 7021 Hollywood Blvd.; 323-465-7900; *www.hollywoodmuseum.com.*

HOLLYWOOD HISTORY MUSEUM: Ensconced in the restored art deco Max Factor Building, this addition to the Hollywood scene salutes Tinseltown, from the silent era of movies to the present, with costumes, props, posters, and more. Admission charge. Open daily. 1660 N. Highland; 323-464-7776; *www.hollywoodhistorymuseum.org.*

HOLLYWOOD ROOSEVELT HOTEL: This historic hotel (built in 1927) was frequented by stars in Hollywood's heyday and was the site of the first Academy Awards ceremony. Vintage photos on the second floor tell the story of Tinseltown from its beginnings at the turn of the century through the silent era and ensuing decades. Great for nostalgia buffs. 7000 Hollywood Blvd.; 323-466-7000.

MANN'S CHINESE THEATRE: Catercorner to the Hollywood Roosevelt Hotel, and better known to movie fans around the world as Grauman's Chinese Theatre, this is probably the most visited site in Old Hollywood. (Ted Mann took it over in 1973.) The theater's forecourt contains the world-famous celebrity handprints and footprints—some surprisingly small—immortalized in cement. Inside is one of the world's most impressive and elaborate movie palaces. Tours of the stars' homes depart from here. 6925 Hollywood Blvd. (for tours, 800-959-3131; for movies, 323-464-8111).

PACIFIC'S EL CAPITAN THEATRE: The Walt Disney Company and Buena Vista Pictures Distribution completely restored this Hollywood Boulevard landmark, formerly the Paramount, and reopened it in 1991. Built in 1926 as a legitimate stage house (Gertrude

Lawrence headlined in the first show, and the film *Citizen Kane* premiered here in 1941), the El Capitan was remodeled in 1942 and became a movie theater. Now moviegoers can enjoy first-run Disney and other films in an atmosphere evocative of another era, but with state-of-the-art projection and sound systems. 6838 Hollywood Blvd.; 323-467-7674.

PANTAGES THEATRE, FEATURING "THE LION KING": A Los Angeles production of the critically acclaimed Broadway musical premiered at this recently restored historic theater in September 2000, and is expected to continue its run through September 2002. Tickets range from $10 to $75 and should be ordered well in advance through TicketMaster, the theater's box office, or the website below. 6233 Hollywood Blvd.; 213-365-5555 (box office); *www.lionkingla.com.*

UNIVERSAL STUDIOS HOLLYWOOD: First-timers to Universal Studios might start with the 45-minute Studio Tour, which passes sets from *Animal House*, *The Sting*, *Psycho*, and *Murder She Wrote*, not to mention King Kong himself. During the ride, you'll encounter a collapsing bridge, an avalanche, an earthquake, and a flash flood.

Other attractions at the park include the Terminator 2: 3-D virtual adventure; Back to the Future, a flight-simulator ride; Waterworld, a live sea-war spectacular; and Backdraft. In Jurassic Park–The Ride, visitors board large river rafts and enter a dense primordial forest with steamy waterways, an 84-foot drop, and impressively lifelike dinosaurs. Tamer by comparison are Rugrats Magic Adventure, an interactive mix of music and magic; Lucy: A Tribute; The World of Cinemagic; and the E.T. Adventure. Admission charge. Open daily; hours vary.

You can eat, shop, and be entertained just outside the park at the Universal CityWalk, an outdoor promenade lined with an eclectic variety of shops, several trendy restaurants, an 18-screen cinema complex, three-dimensional facades, and neon galore; there is no admission charge for CityWalk, but parking is $7. It's open daily. 818-622-4455. Off the Hollywood Freeway (Route 101) at Lankershim Boulevard. 100 Universal City Plaza; Universal City; 818-622-3801; *www.universalstudioshollywood.com.*

THE WEST SIDE

THE J. PAUL GETTY MUSEUM: Part of the bold new Getty Center designed by architect Richard Meier, this facility (five pavilions surrounding a central courtyard) houses most of the collections formerly exhibited at the museum's Malibu villa site, including masterpieces by Rembrandt, van Gogh, Monet, and Cézanne. The recently renovated Getty Villa houses the museum's antiquities collection. The museum has two cafes, a restaurant, bookstore, and children's area. Free admission; weekday parking costs $5 (reservation necessary); local bus transportation is available via the MTA 561 and the Santa Monica Big Blue Bus 14. Closed Mondays and major holidays. 1200 Getty Center Dr.; off I-405 in the Santa Monica Mountains; 310-440-7300 (for information and parking reservations); *www.getty.edu.*

PETERSEN AUTOMOTIVE MUSEUM: In this paean to the car, 200 rare and classic autos, trucks, and motorcycles are incorporated into walk-through dioramas. Highlights include a 1920s service station, a 1950s diner, and a suburban scene. In the museum's learning center, kids get to become human spark plugs. Admission charge. Closed Mondays, except holidays. 6060 Wilshire Blvd. at Fairfax Ave.; 323-930-2277; *www.petersen.org.*

SANTA MONICA

Fifteen miles west of Los Angeles, overlooking the Pacific Ocean, Santa Monica is well-known for its beach (one of the widest in the world), eclectic shops, and animated sidewalk cafes. You can stroll, skate, or jog beside the beach; walk out on the pier to enjoy the amusement park or gaze at the mountains plunging into the sea; or head a few blocks inland to a friendly eatery at the Third Street Promenade. This lively outdoor mall is particularly popular with locals on weekend mornings when it plays host to a farmers' market and artists fair (in the summer months). Montana Avenue is a repository for art, antiques, clothing, and jewelry; Main Street is the place to go for offbeat boutiques, antiques shops, art galleries, and cafes; For area information, call 310-393-7593; *www.santamonica.com.*

Note: One mile south of Santa Monica lies the boardwalk of **Venice Beach**, where outrageous behavior (and attire) is the norm.

LONG BEACH

Only 20 miles from both downtown L.A. and the Disneyland Resort, Long Beach has sandy beaches, picturesque canals, Venice-style gondola rides, a 3,400-slip marina, a museum devoted to the contemporary art of the Americas, tempting shops, and lively cafes. It is home to Southern California's premier aquarium, the **Aquarium of the Pacific**, and it harbors the tall ship **Californian**, the **Queen Mary** (the largest ocean liner afloat, housing a museum, hotel, and restaurants), and the Soviet submarine **Scorpion**. A free shuttle transports visitors to area attractions. Water shuttles depart for Catalina Island throughout the day (see page 145 for details).

For more information, contact the Long Beach Area Convention & Visitors Bureau; One World Trade Center; Suite 300; Long Beach, CA 90831-0300; 562-436-3645 or 800-452-7829; *www.golongbeach.org.*

Shopping

Rodeo Drive, pronounced *"ro-DAY-oh drive"* and located in the heart of Beverly Hills, contains some of the most expensive and exclusive shops in the world (the site of Julia Roberts' "dress for success" excursion in the film *Pretty Woman*), most in just three blocks. The **Beverly Center**, an indoor shopping extravaganza in the heart of L.A., has more than 150 shops and restaurants, plus a 14-screen cinema; it's a great place in L.A. to spot movie stars on shopping sprees. 8500 Beverly Blvd.; 310-854-0070. **Century City Shopping Center**, a fashionable 140-store outdoor complex, is home to Macy's, Bloomingdale's, and the Disney Store, along with a 14-screen cinema and some fun family restaurants. 10250 Santa Monica Blvd.; Century City; 310-277-3898.

Tours & Tapings

See the posh homes of movie stars in L.A. and Beverly Hills with **Starline Tours;** 1-800-959-3131. Explore after-dark hotspots with the **L.A. NightHawks;** 310-392-1500.

These television studios offer tours but only on weekdays: **NBC** ($7; 3000 W. Alameda Blvd.; Burbank; 818-840-3537); **Paramount Pictures**, the only major studio still located in Hollywood proper ($15; 5555 Melrose Ave.; Hollywood; 323-956-1777); and **Warner Bros.** ($32; Hollywood and Olive; Gate 4; Burbank; 818-954-1744). Children under age eight not permitted. Prices subject to change; call for more information.

Tapings: Nab a free ticket to *The Tonight Show* by calling NBC; 818-840-3537. For tickets to other shows, such as *Everybody Loves Raymond*, call Audiences Unlimited; 818-753-3470 or 818-506-0067; *www.tvtickets.com.*

SAN DIEGO

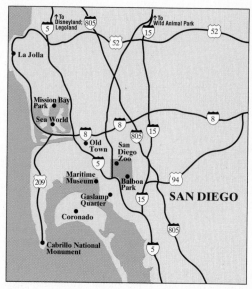

The country's seventh-largest city, and California's second largest, San Diego lies about 100 miles south of Anaheim, a 90-minute drive away on I-5 (or I-15 if I-5 is congested). The city is known for its perennial springlike weather, its sporty lifestyle, and its cultural scene. It's home to ballet, modern dance, opera, theater companies, and a symphony, along with myriad art galleries and museums.

San Diego is also the site of the world's largest military complex. The nation's first warm-weather, year-round, multisport Olympic training complex, the ARCO Training Center, is in nearby Chula Vista. The largest urban park in California, 5,800-acre Mission Trails Regional Park, is eight miles away. Tijuana, Mexico, is 17 miles due south, easily and inexpensively reachable via trolley.

La Jolla (pronounced *La HOY-a*), 12 miles north of downtown San Diego, is actually part of the city. One of the most picturesque communities in Southern California, it is known for its upscale shops, romantic restaurants, ocean views, and theater. La Jolla Playhouse was founded in 1947.

HOT TIP!

Most attractions in the San Diego area may be reached via public transportation—trolley, bus, or ferry—or the highly entertaining Old Town Trolley Tour; 619-298-8687.

For more information about the area, contact the San Diego Convention & Visitors Bureau, Dept. 700, 401 B St., Suite 1400; San Diego, CA 92101; 619-236-1212; *www.sandiego.org.* Also contact the San Diego North Convention & Visitors Bureau, 360 N. Escondido Blvd.; Escondido, CA 92025; 760-745-4741 or 800-848-3336; *www.sandiegonorth.com*; the Carlsbad Convention & Visitors Bureau, 760-434-6093 or 800-227-5722; *www.carlsbadca.org*; the Coronado Visitors Bureau, 619-437-8788; *www.coronadovisitors.com*; and La Jolla Town Council, 858-454-1444.

When you arrive in San Diego, drop by the International Visitor Information Center, at First Avenue and F Street, in Horton Plaza.

BALBOA PARK: This 1,200-acre oasis just north of the downtown area is home to 14 extraordinary museums, which appeal to such diverse areas of interest as art, photography, sports, science, astronomy, aerospace, model railroads, automobiles, Russian icons, and Japanese gardens. The nationally acclaimed Globe Theatres are here, along with the Mingei International Museum of World Folk Art and the recently renovated Museum of Photographic Arts. On Sundays at 2 P.M., the park hosts a free concert on the world's largest outdoor organ.

Park entry and tram service are free, but admission is charged at most museums; each Tuesday night a few museums waive their admission charge. You can save money by purchasing a one-week coupon book for all of the museums. Open daily; museum hours vary. Follow signs from I-5. 1549 El Prado, Suite 1; 619-239-0512; *www.balboapark.org.*

Don't miss the opportunity to dine at The Prado restaurant, a full-service restaurant featuring creative Latin cuisine (619-557-9441); or enjoy light fare in the Sculpture Garden Cafe & Bistro at the Museum of Art (619-696-1990).

BIRCH AQUARIUM AT SCRIPPS: Part of the famous Scripps Institution of Oceanography, this attraction is actually an aquarium and a museum. The two are connected by a plaza with its own man-made tide pool overlooking the Pacific Ocean and Scripps Pier. The aquarium contains 44 marine-life tanks and a giant kelp forest; the museum has interactive displays on earthquakes, climate and weather, plate tectonics, and the "ocean as supermarket," as well as a 12-minute simulated submarine ride. Admission fee, plus $3 for parking. Open daily. 2300 Expedition Way; La Jolla; 858-534-3474.

CABRILLO NATIONAL MONUMENT: Dedicated to the arrival here in 1542 of Juan Cabrillo, and supervised by the National Park Service, it offers exhibits, films, talks by rangers, and tide pools to investigate. A statue of the explorer and a restored lighthouse dating to 1855 are on the grounds. The views are great; you might even spot migrating whales from December to March. Open daily. 1800 Cabrillo Memorial Dr.; San Diego; 619-557-5450.

CORONADO: A separate municipality from San Diego but connected to it by the striking, two-mile-long San Diego/Coronado Bridge—and accessible by car, bus, or ferry—Coronado is a quintessential beach town. The highlight of a visit is the Hotel Del Coronado. Built in 1888, it's one of the largest and most beautiful wooden structures on the West Coast. You can take a self-guided or narrated tour through the hotel's Hall of History and enjoy the old photos (like those taken during the filming of *Some Like It Hot*), then walk on the beach, especially lovely at sunset.

Other attractions include the Coronado Historical Museum, 15 miles of bike paths (bicycle rental is available), 18 public tennis courts, an 18-hole bayside public golf course, professional and community theaters, walking tours, and naval station and aircraft carrier tours. Coronado Visitor Bureau; 1047 B Ave.; 619-437-8788 or 800-622-8300; *www.coronadovisitors.com*.

GASLAMP QUARTER: This 16½-block collection of 90 restored Victorian-style commercial buildings in the heart of San Diego is *the* center for dining, shopping, and nightlife downtown, with traffic jams and numerous valet parking options to prove it (Croce's has long been a favorite for contemporary American cuisine spiced with live jazz and R&B). Most of the buildings in this part of town date from 1870 to 1910. The quarter is bounded by Fourth Avenue, Broadway, Sixth Avenue, and L Street. Horton Plaza shopping complex is adjacent. For more information, contact the Gaslamp Quarter Association; 619-233-5227; *www.gaslamp.org*.

LEGOLAND CALIFORNIA: The first American outpost of the famous Danish park opened in March 1999 on a hill overlooking the Pacific. Six themed areas created from 30 million Lego bricks surround a man-made lake. For the uninitiated, this park has 40 rides and attractions, outdoor and indoor theaters, live entertainment, restaurants, food stands, and even a driving school for kids.

The park's target audience is 2 through 12, but grown-ups are captivated, too, especially by Miniland, with its scaled down Lego versions of New York City, San Francisco, Washington, D.C., New Orleans, a New

PHOTO BY ALICE GARRARD

England harbor and town, and the California coast. Even the people on the streets and in the vehicles of Miniland are made of Lego bricks. Admission charge. Open daily. On the coast, 30 miles north of San Diego, in Carlsbad. To get there, take the Cannon Road exit off I-5; 760-918-5346; *www.legolandca.com*.

MARITIME MUSEUM OF SAN DIEGO: This floating museum is triply blessed, with the full-rigged merchant ship *Star of India* (1863), the steam-powered ferry *Berkeley* (1898), and the steam yacht *Medea* (1904). Each vessel's colorful history begs onboard exploration. From here, you can easily stroll along the Embarcadero to Seaport Village for shopping and snacking, or take the ferry to Coronado Island. Admission charge. Open daily. At the foot of Ash St. on N. Harbor Dr.; 619-234-9153; *www.sdmaritime.com*.

Land-Ho!

As of fall 2001, the decommissioned *USS Midway* was scheduled to be docked at the Embarcadero in a new role: the interactive San Diego Aircraft Museum "Midway Magic," a tribute to those who serve in the U.S. Navy and Air Force. It also houses an entertainment complex bound to make a big splash on the waterfront. 619-702-7700; *www.midway.org*.

MISSION BAY PARK: This 4,600-acre aquatic park has playgrounds, picnic areas, 27 miles of bayfront, 17 miles of oceanfront beach with six designated swimming areas, and paths for biking, jogging, and skating. The bay is popular for windsurfing, sailing, jet-skiing, waterskiing, scuba diving, and sportfishing and whale-watching excursions. Mission Beach draws surfers year-round. Nearby Belmont Park, with its giant wooden roller coaster, is pure California. To get there from downtown San Diego, follow I-5 north to the Clairemont Drive exit; 619-221-8901.

OLD TOWN: The flavor of Mexican California pervades the place where San Diego was born, especially in Old Town San Diego State Historic Park, with seven original and thirteen reconstructed buildings from the 1800s, two museums, and Bazaar del Mundo, a south-of-the-border-style shopping and dining complex. Free walking tours leave from the Visitors Center daily at 11 A.M. and 2 P.M. You can stroll to other historic attractions from here; Mission San Diego de Alcalá is nearby. Open daily. Old Town San Diego State Historic Park; 619-220-5422; and Old Town San Diego Chamber of Commerce; 619-291-4903.

SAN DIEGO ZOO: Home to 4,000 birds and beasts, the 100-acre zoo claims the largest breeding colony of koalas outside of Australia (about 30 of them). A family of giant pandas, Bai Yun (a female, pictured below), Shi Shi (a male), and two-year-old Hua Mei (the first panda ever born at the zoo), on loan from the People's Republic of China until 2008, reside in a lush compound that includes

a large viewing area. (Pandas are solitary creatures, so expect to see them separately.) The zoo is also home to Polar Bear Plunge, Ituri Forest, Gorilla Tropics, Sun Bear Forest, and Tiger River, along with a petting zoo and a baby-animal nursery. There are animal shows, aerial tram rides, and a three-mile, 40-minute double-decker bus tour (best taken early or late in the day when the animals are liveliest). Admission charge. Open daily. Follow I-5 to Park Boulevard. 2920 Zoo Dr.; Balboa Park; 619-234-3153 or 619-231-1515; *www.sandiegozoo.org.*

SEA WORLD: Four-ton killer whales glide through the air, astounding and splashing fans in 7,000-seat Shamu Stadium. Dolphins, sea lions, otters, walruses, and birds steal a few shows. In Wild Arctic, guests spy polar bears, beluga whales, walruses, and harbor seals; in Manatee Rescue, they view the endangered species from an underwater gallery; and in Shipwreck Rapids, they brave churning seas, waterfalls, and a ship's propeller. For $125, visitors can splash with dolphins. Admission charge. Open daily. Exit I-5 onto Sea World Drive and turn right. 500 Sea World Dr.; Mission Bay; 619-226-3815 or 800-325-3150 (in California).

WILD ANIMAL PARK: Here, 3,200 wild creatures roam free over most of the 1,800-acre facility. In the 30-acre Heart of Africa, you can go on a walking safari and actually feed the giraffes. Take a 55-minute monorail ride through remote landscapes of Africa and Asia; or trek through the Hidden Jungle, a replica of a tropical rain forest, or Nairobi Village, a collection of engaging animal presentations. Or join a Photo Caravan tour or a Roar and Snore sleepover (additional charge, reservations required). Admission charge. Open daily. It's 30 miles north of San Diego; follow I-5 to Highway 78 east to I-15; go south to the Via Rancho Parkway exit and follow the signs. 15500 San Pasqual Valley Rd., Escondido; 619-234-6541 or 760-747-8702.

INDEX

The Art of Chinese Brush

by Lucy Wang

*Lucy would like to thank Kathleen Wang, whose help in
creating this book is greatly appreciated.*

Walter Foster Publishing, Inc.
3 Wrigley, Suite A
Irvine, CA 92618
www.walterfoster.com

Contents

Introduction

People of all cultures are drawn to the simplicity, harmony, and unparalleled grace of Chinese brush painting. Characterized by fluidity and economy of line, this style of art bears a unique appearance that suggests both self-discipline and spontaneity. In line with the Taoist philosophy of the East, the focus of Chinese brush painting is capturing an object's essence and spirit rather than reproducing an object as it is seen. Chinese brush artists therefore use brushstrokes, color, and contrast to reflect and reveal the individual character of a subject.

In this book, you will learn the fundamentals of this elegant art style, including how to hold the brush, how to execute basic strokes, and how to use an ink stick and ink stone. And professional Chinese brush painter Lucy Wang will guide you step by step through a delightful collection of subject matter, from a napping kitten to a traditional Asian landscape. With easy-to-follow instructions, helpful tips, and plenty of inspiration to guide you along the way, this book will provide you with a pleasant and approachable introduction to the art of Chinese brush painting.

History and Philosophy of Chinese Brush Painting

Chinese brush painting is a traditional art form that has been around for more than 2000 years. In the year 200 BCE—during the Han Dynasty—the Chinese began to record their history on sheets of silk, bamboo, and other types of wood. They applied these images using tapered paintbrushes made of wolf hair and soaked in ink made from pine soot and water. Though these first Chinese markings were not accurate representations of what they conveyed, each symbol suggested an object, action, or idea within its strokes. It was from this early form of calligraphy that Chinese brush painting evolved, maintaining the importance of essence over realism. In the year 105 CE, the invention of paper brought new possibilities to the art form, offering a thin, absorbent surface for painting. The availability and convenience of paper also helped Chinese brush painting flourish.

The first account of Chinese brush painting theory surfaced shortly after 500 CE. One of the great masters of the art, Hsieh Ho, formulated six tenets that are still respected and followed today. The basic principles are the following:

1. Enliven the painting with a sense of spirit.

2. Use brushstrokes as a means to suggest character.

3. Understand the natural form of the subject.

4. Apply color that is appropriate for the subject.

5. Create a skillful arrangement of the objects and empty space.

6. Copy and pass on the methods of past masters.

Keep these six principles in mind as you complete the projects in this book. Remember that the aim of Chinese brush painting is to portray an essence, so don't be discouraged if your painting doesn't look completely realistic or lifelike; focus instead on capturing the subject's texture, soul, and energy.

Supplies

The art of Chinese brush painting requires four main materials: a Chinese paintbrush, paper, ink, and an ink stone. Called "The Four Treasures" of an artist's studio, these items cover the basics, but there are also several other items that you will need to gather before you begin. When you purchase your supplies, try to buy the best you can afford; better quality products are easier to work with and provide better results than less expensive tools do.

Ink Stick and Ink Stone

The ink for Chinese brush painting comes in the form of a hard stick; it is liquefied with water and ground on the stone. To use an ink stone and ink stick, put about one teaspoon of fresh water in the well of the stone. Then, using a circular motion, quickly grind the ink stick against the bottom of the well of the stone for about three minutes, or until the water becomes thick and dark black. Before each use, make sure your stone is clear of dry ink. Always use fresh water each time you paint, and always grind the same end of the ink stick.

Chinese Paintbrushes

The bamboo brushes used for Chinese brush (sometimes sold under the name "sumi" brushes) are similar to watercolor brushes, but they have bristles that taper to a finer tip. There are two types of bamboo brushes: stiff and soft. The stiff, brown-bristled brushes are more versatile and resilient, making them good for painting leaves and branches. The soft, white-bristled brushes have more flexible bristles, which make them ideal for painting large areas of color and for depicting soft textures, such as animal fur and petals. For best results, use the brushes recommended in each project and that fit the size of your subject. New brushes have sizing in the bristles—a substance that keeps the bristles in their desired shape. Soak your brushes in water to remove the sizing before use.

Papers

You can use many different types of papers for Chinese brush painting. Newsprint is great for practice because it is both absorbent and inexpensive. Watercolor paper is a wonderful painting surface for final artwork because it's versatile and easy to paint on; the paper absorbs the paint just enough without allowing the colors to bleed. Watercolor paper comes in a variety of textures (also called the "tooth"), ranging from coarse to smooth. The three surfaces shown below are the most common. From top to bottom, they are rough, cold-press (medium texture), and hot-press (smooth). As you progress, you may want to try painting on rice paper—the primary painting surface of Chinese brush painters for more than 2000 years. But Chinese brush painting is not limited to paper; you can produce similar fluid effects with surfaces such as wood, pottery, fabric, and silk.

Brush Rest

A brush rest is used to keep the bristles of your brushes protected between uses. Chinese brush rests come in many different styles and are often made of ceramic or metal. Choose whichever type you prefer.

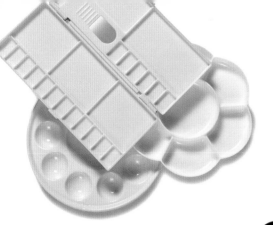

Mixing Palette

Mixing palettes are helpful for diluting your colors and for holding washes for dipping and tipping. (See page 9.) You can also use the sides of the palette wells to help shape the bristles into flattened points. Mixing palettes come in various shapes (round, oval, rectangular, and square) and can be made of a variety of materials (plastic, ceramic, glass, or metal). Plastic palettes are lightweight and reasonably priced, but all types clean up easily with soap and water.

Watercolor Paints

Watercolor paints are often used to add color to Chinese brush paintings. Watercolors are available in several forms and in a range of colors. Tube paints are a popular choice, as they come already moist and ready to use. Just squeeze each color onto a palette well or small dish, and mix it with water to create a wash; the less water there is in the mixture, the more intense the color will be. Pan and cake paints are dry blocks of pigment. To use these paints, add water to loosen the pigment and load your brush with color. Pan colors packaged in a box are convenient, but if you want to mix a lot of color at one time, tube paints are a better choice; you can squeeze out a large amount of pigment quickly and easily.

Water Dish

Chinese brush artists often use small ceramic dishes like the one shown above left to hold clean water for dipping. You should also have an additional jar or bowl for rinsing your brushes between colors. Unless you are double-dipping your colors as directed in a project, always rinse your brush well between colors, and set your brush on a rest when not in use; never let your brushes stand in water.

Other Materials

Aside from the actual painting tools, there are a few extras that will come in handy. Paper towels are great for drying and blotting brushes, as well as for testing colors. You may want to place your paper on felt or use a paperweight to hold it still while you paint to prevent the paper from shifting and curling. To erase any mistakes you make while pencil sketching, use a kneaded eraser rather than a rubber one; kneaded erasers won't damage the surface of the paper, as rubber erasers are prone to do.

Basic Color Palette

Choosing colors can be daunting to beginners, but you don't need to purchase a great array of watercolors to enjoy Chinese brush painting. Just a few basics to add to your black ink will do, and you can always mix just about any other color you may need from these few. Your basic palette of colors should include at least one or two (a warm and a cool version) of each of the primary colors (see page 8), as well as brown and white. As you refine your brush-painting skills and branch out into new subject areas, you will develop your own color preferences. The colors listed below will get you started and are all you need to complete the projects in this book.

- Chinese white
- lemon yellow
- vermilion
- crimson red
- cadmium red
- deep green
- viridian green
- ultramarine blue
- cobalt blue
- indigo blue
- burnt sienna

Color Theory and Mixing

You have already learned that the aim of Chinese brush painting is to convey the essence of a specific subject, and an effective means of capturing this "feeling" on paper is through color. Each color or combination of colors that you select for a subject suggests a particular mood to the viewer; a painting full of reds evokes passion and anger, and a painting made up of soft blues and greens elicits a sense of serenity. Therefore your choice of colors is the key factor in determining whether your painting is a bold, warm piece or a subtle, cool piece. (See "Color Psychology" below.) A basic knowledge of color theory will help you achieve the precise mixes you need for your paintings.

Color Basics

The color wheel provides the perfect starting point for understanding the relationships between colors, which will help you produce the effects you desire. The *primary colors* (red, yellow, and blue) are the three basic colors that can't be created by mixing other colors. All other colors are derived from these three. Each combination of two primaries results in a *secondary color* (purple, orange, or green), and a combination of a primary color and a secondary color results in a *tertiary color* (such as red-orange or red-purple). On the color wheel, at right, the two across from each other are *complementary colors;* they enhance one another when placed together. Groups of adjacent colors are *analogous colors;* when they are used together in a painting, they create an overall feeling of harmony.

Color Wheel

The color wheel is a helpful visual reference that demonstrates color relationships. Knowing the basics of these relationships will help you control the mood and create a sense of unity in your paintings.

Mixing Vivid Secondary Colors

When mixing two primaries to produce a secondary color, you will find that the result varies depending on the hues you choose to mix. Remember that the most vibrant secondary colors are made by mixing two primaries that have the same temperature (i.e., two cools or two warms).

Color Psychology

Colors are often classified figuratively in terms of temperature. The "warm" colors are reds, oranges, and yellows, and the "cool" colors are greens, blues, and purples. But there are variations in temperature within every family of color, or *hue,* as well. A red that contains more yellow, such as cadmium red, is warmer than a red that has more blue, such as alizarin crimson. The temperature of the colors you use can express a mood, season, or the time of day. For example, light pinks, blues, and greens can effectively suggest the fresh air and blooming nature of spring.

Value Scale

Value refers to the relative lightness or darkness of a color or of black. To achieve a range of values with watercolor or ink, simply adjust the amount of water you use in your washes. When creating a wash, it is best to start with the lightest value and build up to a darker wash, rather than adding water to a dark wash.

To get acquainted with the process of creating various values, create a chart like the one above. Apply pure pigment at the left, and gradually add more water for successively lighter values.

Brush Tips

For a flat, dry stroke (near right), dip your brush in color and then press the tip of the brush against the side of a dish or on a paper towel to flatten it and remove excess moisture. Use a flat tip for feathers and flower petals. For a pointed stroke (far right), dip your brush in color and paint with the very tip of the brush. Use a pointed tip for thin lines and details.

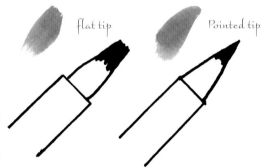

flat tip

Pointed tip

Tipping the Brush

The basic method used in this book for mixing colors on your brush is called "tipping." Start by dipping or fully loading your brush with the first color; then touch the tip of the bristles into the second color. When stroked on the paper, your dipped brush will leave behind an interesting blend of the two colors.

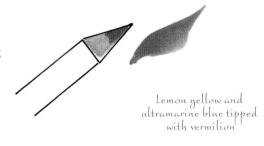

Lemon yellow and ultramarine blue tipped with vermilion

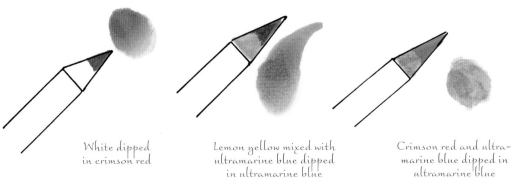

White dipped in crimson red

Lemon yellow mixed with ultramarine blue dipped in ultramarine blue

Crimson red and ultramarine blue dipped in ultramarine blue

Handling the Brush

Chinese brush painting is known around the world for its graceful and expressive brushstrokes. To create the fresh and flowing lines, it is important that you hold the brush correctly. Sit up straight and lay the paper on your table or work surface. Place a piece of felt beneath your paper to keep it from sliding and to protect your table. Then practice making the various strokes on these pages using the vertical and slanted holds shown below. These positions may seem awkward at first, but once you get used to them, you will be able to form the strokes correctly.

Slanted Hold

Hold the brush so it's almost parallel to the paper, and use your thumb and fingers to control the movement of the brush, as shown. The width of the stroke is determined by the angle of and the pressure on the brush. The shape of the stroke is determined by movement of the brush: press and lift, push and pull, turn and twist, or dash and sweep.

Vertical Hold

Hold the brush so it's perpendicular to the paper. Grasp the handle just below center, placing it between your thumb and index finger and resting the lower part on the nail of your ring finger. Rest your middle finger on the handle just below your index finger. Support your third finger with your pinkie, and brace the handle with your thumb.

Creating Strokes

Each stroke requires one fluid movement—press down, stroke, and lift. All your brushstrokes should move in a definite direction; you should always be either pushing or pulling your brush. Use your second finger to pull and your third finger to push. Hold the brush gently, letting it lightly touch the paper. Pressing too hard releases too much ink and makes the strokes difficult to control. Practice applying only as much pressure as is needed to create the shape and width of your brushstrokes. It is important to thoroughly practice each stroke and brush position before you begin following the lessons in this book; Chinese brush painting calls for a minimal number of strokes, so each one must be carefully and confidently placed.

Slanted Strokes

Hold the brush almost parallel to the paper and, in one smooth movement, press down, stroke, and lift, using your thumb and fingers to control the movement of the brush. Use slanted strokes to paint large areas and thick shapes.

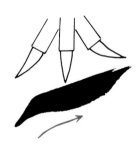

Vertical Strokes

Hold the brush perpendicular to the paper and stroke from top to bottom, thickening your line by gradually pressing the brush down on the paper. Because this stroke can produce thin lines, it is perfect for outlines, branches, clothing, and other detailed lines.

Chinese painting strokes were developed from the strokes of traditional calligraphy (Chinese writing) thousands of years ago. There are three basic strokes derived from calligraphy that you will use throughout this book: the water-drop stroke, which is made by holding the brush in the slanted position, and the bone stroke and the hook stroke, which are both made by holding the brush vertically. Below are a few examples of eight different variations of these strokes for you to follow and practice—remember to keep your wrist and hand loose and flexible as you paint!

Short water-drop
stroke: top to bottom

Long water-drop
stroke: top to bottom

Reverse water-drop
stroke: thicker at top

Water-drop stroke
with a thick end

Horizontal bone stroke

Vertical bone stroke

Combined vertical and
horizontal bone strokes

Hook stroke: vertical
line with a water-drop
stroke at the end

Petal and Leaf Strokes

Follow the arrows with your brush to re-create each brushstroke. For thicker lines, press down harder on the brush; for thinner lines, use a lighter touch.

1. Triangle (press down at start, lift for tip)

2. Reverse teardrop (touch tip of brush from top and press down to paper, lifting for tip)

3. Teardrop (press entire brush to paper and lift without moving the brush)

4. Short water-drop

5. Long water-drop

6. Rectangular (even stroke, top to bottom)

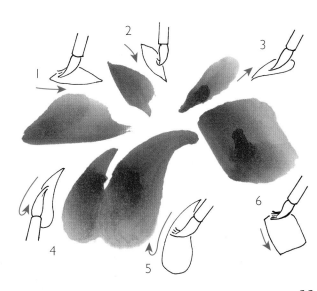

Using Basic Strokes: Bamboo

Bamboo was one of the first subjects to be studied and painted in the Chinese style, so it is fitting that you should begin your practice and preparation with this traditional Chinese plant. Bamboo provides an excellent starting point; the tall, sectioned stalk and long leaves can be easily re-created using the three basic strokes of Chinese brush painting: the bone stroke, the water-drop stroke, and the hook stroke.

Step 1

First saturate a stiff brush with light ink and tip it with dark ink. Then, to paint each section of the stalk, move the brush from the bottom to the top without lifting it off the paper. At the end of each section, stop the brush and lift as you drag slightly to the left to create a bulge or a knot.

Step 2

Using a stiff brush dipped in medium ink and tipped with dark ink, paint bone strokes for the thin branches that grow out of each knot. Paint from bottom to top and add a slight curve to each branch.

Step 3

Now dip a stiff brush into medium ink and tip it with dark ink. Using long water-drop strokes, hold the brush at a 45° angle and move only the wrist as you paint two long leaves growing from each branch end. Make the leaf clusters fuller by adding a few small leaves.

Step 4

To finish, tip a soft brush with dark ink and paint a thin, curving hook stroke (shown above) across each knot.

Painting flowers

The vibrant colors and soft, curving forms of flowers make them a favorite subject of Chinese brush painters. A great range of brushstrokes and techniques can be used to re-create the various shapes and textures of leaves and petals. Follow the demonstrations below to learn the methods for painting three distinct flowers. As this is the first exercise that involves tipping the brush, notice how the colors interact and blend as you stroke and how the variations in tone create a sense of depth.

Camellia

Step 1

Load a large soft brush with a thin white wash and tip it with crimson red. Allow the wash to mix on the brush and then paint two water-drop strokes side by side for each petal, moving from the outer tip of the petal toward the center.

Step 2

Paint five petals in a circular formation to develop the flower, leaving the center unpainted. You may want to rotate the paper as you complete each petal; this way you will not have to change the angle and direction of your strokes.

Step 3

Now load a soft brush with a wash of lemon yellow and deep green and fill in the flower's center. Using a detail brush loaded with thick Chinese white, paint the stamen with thin bone strokes from the tips to the center.

Step 4

Using a very small brush tipped with thick yellow paint, apply dots of pollen in the center of the flower, around the tips of the stamen.

Painting Leaves and Stems

 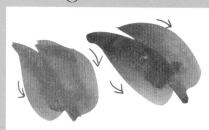 

For a blue-green leaf, mix lemon yellow and deep green and load a small stiff brush; then tip it with ultramarine blue and paint two short water-drop strokes. Repeat this process with yellow-green tipped with burnt sienna for a browner leaf, and use less blue for greener leaves. Use a very small brush tipped in a yellow-green wash to paint the stem with bone strokes.

Poinsettia

Step 1

Soak a small stiff brush with a mix of lemon yellow and deep green and tip it with ultramarine blue. Paint a cluster of four round buds, then tip the brush with yellow and add more buds to create an oval shape.

Step 2

Using a soft brush dipped in a vermilion wash and tipped with crimson red, hold the brush at a 65° angle and paint the petals using water-drop strokes. Add a small tip to the middle edge of each petal.

Step 3

Paint the next two petals using the same method as in step two. As you paint each petal, be sure to point the tip of the brush toward the flower's center. Again, it may be easiest to rotate the paper as you paint.

Step 4

Add three more leaves, making each leaf a slightly different length and shape. You may have to apply more than one water-drop stroke for each petal in order to achieve the desired shape.

Step 5

The poinsettia is a full flower, so be sure to fill in any gaps or empty spaces with petals. When you have completed the petals, paint crimson red dots on the green buds with the tip of a small stiff brush.

Bird of Paradise

Step 1

Dip a soft brush in vermilion and tip it with crimson red. Then hold the brush at a 65° angle with the tip facing away from you. Lift up the brush gradually while stroking toward you, controlling the brush's movement with your finger; the angle of the brush will change as it moves.

Step 2

Load a stiff brush with blue, tip it with a small amount of crimson red, and paint water-drop strokes for the petals. Begin with the tip of the brush on the paper and gradually press down at the end. Then hold the brush vertically and add bone strokes for the stem.

Step 3

Mix deep green and lemon yellow with a soft brush and tip it with blue. Allow the washes to blend in the brush and tip it again with crimson red. Holding the brush at a 45° angle, press down from the tip of the sepal and lift the brush up to taper the stroke and finish the sepal.

Step 4

With the same color combination as in the previous step, hold the brush straight up and down and paint the stem with a bone stroke. To create the dry, coarse effect shown at the bottom of the stem, blot the brush on a paper towel before you stroke.

Painting Insects

A common element in Chinese brush paintings, insects usually complement flowers and serve as colorful, intricate focal points. The thin lines and delicate details provide a dynamic contrast to the large, smooth areas of color used to paint flowers. Follow the demonstrations below to practice executing fine details and to gain confidence in using the very tip of the Chinese paintbrush. During this process, remember to keep a fluid simplicity to your brushstrokes and avoid overworking your insects.

Butterfly

Step 1

Use a soft brush with a light ultramarine blue wash tipped with a darker blue wash to paint three water-drop strokes toward the body.

Step 2

Using the tip of a dry stiff brush loaded with black ink, hold the brush vertically and paint the veins of the wings with bone strokes.

Step 3

Holding the brush vertically, paint a dot for the body and bone strokes for the stomach. Create the legs and antennae with bone strokes.

Step 4

To add markings to the butter-fly, dot on small areas of thick white paint. Remember that a butterfly's wings have symmetrical markings.

Dragonfly

Step 1

Saturate a stiff brush with burnt sienna and tip it with crimson red. Paint small water-drop strokes for the eyes and mouth. Using the same color, paint two slanted strokes for the dragonfly's thorax.

Step 2

Using the tip of the brush, paint bone strokes from the thorax to the tip of the abdomen, making the abdomen appear to consist of several segments. The abdomen should be about five times longer than the thorax.

Step 3

Load a soft brush with light ink and tip it with medium ink. Allow the ink to blend within the bristles and then blot the brush on a paper towel. Paint long, rapid water-drop strokes down toward the top of the thorax.

Step 4

Saturate a dry stiff brush with black ink and use the tip to paint thin lines on the dragonfly's wings. Finally tip a clean, dry stiff brush with vermilion and crimson red and paint bone strokes for the legs.

Bees

Step 1	Step 2	Step 3	Step 4	Step 5
Create a thick yellow wash, load a small soft brush, and tip it with burnt sienna. Paint a small square shape with the tip.	Prepare the brush as you did in the previous step, and paint the body of the bee with a fat, rectangular water-drop stroke.	Tip the stiff brush with medium ink, blot it on a paper towel, and add the wings with two pairs of thin water-drop strokes.	Now add the eyes, antennae, and lines along the wings using a dry stiff brush tipped with dark ink.	Finally paint the six legs with black ink using bone strokes and the tip of a detail brush.

Step 1	Step 2	Step 3	Step 4	Step 5
Dip a small soft brush in thick yellow and tip it with burnt sienna. Using only the tip, paint a small square shape.	Load the brush again as you did in the previous step. Then paint the bee's body with one small, fat water-drop stroke.	Using a dry stiff brush tipped with medium ink, paint two water-drop strokes on each side of the body for the wings.	Use a dry stiff brush and dark ink to paint the eyes, antennae, and lines along the wings. Add stripes on the body.	Load a very small, dry brush with black ink, blot it on a paper towel, and use the tip to paint six legs with bone strokes.

fish

Step 1

To paint the body of the fish, load a stiff brush with a vermilion wash and tip it with crimson red. Hold the brush at a 45° angle and swish it in a smooth stroke from the head to the tail, gradually lifting the brush up as you stroke. The curve of the stroke will suggest the movement of the fish's body.

Step 2

With small water-drop strokes, paint two pairs of fins as shown. Then add two water-drop strokes of equal size for the tail, pressing down on the brush at the end of each tail fin.

Step 3

Tip a stiff brush with dark ink and, holding the brush in the vertical position, paint two dots for the eyes. Then paint a dark line down the center of the back as shown.

Painting the Vegetation

Load a small soft brush with thin deep green tipped in crimson red. Then, holding the brush horizontally, apply dots of varying size to suggest the vegetation on the water. Next mix a cooler green by adding a touch of blue to the thin green wash, and randomly apply some more dots, slightly varying the size and shape, as shown in the example. Don't add too much vegetation; you just want to create the essence of the plants to add interest to your composition.

Step 4

To make the black fish, follow the same procedure using medium ink tipped with dark ink for the body.

Step 5

Now use your knowledge of painting fish to create a final composition. Fish should be painted in odd numbers or in pairs, and all the fish should swim in the same general direction. Add a few dots sparingly between the fish to suggest vegetation (see the box on page 18), being careful to preserve the simplicity of the painting.

Cocker Spaniel

Step 1

First lightly sketch the shape of the dog with a pencil. Then use a dry stiff brush tipped with black ink to paint a small dot for the dog's eye and a triangle pointed downward for the nose. Wash out the brush and saturate it with medium ink. Wipe the brush on a paper towel to dry it slightly, and then use the tip to outline the shape of the dog's head, holding the brush vertically.

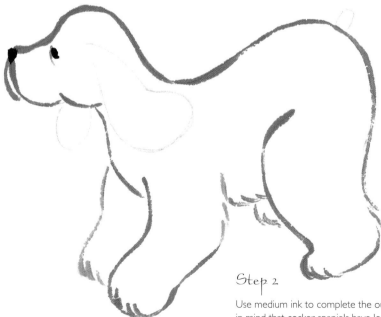

Step 2

Use medium ink to complete the outline of the dog's body. Keep in mind that cocker spaniels have long hair on their legs, making them look wider than they really are. To show the hair on the feet, behind the leg, and on the belly, apply a few short strokes, rather than making a smooth, continuous line.

Step 3

With a soft brush loaded with medium ink and dipped halfway into dark ink, paint a curved water-drop stroke. Start by placing the tip of the brush at the top of the dog's ear, gradually pressing down more on the brush as your hand turns, following the shape of the ear. Finally paint a short black line with the tip of your brush for the tail.

Step 4

Soak a soft brush with medium ink and tip it with dark ink. Dry the brush slightly on a paper towel and paint the dog's coat markings using three connecting water-drop strokes for each pattern.

Panda

Step 1

Begin by using a pencil to lightly sketch the shape of the panda's head, body, and limbs. Then saturate the soft brush with dark black ink and paint oval-shaped eye patches that slant at a 45° angle. Add a triangular nose and two C-shaped ears, leaving a white space in the center for the opening of the ears.

Step 2

Next load the dry stiff brush with medium-dark ink and use it to paint a thin outline of the panda's face and body. Make sure that the wash is noticeably lighter than the dark ink used for the eye patches and ears; this will ensure that the outline doesn't stand out too much compared to the panda's markings.

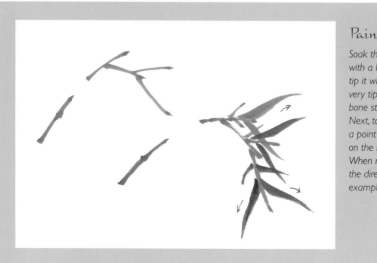

Painting the Bamboo

Soak the very tip of the stiff brush with a light green wash and then tip it with dark green. Then use the very tip of the brush to paint thin bone strokes for the branches. Next, to form the leaves, begin with a point on the branch, press down on the brush, and quickly lift up. When making your strokes, follow the directions of the arrows in the example.

Step 3

Next paint the front and back legs on the panda's left side using the soft brush. Saturate the brush with medium ink and dip it in dark black ink; then press down firmly. Soak the brush with dark ink and dip the tip into a small amount of water; then dry the brush on a towel to create a medium-dark ink. Now paint the two legs on the panda's right, starting from the top and moving the brush down to the end of the foot. Be sure to leave a small white gap between each leg to keep them from blending into one another.

Step 4

Now add the bamboo stalk, starting with the branch. Each branch should hold only two large and two small leaves. You may want to add another layer of black ink to the darkest areas of the panda; this will create a stronger contrast against the white.

Kitten

Step 1

Begin by outlining the kitten with pencil. Then dip a stiff brush into a dark wash of dark ink and blot the brush on a paper towel before tracing over the sketch of the kitten's ears, eyes, nose, and mouth with long, fluid bone strokes. Next wash out your brush and mix some medium-light ink. Outline the head with bone strokes and paint several light dots on the kitten's mouth to suggest the base of the whiskers.

Step 2

Now use light ink to outline the body with bone strokes, beginning with the shoulder. Trace over the rest of your pencil marks with a dark gray ink wash, making sure that the brush is not overloaded with ink. Then saturate a soft brush with light ink and dip it in dark ink. Dry the brush and hold it at a 45° angle to paint the tip of the tail with one quick stroke.

Step 3

Saturate a small soft brush with a light wash of black ink and tip it with dark ink. Dry the brush on a paper towel and hold it at a 45° angle to paint black stripes on the head, body, and tail. Begin painting these stripes at the edge of the back, curving down to the right to suggest the rounded upper body. Do the same for the hind leg, beginning the strokes at the left and curving them over and down.

Step 4

Next saturate a small soft brush with a medium wash of black ink and stroke light gray over the black marks. (Be careful not to paint over areas that should remain white, such as the ears, face, and lower leg.) Now create the kitten's whiskers using a stiff brush. Load it with very black ink and blot it well on a towel, forming the tip to a dry and straight point. Then hold the brush upright and stroke outward from the little dots on the sides of the mouth. Paint rapid bone strokes with the tip of the brush and keep them simple, with only three whiskers on each side. For the pink areas, load a soft brush with a thin wash of crimson red and blot away excess moisture. Then paint a small pink dot on the nose, line the lower lid of each eye, and add a little pink in the center of both ears.

frog

Step 1

First lightly draw the shape of the frog with a pencil. Then use a stiff brush tipped with dark ink to paint two water-drop strokes for the circular eye, leaving a small white highlight at the top, between the two strokes. After allowing the ink to dry, saturate the soft brush with a vermilion wash and tip it with crimson red. Blot the brush on a paper towel; then paint the top of the head using water-drop strokes, surrounding the eye with color.

Step 2

Using a soft brush dipped in a vermilion wash and tipped with crimson red, paint a long water-drop stroke from the neck to the frog's rear. Then add a series of water-drop strokes along the frog's back, sweeping downward and over the foreleg. Next saturate the soft brush with light ink tipped with a vermilion wash and paint a water-drop stroke from the chin down to the top of the chest, leaving a white spot at the corner of the frog's mouth.

Painting the front Leg

Using a stiff brush dipped in light ink and tipped with dark ink, paint the remainder of the forelegs with water-drop strokes. Add the toes using small bone strokes, pressing down the brush tip at each joint. To paint the legs farthest from the viewer, use light ink.

Painting the Back Leg

Dip the stiff brush in light ink, tip it with dark ink, and paint the hind leg with two overlapping water-drop strokes. Reload the brush and blot the excess wash on a paper towel. Holding the brush vertically, paint the toes with bone strokes.

Step 3

Paint the legs and feet following the instructions in the box on page 26. Then tip a dry soft brush with light ink and fill in the empty space on the frog's chest. Rinse the brush and load it with a light wash of deep green for the frog's underside. After rinsing the brush again, load it with light ink and outline the belly of the frog. Paint two dots on the frog's backside and add spots to the forearm. Then dry the brush, tip it with dark ink, and paint a dot for the nostril. Add a thin line to define the mouth and another thin line that extends from the corner of the eye outward.

Step 4

Now create a background for the frog by placing him on an anthurium leaf. First add the *spadix*—the curved spike at the flower's center. Saturate a stiff brush with a medium crimson red wash and tip it with a darker, thicker crimson red wash; then apply a long water-drop stroke from the top curving down to the center of the leaf. Use the point of a clean stiff brush tipped with a thick wash of lemon yellow to add equally spaced dots to the crimson spadix. Next tip a dry stiff brush with medium ink and outline the main leaf with long, gently curving strokes. Then rinse out the brush, load it with a wash of lemon yellow and deep green, and highlight areas of the outlines. Tip the same brush with a crimson red wash and add one thick stroke for the stem.

Rabbit

Step 1

Load a soft brush with medium black ink and tip it with dark black ink to paint a water-drop stroke from the nose to the back of the head.

Step 2

Then paint a water-drop stroke beginning at the left point of the first stroke and sweeping under the eye. Add a triangular nose with a brief, downward stroke.

Step 3

Use a soft brush dipped in medium ink and tipped with dark ink to paint the rabbit's ears, using long water-drop strokes. Then add a thinner stroke that connects the tip to the base of the rabbit's right ear, leaving a slender space of white that suggests a fold.

Step 4

Use a dry stiff brush tipped in dark ink to add the eye, leaving a space between the eyeball and the eye socket. Finally paint the mouth, cheeks, and whiskers with bone strokes using medium ink.

Painting the flowers

Load a soft brush with a wash of lemon yellow and deep green tipped with a pure lemon yellow wash. Hold the brush with the handle nearly parallel to the paper, press down, and lift to create the stamens of the flowers.

Dip the brush into a light wash of white, tip it with ultramarine blue wash, and then tip it again with a small amount of crimson red wash. Flatten the brush tip and paint the petals from the outer tips to the edge of the stamen.

Load the brush with a wash of lemon yellow mixed with green deep; then tip it with a wash of ultramarine blue. Use thick, fat water-drop strokes to paint leaf clusters. Vary the size and shape of each leaf to add interest.

Dip the brush into a wash of lemon yellow and tip it with a crimson red wash. Use a series of thin bone strokes to create the stems. Alter the direction of the brush after each bone stroke to give the appearance of knots at the joints.

Step 5

Dip a soft brush in medium ink and blot it on a paper towel. Then outline the rabbit's body using curved bone strokes. Begin each stroke with pressure on the brush tip, and then lift up slightly as you pull the brush along. As each stroke comes to a finish, apply more pressure again at the tip.

Step 6

Load a soft brush with medium ink and tip it with dark ink. Create the rabbit's black markings with large water-drop strokes, beginning at the back and sweeping down.

Step 7

Finally add color and balance your painting with a few blue flowers, following the steps shown in the box on page 28.

Lotus flower and Bees

Step 1

First sketch the lotus flower and bees in pencil. Then load a large stiff brush with a wash of lemon yellow and deep green, tip the brush with ultramarine blue, and paint a dot in the middle of the leaf. Next paint the leaf in three equal sections, using three long water-drop strokes for each section. Paint outward from the center dot, leaving a small white space between the dot and the leaf.

Step 2

To finish the leaf, tip the brush in a yellow or burnt sienna wash (to add variety to the green) and fill in the areas between the three sections of the leaf.

Step 3

Now saturate a large soft brush with a thin white wash and tip it with crimson red. Then apply the front layer of the flower petals with water-drop strokes, following the directions of the arrows.

Step 4

Tip the brush again in the crimson red wash and outline the petals that are farthest from the viewer. Now load a soft brush with a yellow-green wash and fill in the seedpod inside the flower.

Step 5

Still using crimson red, add the two flower buds; then tip some yellow-green on the tip of the bud on the left to indicate the seedpod. Next use a large stiff brush soaked in a yellow-green wash and tipped with ultramarine blue to paint some of the stems with long bone strokes. Paint the remainder of the stems in the same manner using a stiff brush loaded with yellow-green and tipped with crimson red. Then paint the profile of a leaf above the flowers. Add a leaf bud below the large central leaf.

Step 6

Use a stiff brush tipped with deep green to paint dots along the stems. Next outline the seedpod with a very small brush dipped in dark ink. After rinsing out the brush, tip it with lemon yellow and paint small, fat water-drop dots for the stamens around the seedpod. Finally paint the bees by following the chart on page 17.

Horse

Step 1

First sketch the horse's body in pencil. Then load a soft brush with a thinned mix of burnt sienna and medium ink, dip the tip into a pure burnt sienna wash, and paint a diamond-shaped outline for the star on the horse's forehead. Tip the brush with burnt sienna again and paint the nose with two water-drop strokes. Add another small water-drop stroke for the chin.

Step 2

Now dip the tip of the brush in a burnt sienna wash and paint a long water-drop stroke with a crisp, curved edge to create the cheek. Connect the nose and chin with a short stroke.

Step 3

Next tip the brush with black ink and paint two water-drop strokes for the ears. Tip the brush with dark black ink, blot the brush on a paper towel, and paint the nostril and the eye.

Step 4

Rinse the brush well and saturate it with a mix of thinned burnt sienna and medium ink. Apply two long water-drop strokes from the top of the head to the bottom of the neck, using small strokes where needed to connect the neck and head.

Step 5

Load the brush with a wash of burnt sienna and medium ink and tip it with a thicker wash of burnt sienna. Holding the brush at a 65° angle, paint from the top of the back to the bottom of the horse's sides with slightly curved strokes. Leave the stomach white.

Step 6

Now mix light ink with a wash of burnt sienna and tip the brush with black ink. Paint two water-drop strokes to create the chest. Next tip the brush with a pure burnt sienna wash and paint the horse's front left leg from the shoulder to the knee with bone strokes, turning the brush to create the lower section of the leg. When you paint the horse's knees, press down on the brush tip a bit harder to create a knotlike form. Then use the same brush to outline the horse's hoof. Paint the other legs the same way, but use a lighter wash for the two legs farthest away to suggest distance. Next add a thin stroke under the stomach.

Step 7

Load a stiff brush with dark ink. Flatten the tip of the brush by stroking the brush along the rim of a dish or palette well. For the mane, paint strokes from the top of the neck outward, lifting the brush as you stroke to taper the ends of the hair. Next mix light ink with a small amount of burnt sienna and load the brush. Tip the brush with dark ink and paint several curved water-drop strokes, starting with the tip of the brush at the horse's rear and gradually pressing down as you stroke. At the end of each stroke, quickly lift up the brush. When you paint the background, you'll want to cover the top half of the horse with a paper towel so that you don't accidentally splash it with color. Soak the brush with a wash of deep green and hold the brush a few inches from the paper in a horizontal position. Tap the end of the brush handle with your index finger so that tiny droplets of paint spatter over the paper. Then repeat this same process using a wash of crimson red and ultramarine blue (a blue-violet color). When the colors are dry, paint horizontal strokes of a lighter wash of deep green for the ground.

Penguins

Step 1

First determine the position and form of each penguin by creating a light sketch in pencil. Make sure that each penguin is slightly different from the others so the composition isn't too symmetrical.

Step 2

Then paint the head of one penguin with a soft brush dipped in medium ink and tipped with dark ink. Start with a water-drop stroke from the forehead to the back of the head. Holding the brush vertically, paint the beak with the point of the brush and follow with a water-drop stroke down through the throat.

Step 3

Now, still using the soft brush that has been dipped in medium ink and tipped with dark ink, apply a water-drop stroke from the base of the penguin's head over the shoulder and down the side of the body. With the same brush dipped in dark ink and held vertically, sweep from the shoulders to the tips of the wings.

Step 4

Next load a stiff brush with light ink, tip it with medium ink, and paint the outline of the body, legs, and tail with quick, brisk strokes.

Step 5

Repeat steps 2–4 for the other two penguins.

Step 6

Using a soft brush tipped in a vermilion wash, apply short strokes for the bottom of the legs and webbed feet. To paint the glacier, dip a stiff brush in medium ink, tip it with medium-dark ink, and wipe the brush on a paper towel until it is only moist. Holding the brush at a 30° angle and beginning at the peaks, paint the outline of the mountains with downward strokes. Then use a soft brush dipped in a very light wash of ultramarine blue to stroke in icy blue shadows in the snow.

Calico Cat

Step 1

First sketch the outline of the cat. Then saturate a small stiff brush with a lemon yellow wash, blot it on a paper towel, and paint a dot for the eye with a small, rounded water-drop stroke. Using a soft brush tipped in dark ink, outline the eye with the brush point and add dots for the base of the whiskers. Tip the brush with medium ink and finish the outline of the cat's face and body with a series of bone strokes.

Step 2

Saturate a soft brush with light ink tipped with dark ink and dry the brush slightly on a paper towel. Apply a water-drop stroke from the top of the head around the ears, leaving the ears unpainted. Continue to add markings along the top of the cat's back with water-drop strokes. Using the same brush dipped in light ink and tipped in dark ink, start at the tip of the tail and stroke in a curved line to meet the cat's rear marking. For the whiskers, use a dry stiff brush moistened with dark ink to paint several thin bone strokes from the side of the cat's mouth outward. Then add the dark spot for the nose and the short line indicating the mouth. Finally, using the same brush, paint a thin vertical line to indicate the cat's pupil.

Step 3

Rinse the soft brush and load it with a light wash of burnt sienna tipped with darker burnt sienna. With water-drop strokes, paint reddish-brown markings on the cat's ears, face, and back.

Painting the flowers and the Butterfly

To create the blossom, dip a soft brush in a light crimson red wash, tip it with a darker crimson red, and paint five rounded water-drop strokes for the petals. For the flower's stamen, saturate a stiff brush with dark ink and blot it on a paper towel. Use only the tip of the brush to paint a small circle in the center and several lines radiating out.

To paint the sepal—which can be seen only on buds and flower profiles—use dark ink to add a short stem and two small water-drop strokes at the base of the flower. The water-drop strokes should curve slightly and rest perpendicular to the stem. Use only three petals to show flowers from a side view. For each bud, simply paint one dot.

For the butterfly, soak a stiff brush in a wash of lemon yellow, tip it with burnt sienna, and paint four water-drop strokes as shown, making the top two sections of the wings longer than the bottom sections. For the butterfly's body, tip a stiff brush in dark ink and indicate the antennae, body, legs, and black markings on the wings.

Step 4

Now add a colorful plum branch and butterfly (demonstrated in the box above) to complement this adorable cat. For the branches, load a stiff brush with light ink and tip it with dark ink. Holding the brush vertically, paint the branches with bone strokes.

Tiger

Step 1

First lightly sketch the tiger with a pencil. Copy what you see, being careful to imitate the angle of the head, the folds in the skin, and the stripes on the face.

Step 2

Now use the fine point of a dry soft brush and medium-dark ink to outline the entire tiger. Start with the eyes, and then paint the nose, mouth, ears, and body. Use more pressure for thick lines and lift the brush to taper the stroke for thin lines.

Step 3

Use the same brush and dip it in medium-dark ink to paint stripes that curve down from the top of the back to the side of the body. Keep in mind that the markings do not necessarily connect from top to bottom; the stripes appear more realistic when broken up. For the tail, paint curved black stripes that continue to the solid, dark tip.

40

Step 4

Next mix a light yellow wash with small amounts of burnt sienna and light black or ink. Use a soft brush to layer this color on the tiger's head and body. Begin from the top of the back and continue down the side of the body, but leave the stomach and the area around the eyes white. When the color dries, stroke burnt sienna over the face and the black stripes. The forehead, nose, cheeks, and top of the back should all be darker. (If the color bleeds into areas that are meant to be white, use white paint to cover the color.) Mix a thin wash of lemon yellow to fill in the eyes.

Step 5

With a dry stiff brush saturated with dark ink, retrace the outline of the face and some of the stripes on the body to make them more distinct and to create variations in the stripes' values. It is not necessary to highlight every stripe; make the markings most intense on the back and keep the markings on the stomach medium gray. For the whiskers, use a dry stiff brush with black ink and begin painting from the black markings above the mouth. Be sure to use rapid strokes to create thin dry lines. To finish, dip the tip of a dry brush into dark ink to paint the pupils of the eyes. Then use thick white paint to add a light reflection in the upper edge of the pupils.

Monkey

Step 1

First draw the outline of the monkey in pencil. Mix a wash of ultramarine blue and paint a horizontal stroke across the monkey's forehead with a stiff brush; then trace around the heart-shaped nose (A). Next rinse out the brush and paint the eyes, ear, and outline of the nose with dark black ink (B).

A

B

Step 2

Now load a soft brush with a wash of burnt sienna and light ink and tip it in black ink; brush on a semi-circle for the head and two water-drop strokes for the shoulders. Tip the brush again with dark ink and paint a horizontal line across the forehead for the hairline. Then load a stiff brush with a light wash of burnt sienna and black ink, blot the brush well on a paper towel, and add small swipes of the brush along the monkey's face to suggest wisps of hair.

Step 3

Load a soft brush with a wash of burnt sienna and tip it with dark ink for the monkey's coat. Begin your first stroke at the lowest point of the back—between the shoulders—and sweep up and around the monkey's rear, keeping the darker tip of the brush along the pencil outline. Then paint several strokes from the monkey's back across and down the side of the body, lifting the brush after each stroke to create a coarse trail. Now dip the brush into the burnt sienna wash and tip it in a thicker wash of burnt sienna to add multiple shades of brown to the brush. Paint the tail in one long, continuous stroke from the tip of the tail to the monkey's rear.

Painting Peaches

Using a thin mix of yellow and green tipped with crimson red, paint two water-drop strokes beside one another to make each peach. Then use a mix of yellow and green tipped with blue to create the leaves with small water-drop strokes.

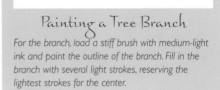

Painting a Tree Branch

For the branch, load a stiff brush with medium-light ink and paint the outline of the branch. Fill in the branch with several light strokes, reserving the lightest strokes for the center.

Step 4

Saturate a soft brush with burnt sienna mixed with light ink. Tip the brush in dark ink and paint water-drop strokes from the shoulder to the hand. Then use the tip of the brush to paint a thin, curved line along the outline of the stomach.

Step 5

Use the same wash from step three to paint the monkey's legs, starting from the top and lifting the brush slightly as you taper down to the feet. Then tip the brush with a darker wash of burnt sienna mixed with dark ink and paint the individual toes and fingers with thin, controlled strokes. Add colorful background elements, following the instructions in the box above.

43

Elephant

Step 1

After lightly outlining the elephant in pencil, load a soft brush with a thin mix of burnt sienna and a bit of black ink. Tip it with medium-dark ink and, holding the brush vertically, make a fluid, sweeping stroke from the tip of the trunk to the forehead.

Step 2

Now paint a large water-drop stroke from the elephant's mouth to the chin, finishing the head.

Step 3

Next tip the brush with medium-dark ink and paint a heart shape for the right ear, holding the brush at a 45° angle. Tip the brush with a wash of burnt sienna and paint the left ear with one stroke, leaving a small white space between the ears and the head.

Step 4

Now load a stiff brush with dark ink and paint the eye with a small water-drop stroke. Add two small moon-shaped marks for the eyelids.

Step 5

Saturate a soft brush with burnt sienna and tip it with medium-dark ink. Paint the right front leg from the top of the leg to the base, using a few strokes to copy the shape. Then paint the back leg, beginning from the top of the leg and stroking down to the bottom. Again you will need to use more than one brushstroke to fill this area, so be sure to apply each new stroke while the previous one is still wet. Otherwise the edges will dry, creating streaks within the painted areas.

Step 6

Using a soft brush saturated with burnt sienna and tipped with medium-dark ink, paint several large water-drop strokes, swooping from the neck and curving over the elephant's backside. Add one stroke from the elephant's back curving down to the underside, but be sure to leave a gap of white between the legs and the stomach. Then use a dry stiff brush tipped with dark black ink to paint the tail with a long, thin, continuous stroke.

Painting the Trees

Saturate a dry stiff brush with a medium value of black ink and tip it with a dark value of black ink. Then paint the tree trunk and branches using bone strokes. To create the illusion of a round trunk with dimension, use a lighter value of ink in the center of the brush and a darker value in the outer bristles.

For the green leaves, load a small stiff brush with a mixture of lemon yellow and deep green, and then tip it with ultramarine blue. Next flatten the brush tip on the side of a dish or mixing palette. Hold the brush at an 80° angle, and paint small clusters of leaves by dotting the brush on the paper. Overlap the dots to create depth and texture. Paint the red leaves the same way you painted the green leaves, but use vermilion tipped with crimson red.

Step 7

Using a soft brush dipped in thinned burnt sienna and a small amount of light ink, stroke from the top of the elephant's left leg to the bottom of the foot with a slight water-drop motion. Then paint the right front leg with one small water-drop stroke. For the elephant's toenails, tip the brush with medium-dark ink and paint a few dots along the bottoms of the feet. Load the tip of a stiff brush with a very light wash of thinned ultramarine blue and paint small droplets of water, starting at the tip of the trunk. For the mountain, load a soft brush with a light ultramarine blue wash and tip it with medium blue. Place the brush bristles onto the paper so that the tip is away from you and the bristles are lying flat against the paper. The handle should be leaning toward your face. Then pull the brush to the left and slightly toward you while slowly lifting the brush back to the vertical position. Using a stiff brush loaded with a wash of burnt sienna and black ink, paint thin bone strokes for the surface of the ground. Then use a mix of lemon yellow and deep green tipped with pure deep green to fill in the area below this line. Finally add the trees and flowers as shown in the box on page 46.

Iris and Hummingbird

Step 1

After sketching the whole scene in pencil, prepare a violet wash using a mix of cobalt blue and crimson red. Load a soft brush with the mixture and then dip it in pure water, creating a medium violet wash within the brush. Tip the brush with the initial violet wash, hold the brush at a 65° angle, and paint the first petal from top to bottom with a long, curved water-drop stroke. To modify the size and shape of the petal, add water-drop strokes to either side of the initial stroke.

Step 2

Using the same strokes that were used in step 1 and following the arrows in the example, paint a second petal to the right of the first. For the third petal (at the top), tip the brush with a bit of water before applying the color. (Remember that each petal grows from the center point.) For the fourth petal (at the bottom), use a series of water-drop strokes to create the shape, gradually making each stroke shorter.

5

6

Step 3

Tip the brush with cobalt blue to paint the fifth petal (on the left). Then tip the brush with violet to alter the color for the sixth petal (on the right). This variation in color within the flower will give the blossom a sense of depth and keep it from appearing flat on the paper.

Step 4

Mix a lemon yellow and deep green wash with a large stiff brush and tip it with crimson red. Paint the sepals from the base of the flower outward with water-drop strokes; then paint the stems with long, thin bone strokes. Load a soft brush with a violet wash to add a round bud, placing a bit of lemon yellow wash in the center of the flower petals for the stamen.

Step 5

Tip a stiff brush in dark ink and blot it on a paper towel. Then hold the brush at a 65° angle and paint a water-drop stroke from the tip of the bird's beak toward the face, adding more pressure to the brush at the end of the stroke. Use the same brush to paint two small dots for the eye, leaving a white space for the highlight. Finally paint the wispy black feathers around the eye with short, quick strokes.

Step 6

Load a small soft brush with a blue-green wash of viridian green and cobalt blue. Tip the brush with a pure cobalt blue wash and paint the top of the head with a water-drop stroke, starting from the beak. Add two smaller water-drop strokes to form the back of the neck. Then paint several water-drop strokes for the base of the wings, dipping again in the light blue-green and tipping in cobalt blue.

Step 7

Now load a stiff brush with medium ink and flatten the tip by running the brush along the edge of a dish or palette well. Starting from the end of the beak, paint outward strokes to create a triangular throat. Use the same brush to outline the stomach. Then dip a stiff brush into medium ink and tip it with dark ink to paint feathers on the wings using long water-drop strokes, pressing down at the end of each stroke.

Step 8

Next load a soft brush with a light blue-green wash and paint water-drop strokes within the tail. Then, without rinsing the brush, tip the brush in light ink and fill in the layer beneath the tail with gray strokes. Now tip a stiff brush in dark ink and paint the bird's feet with small bone strokes.

Step 9

Mix a thick wash of white paint and use a stiff brush to paint rows of dots on the bird's head. Then apply a thin layer of cobalt blue on the top of the head. Now use a soft brush tipped with burnt sienna to add a light brown to the bird's underside.

Step 10

To create the leaves, mix a wash of lemon yellow and deep green with a large stiff brush and tip it with ultramarine blue. Paint each leaf from top to bottom, lifting the brush as you stroke down. Then tip the brush with a crimson red wash and add the leaf in the background.

female figure

Step 1

Begin by sketching the outline of the figure on paper. Next use a very small brush dipped in medium ink to retrace the image with long bone strokes, blotting the brush on a paper towel to create a coarse, controlled line. (If you wish to trace the exact figure from this project, you can make an enlarged photocopy of step one and place rice paper on top for tracing.)

Painting the Head

Create a light vermilion wash to produce a pale peach color. Saturate a small soft brush with the peach wash, and fill in the woman's face and neck. Leave the nose unpainted to suggest a highlight.

After the face dries completely, load the same brush with a light crimson red wash and blot it on a paper towel to dry it slightly. Then stroke the brush lightly over the upper cheeks, giving the woman a blushed appearance.

Next paint the eyes with a very small, dry brush and thick, dark ink. Then, using thick white paint and the tip of a brush, dot highlights on each eye. Paint the hair with short strokes of dark ink and the flattened tip of a small soft brush.

Step 2

Paint the head as demonstrated in the box on page 52; then fill in the hands with the same light vermilion wash used on the face. Load a large soft brush with a cadmium red wash and apply color generously within the outline of the robe. Then, using a small soft brush, paint the edge of the robe with black ink and paint the ribbon with a cobalt blue wash.

Step 3

Next go over the outline of the robe again with a very small brush dipped in dark crimson red. Apply a wash of light burnt sienna over the folds of the skirt with a soft brush. To create the skirt cover, use a soft brush dipped in a dark wash of cobalt blue. Now paint on the woman's bracelet with a light blue-green wash and a very small brush; then add the hair ornaments using cobalt blue, light blue-green, and cadmium red.

Step 4

Fill in the fan using a small soft brush dipped in light ink. After the ink dries, tip the brush in dark ink to create the frame of the fan and to paint the small bamboo design. Next add the cluster of bamboo leaves above the figure using the tip of a small stiff brush dipped in a yellow and deep green wash and tipped with ultramarine blue. Paint each leaf with a long, thin water-drop stroke that tapers to a fine point, making some of the leaves cross and overlap. To add the two butterflies, follow the instructions on page 16.

Step 1

After marking the position of each element of the painting in pencil, begin painting the chicks. Load a soft brush with light black ink and tip it with dark ink. Holding the brush at a 65° angle, paint four fat, egg-shaped water-drop strokes for the head, back, and wings. (For the yellow chick, repeat this process using a lemon yellow wash tipped with burnt sienna.)

Step 2

Dip a very small brush in dark ink, blot the bristles on a paper towel, and hold the brush at a 65° angle to paint the beak and eye. Then use a small stiff brush tipped in dark ink to paint four water-drop strokes along the tip of each wing. The largest stroke should be the farthest from the body. (For the yellow chick, use burnt sienna tipped with medium ink to paint the beak and burnt sienna to paint the tips of the wings.)

Step 3

Saturate a large soft brush with light ink tipped with medium ink and paint one water-drop stroke from the corner of the beak around the bottom of the eye. Apply another water-drop stroke for the chick's chest. (For the yellow chick, use lemon yellow tipped with burnt sienna.) To paint the legs and feet, use a very small brush tipped in dark ink and bone strokes. (For the yellow chick, use burnt sienna tipped in light ink.) Finally add a small stroke of a vermilion wash for the tongue.

Step 4

Now that the chicks are complete, begin painting the flowers. Use a large soft brush loaded with vermilion and tipped with crimson red to paint the petals with round water-drop strokes, giving each flower five petals and leaving the center unpainted. To make each stroke, flatten the bristles, hold the brush at a 65° angle, and paint downward.

Step 5

Without rinsing the soft brush, tip it with lemon yellow and paint the cone-shaped bulbs at the base of each slight- or full-profile flower using several side-by-side strokes. Then soak the brush with a vermilion wash and tip it with lemon yellow to paint the buds with small water-drop strokes.

Step 6

Next use a large stiff brush dipped in light ultramarine blue and tipped with darker blue to paint the leaves with water-drop strokes. You may want to add multiple strokes to achieve the desired shape.

Step 7

Load a very small brush with a wash of lemon yellow and ultramarine blue. Holding the brush upright, paint branches with bone strokes and connect the flowers to the leaves with short strokes. Add a long vine sweeping down from the main cluster of flowers and curving to the right; you may want to add more blue leaves growing on the vine. Then paint the ladybug as shown in the box at right.

Painting the Ladybug

Saturate a very small brush with cadmium red and tip it with crimson red. Paint two small water-drop strokes for the wings. Rinse out the brush.

Tip the brush with dark ink, and paint one small stroke between the wings for the body. Then add dots for the eyes, antennae, and spots.

Landscape

Step 1

First lightly sketch the scene on paper with a pencil. When there are several elements in a composition—such as a landscape with trees, mountains, sky, and figures—it is important to mark the position of each element before applying ink so you can make proportion adjustments.

Step 2

Next use a small stiff brush dipped in light ink and tipped with dark ink to paint the tree trunk with downward bone strokes. Holding the brush straight up and down, paint the branches with smaller bone strokes. Then add texture to the trunk by filling in the spaces with short bone strokes. Next paint two more trees in the same manner, and add the foliage as shown in the box below. Then, using a very small brush dipped in dark ink, outline the figures in your scene.

Painting the Needles and Leaves

Load a small stiff brush with medium ink and tip it with dark ink. Holding the brush upright, paint the pine needles with downward strokes. Arrange the needles in bundles, allowing some needles to overlap each other.

For the tree on the far right, use a small stiff brush dipped in medium ink and tipped with dark ink. Paint two lines for each downward-turning leaf, holding the brush upright.

Step 3

Paint the outline of the rock as demonstrated in the first step below. Then load a stiff brush with medium ink, tip it with dark ink, and dry the brush slightly on a paper towel to remove some moisture. Apply a series of horizontal strokes to suggest the ground. To give your landscape a sense of space and depth, add the distant mountains and the ground. Reload the stiff brush as described above and trace over the nearest mountain outline; then, holding the brush at a 30° angle, suggest streams of water by sweeping a series of lines from the top of the waterfall to the bottom.

Painting the Rocks

Using a large stiff brush dipped in light ink and tipped with dark ink, paint the outline of the rock. Add shading with a small soft brush dipped in light ink.

Then use a small soft brush dipped in burnt sienna and tipped with light burnt sienna to paint the lower part of the rock around the base, as shown.

To give the rock a cool, stonelike hue, apply a thin wash of indigo blue down the center of the rock. Then add a light blue-green wash to the top surface of the rock.

Step 4

Add the far mountain by retracing the sketch with the stiff brush dipped in medium ink and tipped with dark ink. Now apply a layer of shading to the ground and various planes of the mountains with a light ink wash. To add the colorful hazy mountains in the distance, load a large soft brush with a light burnt sienna wash for the mountain on the right. Hold the brush at a 30° angle and move it from right to left repeatedly to create different shades within the strokes. Paint the blue mountain in the same manner but using a light ultramarine blue wash.

Step 5

Next apply the first layers of color to the other elements in your landscape. Using a soft brush dipped in burnt sienna and tipped with light burnt sienna, stroke the wash on the lower areas of the rock, the mountain, the ground, and the tree trunks. Be sure to leave the waterfall area unpainted. Now use a small stiff brush to add color to the leaves and the needles of the trees with a light blue-green wash (for example, viridian green mixed with cobalt blue). To add color to the waterfall, mix a light blue wash and paint over the water with a soft brush.

Conclusion

Now that you've completed the projects in this book, continue practicing and experimenting with your newfound knowledge of Chinese brush painting. The more you practice, the sooner you'll develop your own unique style and approach. As long as you adhere to the fundamental principles of this timeless art, you can turn any subject into a dynamic Chinese brush painting. Still lifes, landscapes, figures, and animals can all be used to create expressive masterpieces, painted with graceful, deliberate strokes and splashed with vibrant color. We hope you have enjoyed learning about the tools and techniques that make Chinese brush painting such a unique art form, and we wish you the best of luck with your artistic efforts!